Ronald Harwood's
Tragic Vision

Ronald Harwood's Tragic Vision

*A Critical Analysis of His Novels,
Plays, and Screenplays*

Ann C. Hall

University of Iowa Press, Iowa City

University of Iowa Press, Iowa City 52242
Copyright © 2024 by the University of Iowa Press
uipress.uiowa.edu
Printed in the United States of America

ISBN 978-1-60938-977-2 (pbk)
ISBN 978-1-60938-978-9 (ebk)

Text design and typesetting by Jessica Shatan Heslin/Studio Shatan, Inc.

No part of this book may be reproduced or used in any form or by any means without permission in writing from the publisher. All reasonable steps have been taken to contact copyright holders of material used in this book. The publisher would be pleased to make suitable arrangements with any whom it has not been possible to reach.

Printed on acid-free paper

Cataloging-in-Publication data is on file with the Library of Congress.

To all my students over the years.
You challenged me, taught me, and made me laugh.
May you continue to do so in the future.

Contents

Preface ix

Acknowledgments xi

Introduction: "Art Has a Lot to Answer For" 1

Chapter One: Sir Donald Wolfit 24

Chapter Two: The Novels 36

Chapter Three: The Plays 67

Chapter Four: The Screenplays 130

Conclusion 165

Notes 171
Works Cited 175
Index 187

Preface

I first met Ronald Harwood through my interactions with Donald Freed and indirectly through Harold Pinter. Donald Freed was a resource and incredible cheerleader as I organized an International Harold Pinter Conference in London. We talked frequently about featured speakers, the challenges of herding a group of international academics into the Russell Square Hotel, what to serve as snacks, and the various dinners and other activities accompanying the conference. Along the way, Freed mentioned Ronnie and, during one of the breaks, introduced me to him. We sat with tea, scones, and clotted cream, while Ronnie smoked, joked, and entertained. Later, Donald commented, "someone should write a book about Ronnie." Having met Ronnie, I concluded that person would be me.

With a sabbatical from Ohio Dominican University, I spent a week in London in the British Library reviewing Harwood's papers. Jamie Andrews, who managed Harwood's papers at the time, was an invaluable resource, and he and Ronnie allowed me to witness Ronnie contributing more papers to the archive.

During this time, I also spent several days in February 2010 interviewing Ronnie in person, and I had the honor of having him help me with my coat, a gesture he learned in his role as a dresser for Sir Donald Wolfit. He continued to perform that service for many celebrities and ordinary folks like me throughout his life. The gesture struck me as not only charming but as a symbol of Harwood's humility. Though blustery and hardheaded at times, he was always generous and empathetic. Early on in conversation with new acquaintances, he always let them know that he was Jewish—not to protect himself from anti-Semitic comments, but to protect the speakers from making embarrassing remarks they might later regret. Such an optimist.

Natasha served us lunch one day, and both she and Ronnie smoked throughout the meal. I had quit, but I was tempted to join them, especially as I inhaled at least the equivalent of a pack of cigarettes from their secondhand smoke. Happily, I refrained. The lunch was delicious, though Natasha was unhappy with the lamb, and the two carried on with their domestic habits. Natasha was working on her calendar, indicating that she had to write everything down or she would forget important details and implying that this was a new development in her life. Their behavior confirmed that they were a loving, long-term married couple who had found one of life's greatest gifts: a lifelong partner. Later, Ronnie hinted at some marital difficulties one of his children was having or had had, concluding that having parents who were so successfully married made it difficult for the children—they had set such a high standard for partnerships. When I asked him about the secret to their marriage, without missing a beat he struck a match, lit another cigarette, and responded: "She ignores me." He then went on to tell another story.

Harwood was full of stories. Stories for novels. Stories for television. Stories for the theatre. Stories for films. Stories about South Africa, theatre, religion, anti-Semitism, gender, cigarettes, writing, Hollywood, music, family, critics, and more. His curiosity and interests were expansive. He read voraciously. Whenever I talked to or emailed him, he was always reading and writing something new.

It has been an honor to discuss many of Ronnie's stories in these pages, and I hope you see here something of the passion, energy, and vision at work in all his writings.

Acknowledgments

I have received much support for this project, and I am grateful. Jamie Andrews of the British Library was curating Harwood's papers while I was visiting Harwood. We had a lovely tea in the backrooms of the British Library to commemorate Harwood's contributions to the archives. The University of Louisville provided me with a sabbatical to finish the project. Dr. Tyler Fleming offered an excellent suggested reading list on Jews in South Africa, South African history, and apartheid. Dr. Russell Vandenbroucke read a version of the manuscript, offered suggestions gently and supportively, and recommended histories of South Africa, even sharing his notes from his time in South Africa when he began his study of the country and of Athol Fugard. Dr. Katherine Burkman, one of my biggest supporters in all things, read an early draft, and the Wild Women Writing Group in Columbus, Ohio, offered me suggestions when I read aloud an excerpt. Dr. Judith Roof offered suggestions, support, and encouragement, as did Dr. Burkman. Other supporters included Lady Antonia Fraser, members of the International Harold Pinter Society, and my colleagues at Ohio Dominican University and the University of Louisville. Great thanks to Meredith Stabel of the University of Iowa Press for her faith and support of this work and to Susan Boulanger for her precise, conscientious, and incredibly helpful editing. She has saved me from many errors, and the ones that remain are mine. To my husband, Geoffrey Nelson, daughter, Sarah Hall Nelson, and son, Zachary Hall Nelson, who cheer me on. You are the best, my greatest treasures. A special mention to my father, Robert E. Hall, who offered suggestions and encouragement while he was in hospice and, later, from the great beyond.

INTRODUCTION

"Art Has a Lot to Answer For"

IN HIS BIOGRAPHY OF SIR DONALD WOLFIT, SIR RONALD HARWOOD NOTES that a "once well-known West End actor" asked him, "Now why would anyone want to write a book about *him*?" (*Wolfit*, xi). The same might be asked of this book on Harwood: Why would anyone want to write a book about *him*? Despite having written more than twenty major plays, eight novels, nineteen screenplays, four edited collections on theatre, numerous articles, and received a Tony nomination for *The Dresser* (1980), an Oscar for *The Pianist* (2002), a BAFTA for *The Diving Bell and the Butterfly* (2007), and the participation and respect of performers such as Albert Finney, Tom Courtenay, Maggie Smith, Anthony Hopkins, Ian McKellen, Michael Caine, Annette Bening, Alan Bates, and Tilda Swinton, Harwood remains relatively unknown, and his work has not received extensive critical analysis. This book presents the first extensive study of his works. Because he was so prolific and his writing career was so long, certain works, of course, will be excluded, namely the edited collections, rare early works, and several plays and film screenplays that repeat themes better represented in more successful and accessible works. It is hoped, too, that this book will encourage publishers to release or rerelease Harwood's significant novels, plays, and screenplays.

Harwood is worth studying, too, because the incredible range of his work illustrates, reflects, and critiques the wide spectrum of shifts that occurred in the arts over the course of his career. His work with actor Donald Wolfit not only inspired Harwood to write his famous play *The Dresser*, but it also connected him to Victorian theatre, a particular understanding of

Shakespeare and tragedy, and the role of the now-extinct actor-manager, a position demanding incredible will power and vision from the incumbents and blind obedience from those performing under them. While Harwood's novels follow a straightforward (some say old-fashioned) narrative structure, they resonate with contemporary themes and issues that include the role of art in society, totalitarian abuses of power, and racial injustice. The sources and impact of his work thus span the nineteenth to the twenty-first centuries, keeping pace with some of the most tumultuous, innovative, and compelling changes and developments in history, politics, and the arts.

So why has Harwood been overlooked? Theatre trends of the 1950s and 1960s, including the absurd, explicit political dramas, and other experimental forms, overshadowed his more traditional dramatic pieces. More importantly, while the Chichester Festival Theatre called him "one of the major playwrights of the twentieth century" (Hewitt), many theatre critics misread, dismissed, and, in some cases, savaged his work because they did not understand his artistic perspective—what I call his "tragic vision." Harwood developed his sense of tragedy and its structure during his time with Wolfit, and it set him apart from other artists and often caused critics to overlook his work. His characters live in tragic worlds and face terrible choices. Many are artists who must make difficult decisions to pursue their art. As Sarah Bernhardt proclaims in his play *After the Lions* (1982), "Art has a lot to answer for." But like Bernhardt and mentor Wolfit, Harwood repeatedly demonstrates that while the practice of art may be hell, it also sustains and ennobles both those who pursue it and those who value it.

Biography

Born Ronald Horowitz to Isaac and Isobel (née Pepper and known as Bella) Horowitz in Sea Point, "a modest suburb of Cape Town," South Africa, on November 9, 1934 (Robinson, 8), Harwood was the youngest of three children, following by several years his sister Evvy Leonora, who was born in 1922, and his brother Harold Ralph, who was born in 1928. Called "the afterthought" (Robinson, 8), Harwood was raised as an only child, and in his novel *Home* (1993) he cast the fictional version of himself as an only child.

Harwood's parents adored him, but he recalled their marriage as "tormented, painful" ("Memoir," 3). Though both were Russian Jews, their religious commitments, practices, and cultures clashed. Isaac's family was more resolutely "Litvak," Lithuanian Jewish. They were "strict, Yiddish-speaking and Orthodox" and often considered "uneducated, rural, and non-European," while his mother's family identified with the established South African Jewish community, which was highly educated, liberal, and secular (Robinson, 8).

Bella's father, who had been in England for a time, came to South Africa by choice: he found a job in the ostrich feather business, and the climate suited his health (Lockwood, 11); he and his family identified with the liberalism of the existing Jewish community. Isaac's family, on the other hand, had come to South Africa during the great migrations of Litvaks—Lithuanian Jews who fled Russia to escape the pogroms; they were more conservative. The tensions in the Horowitz household thus reflected those between the established Jewish community and the immigrants: "with the Yiddish-speaking immigrants regarding the Anglo-Germans as irreligious and ignorant and the Anglo-Germans accusing the Eastern Europeans for crudeness and unmannerly behavior, but gradually the new immigrants overwhelmed the smaller communities and began to redefine their character" (Lockwood, 15).

South Africa's growing economy smoothed over many differences between the two Jewish communities: "as whites in an expending capitalist economy, Jewish immigrants were well positioned," ultimately abandoned Yiddish for English, and identified with white "South Africanness" (Mendohlson and Shain, 83). Under apartheid, the differences among the Jewish communities would be eliminated by the apartheid act of 1948. Simply, Jews were "white" and superior to the "non-white" (Mikel-Arieli, 22), so to a certain extent, Jewish identity was clarified.

Neither the Horowitzes nor the South African Jews maintained such unity. In addition to their religious and cultural differences, Isaac and Isobel faced financial hardships, which strained their marriage. Isaac had trouble earning a living. He worked as a salesman, but later he went bankrupt after making a bad business investment. His health also complicated matters. After the death of his mother, he became paralyzed, which many, particularly Isobel, thought to be psychosomatic. When he died, however, an autopsy revealed that he had a non-malignant brain tumor that caused the paralysis. While he was alive, Isobel blamed him for every disappointment in her life. The marriage was so dysfunctional that the couple communicated with one another through Hardwood, which he found extremely difficult.

4 | Introduction

Unwilling to divorce, resentful of Isaac's business failures, and ignorant of Isaac's illness, Isobel dedicated her life to her children, especially Harwood, whom she considered exceptionally talented. She introduced him to theatre, music, literature, and film. However, as Harwood jokes, "She was lacking when it came to visual art. Her taste for interior design was non-existent. These deficiencies I have inherited" ("Memoir," 42). She was an unapologetic Anglophile who enrolled all her children in diction lessons to eliminate their South African accents. Aunt Rose in Harwood's play *Another Time* (1989) summarizes his mother's sentiments toward the British Empire and its language: "English is a language. And thank God for the Empire. Without the British Empire you'd be talking Zulu. . . . But English. Oh . . . what a language. Take time to read, I beg you" (221).

Such views may seem surprising in the light of the Boer War and may seem old-fashioned and incompatible with current political and artistic emphases, but they reflect the attitudes of many Jews in South Africa at the time. During the 1930s, English and Jewish businesses were thriving, while those of Afrikaners were not. Tensions rose, and Afrikaners intimidated, illegally intervened, and generally harassed their rivals: "such hostility entrenched Jewish identification with English-speaking whites" (Mendelsohn and Shain, 118). Novelist Dan Jacobson remembers sharing Isobel Horowitz's admiration for the English. He says, South African Jews who lived:

> under the British crown . . . could think of themselves as attached to, a part of, a political system that exercised worldwide power and was held in worldwide esteem . . . the crown, the coinage . . . the playing of "God Save the King" at the end of cinema performances . . . was a source of an enlarged sense of selfhood, even for those who could at best claim to have been stepchildren of the Empire. The British offered the best education, literature, art, music, culture, and accent, and Isobel went to great pains to have all her children experience and learn about British culture. She even sent them to classes to anglicize their accents to avoid the distinctive South African accent she was sure would hinder their upward mobility. (qtd. in Mendelsohn and Shain, 118).

In addition to developing an appreciation for the English language, Harwood developed a love for music and watched films about orchestras such as

Carnegie Hall (1947). He says, "music invaded my innermost being" ("Memoir," 39), a feeling he expressed throughout many of his later works, such as *César and Augusta, Taking Sides, Mahler's Conversion,* and *The Pianist.*

Theatre, however, was his passion. When his sister gave him the sound recording of Sir Laurence Olivier's 1948 film *Hamlet,* Harwood memorized the entire script. He later learned that Olivier had cut Shakespeare's Rosencrantz and Guildenstern sections, experiencing it as an early lesson in the art of adaptation that he would master later in life. In his memoir he cites Olivier's *Hamlet* "as an example of the major cuts that have to be made in an adaptation of any novel or play to the screen" ("Memoir," 76).

In addition to Shakespeare, during his senior school years, Harwood was introduced to several American dramatists. Harwood was overwhelmed by Arthur Miller's *Death of a Salesman* (1949), for instance, a response he saw as "only to be expected given that I was the son of an unsuccessful salesman. I had been moved by other playwrights, carried along by the stories they had to tell, my senses alert to their language, but never before had I felt so personally involved. This was a play about me and my world." After seeing a touring performance of Tennessee Williams's *Streetcar* (1947), however, he concluded that Williams was the more "universal playwright, with a poetic gift for metaphor, language that outshone Miller, and [who] enhanced the possibilities of dramatic literature" ("Memoir," 73).

Though Harwood admits that while in school he preferred to read *Theatre World* rather than study (Robinson, 16), he was a voracious reader who appreciated the British giants of the modern novel, particularly E. M. Forster, Evelyn Waugh, and Somerset Maugham. During a personal interview in February 2010, I asked Harwood what work influenced him the most besides Shakespeare's plays. Without hesitation, he said Graham Greene's 1940 *The Power and the Glory,* the story of a "whisky priest" who provides salvation to others despite his own sinful nature and a police officer who heartlessly follows the letter of the law. The choice may surprise some, given Harwood's Jewish upbringing, but the integration of Jewish and non-Jewish literature and culture characterized his world and education.

Perhaps due to this milieu, the tensions around religion in his household, and the openness to Christianity in South African Jewish communities, Harwood had a complicated relationship to religion in general and Judaism in particular. He notes in his memoir that he had a teacher in junior high school who tried to force Jewish students to convert to Christianity (18), and later he had a flirtation with Catholicism. He describes ultimately discovering a profound reverence for Jewish spirituality, which he qualified as "indeed spirituality of every kind" ("Jewish Spirituality," 3).

Harwood ultimately identified as Jewish and embraced the history and legacy of his ancestors, a legacy contributing to his identity as an outsider. While seen in the South Africa of his boyhood as being superior to non-whites, Jews still faced anti-Semitism and were not fully integrated into the prevailing white Christian culture and government. Following the Quota Act of 1930, which discriminated against the Litvaks, the formation of the South African Gentile National Socialist Movement in 1933 sanctioned anti-Semitism under the euphemism the "Jewish Question." The movement mirrored the Nazi movement in Germany, but rooted it in the local context by claiming that South African Jews "fomented the Boer War, incited blacks against white civilization, controlled the press, dominated the economy, and exploited Afrikaners" (Mendohlson and Shain, 106). With the establishment of the National Party in 1948, the Jewish Question was set aside, and the more complicated question of the South African Jewish community's support of or resistance to apartheid arose.

Harwood describes his youthful experiences with anti-Semitism in South Africa:

> I cannot remember a time when I was not conscious of its dangers or sensitive to its cruelty. During the war, anti-Semitism took on a new, more frightening dimension, sharpening my awareness [as] to what the verbal insults, the snide remarks, the thousand-and-one insidious references can eventually lead. To this day I find it necessary . . . to slip into conversation as soon as possible that I am a Jew. It is not admirable, but it is a psychological quirk. . . . Why do I do it?
>
> To avoid having to make a stand and to save anti-Semites from embarrassment, I suppose. That is my rationale, but the real reason, I suspect, is my own insecurity. ("Memoir," 63)

Harwood admits "the dreadful images—the skeletons passing for human beings, the bulldozers shifting mounds of corpses into mass graves—have haunted me ever since" seeing them ("Memoir," 62), and anti-Semitic comments serve as triggers, returning him to the horrifying images from his childhood. As Harwood's work progressed, his identification with his Jewish heritage grew more robust, and some of his best works address systemic anti-Semitism—the subtle forces that made the Holocaust possible then and could make it happen again today.

Despite the war, anti-Semitism, parental strife, and tensions over religious observances, Harwood's family provided love. While his parents no longer loved one another, the mismatched pair loved their children deeply, which they all felt. Harwood opens his unpublished autobiography with his father, giving him a place of honor. The writer's relationship to his mother was more complicated. When Harwood prepared to leave for London in 1951 to audition for the Royal Academy of Dramatic Arts (RADA) following his father's death, he was advised to change his name from Horowitz to Harwood. His mother changed hers at the same time, and while it may be innocent enough, perhaps even a sign of support, it must have been an odd experience to have his mother relinquish her married name to take his. His play *Another Time* (1989) offers further insight into this maternal relationship through the character of Belle Lands. But the most succinct description of Harwood's relationship to his mother comes through a comment from John Osborne. In his autobiography, Harwood reports having commented to John Osborne that reading Osborne's autobiography, *A Better Class of Person* (1981), made him realize that, in contrast to Osborne, he had portrayed his own mother in an unflattering light in his work. On mentioning it to Osborne, the latter replied, "You're Jewish, aren't you?" ("Memoir," 27).

While Harwood has been criticized for changing his name, he defended his decision, saying it was expected at the time and was not intended to disguise his identity as a Jew. He explained further in Robinson's biography: "I have been reproached for changing my name . . . as though I were trying to hide my Jewish origins; an accusation I find offensive" (17). He goes on, quoting Joseph Roth, to argue that Jewish names are arbitrary anyway: "They have compulsory aliases. Their true name is the one by which they are summoned to Torah on the Sabbath . . . their Jewish first name" (qtd. in Robinson, 17). Whatever the rationale, Harwood continued to identify himself as Jewish.

Ronald Horowitz, now Harwood, auditioned for RADA but was assigned to the Preparatory Academy for two semesters. When he finally entered

RADA, he was welcomed by Sir Kenneth Barnes, who had been principal when the school began fifty years earlier. As an example of Barnes's disengagement from his art and his students, Harwood notes that Barnes welcomed the new students, saying, "The most important thing in acting . . . is to become familiar with each other's parts" ("Memoir," 97). The co-ed audience understood the double entendre, though, according to Harwood, the speaker did not. Harwood jokingly describes "the most famous academy of acting in the world" as "like a genteel finishing school," which was, at this time, "outdated, sterile, and lifeless" (Wolfit, xii). Yet Harwood was disappointed when he had to drop out for financial reasons. His mother could no longer pay for his tuition (Robinson, 80).

Thanks to a personal contact, Harwood landed a job with Sir Donald Wolfit's theatre company. He worked with Wolfit from 1953 until 1958 as an actor in small parts and later as Wolfit's dresser.[1] Harwood's experiences with the company inspired both his biography of Wolfit and his hit play *The Dresser* (1980).

When Wolfit announced his retirement in the late 1950s, Harwood struggled in his personal and professional life, but landed a job with Richard "Dicky" Scott, who was doing repertory theatre in Derbyshire. With most of the cast and crew established, Scott still needed to hire a stage manager, but he was torn between a more experienced woman and a beautiful novice. Harwood advised Scott to hire the beautiful one, Natasha Riehle, and as Harwood later wrote, "Reader, I married her" ("Memoir," 168).

Riehle and Harwood came from different backgrounds: his family from peasant Jewry, and hers from Russian Catholic nobility. Harwood later explored these histories in his novel *Home*. Married in 1959, they remained so until Natasha died in 2013; Harwood never remarried. Theirs was a happy marriage.

They had no work when they returned from their honeymoon. After signing onto the dole, Harwood "contemplated a future either building the Hammersmith flyover or joining a traveling circus—suggestions put to him by the officials at the Labour Exchange" (Robinson, 69). Natasha became pregnant with their first child, Antony; two children, Deborah and Alexandra, subsequently followed. During Natasha's first pregnancy, and seeing their situation, Harwood's father-in-law, who ran an office supply business, gave Harwood a typewriter. Harwood began working on his first novel, published under the title *All the Same Shadows* in Great Britain (1961) and as *George Washington September, Sir!* (1961) in the United States ("Memoir," 181).

With strong reviews coming in from the novel, Natasha suggested that Harwood begin working on a play. After writing *The Barber of Stamford Hill* (1960), he sent it along to Casper Wrede, with whom Harwood then collaborated on the highly successful television play *Private Potter* (1961).

The timing was perfect. Both plays were presented as part of what was known as an "unholy alliance between theatre and television" produced by Hugh "Binkie" Beaumont (Robinson, 80). Known as "Binkievision," the series included some of the United Kingdom's greatest talents, including Maggie Smith, Tom Courtenay, Donald Pleasence, Sean Connery, Alan Bates, and Oliver Reed, performers he would know for a lifetime. Harwood went on to write a number of plays for television through the 1960s to the early 1980s, including adaptations for a series of Roald Dahl stories from *Tales of the Unexpected*. After this series, however, Harwood's television work diminished considerably, although *Mandela* appeared on HBO in 1987 and a screen version of Harwood's play *Countdown to War*, starring Ian McKellen, appeared in 1989.

Though this analysis does not consider the television plays, it is important to mention that Harwood's diminished output for television represents a shift in the ideological and cultural purposes of television, as well as Harwood's own disenchantment with the medium. During the early 1960s, Harwood, like many artists, thought that the medium could do what touring companies like Wolfit's did—provide culture to the masses. Television audiences were captives, and though Harwood admits that audiences could change the channel at any time, once they were watching a television drama, most did not. In his 1968 lecture "Writers and Television," Harwood expresses his belief in and hope for the new medium:

> The film industry has never apologised for being entertaining, although it pats itself on the back if a so-called serious film slips through the net and takes a fortune at the box office. The theatre, on the other hand, has become unashamedly serious: it has become a platform and pulpit, psycoological [sic] textbook and social manifesto depending on the views of the authors it employs and both these media, the cinema and Theatre,

contain an element of choice and the performing of a conscious act in order to enjoy them.

Harwood's disillusionment with the theatre of the time gave rise to his hopes for television—that it could become a "testing ground for the new writer and scores of dramatists."
Thirty years later, Harwood reconsidered television's role and popular culture in general. In an unpublished lecture, he expressed concern over what he termed "pop virus":

> The virus feeds on the demands of the market-place, to some extent on lower and lower educational standards and, most unfortunately, on those who believe that popularity is preferable to anything else. Popularity makes them feel better. And, of course, it makes them richer. . . . The secondary symptoms are to be observed when governments and the media begin to talk of elitism, by which is meant that art, in its highest form, is a luxury item and those who wish to purchase it must necessarily be rich, privileged and, yes, here is the echo of totalitarianism, asserting their individuality at the expense of the general good.
> Anyone who seeks to defend high standards in art is immediately branded old-fashioned or even fascist but, oddly enough, never Marxist. Quality is measured by the number of consumers. . . . I will only refer to television in passing. The best that can be said of it is that the more television there is, the less there is to watch. Television is to culture what MacDonald's [sic] is to *haute cuisine*. ("Pop Virus,"1).

Harwood's writing career reflects television's unrealized promise, with his participation in the medium declining over the years as its artistic standards diminished.
His early work in television, however, opened up opportunities for him. Following *Private Potter*, he worked on his novel *The Guilt Merchants* (1963) and a wildly successful 1966 film, released as *Arrivederci, Baby!* in the United States and *Drop Dead Darling* elsewhere. As Robinson notes, by the end of the 1960s, "Harwood's own journey to a state of material comfort and ease was complete" (104). He was able to purchase a "large country home" where he and Natasha raised their three children: "Greatest of all his financial windfalls, though, was the £10,000 delivered to him by Richard

Burton for the film rights to *The Guilt Merchants*: a fortune undiminished by the fact that the film never went into production" (Robinson, 104).[2]

With his finances secure, Harwood worked toward becoming a "respected literary figure," and nothing solidified that dream and its attainment more than Harwood's membership, initiated in 1966, in the Garrick Club, a gentleman's club inhabited by only the "brightest stars in . . . law and the arts" (Robinson, 104–6). He had had success writing films and novels, and following the actor-manager's death in 1968, Harwood began writing his biography of Wolfit.

In the 1960s, Harwood wrote the plays *March Hares* (1964) and *Country Matters* (1969), but he needed to make a living so he took on ghostwriting projects, screenplays, and other work. It wasn't until *The Ordeal of Gilbert Pinfold* (1977), based on the 1957 novel by Evelyn Waugh, that he received real critical attention for his stage writing.

He explains that his Oscar for writing the screenplay of *The Pianist* was a "recognition for a long struggle. . . . There were many times when I was offered some pretty rough things, and one had to do them, what with bringing up a family, paying mortgages. You have to make a living. I've made a living writing in different forms, and I'm immensely proud of that" (qtd. in Gritten). His collection of short stories on working in film, *One. Interior. Day* (1978), published twenty-five years before his Oscar, offers some insights into what these "rough things" were. This is how in one story, Harwood introduces Edward Lands, the collection's protagonist and writer-for-hire:

> For a year or more of his life, Edward Lands was engaged by Italian producers to work on their projects, polishing scripts, improving the English translations, contributing where he could. . . . Edward, therefore, was flying back and forth to Rome, sometimes as often as twice a week, and although there was much activity in his life, there was, he realised desolately, very little movement. (33)

Fortunately, Harwood's career, which did include a stint as a screenwriter for an Italian film company, did not stagnate. Even as Harwood established his reputation in theatre, he also edited several essay collections: *A Night at the Theatre* (1982), *The Ages of Gielgud: An Actor at Eighty* (1984), *Dear Alec: Guinness at 75* (1989), and *The Faber Book of the Theatre* (1993). He became politically active, as well. Thanks to an invitation from a good friend, Lady Antonia Fraser, Harold Pinter's second wife, Harwood joined English PEN and served as president from 1989 to 1993; he served as president of International PEN from 1993 to 1997. In addition to addressing the *fatwa* against Salman Rushdie, Harwood had the onerous task of fundraising. Numerous good-natured letters in his British Library archives indicate that while the organizations were seriously underfunded, his requests were always charming.

Harwood's success stemmed from his discipline and an almost maniacal need to write: "I work mornings, from 8:30 to about 12:30, then have lunch with my wife. I always take a siesta in the afternoons . . . sleep for an hour. Then I get up, have a cup of tea and a biscuit, and from five to seven, I look back at what I've written that morning and edit myself" (qtd. in Gritten). When asked about his prolific output in a variety of genres, he explains, "My energy is too much for me . . . I can't contain it. . . . I hoped that as I got older, I'd get calmer, but I can't stop writing. I'm an obsessive writer and you know, if you write a play and that finishes, you have to find something else, or something compels you to find something else; it may be a novel, it may be non-fiction" (qtd. in "Ronald Harwood"). His work ethic and passion earned him not only the Oscar but France's Chevalier National Order of Arts and Letters (1996), and the title Commander of the Order of the British Empire in 1999. Harwood was knighted in 2011 as part of the Queen's birthday honors. Harwood's beloved Natasha died in 2013, and he died on September 8, 2020.

The Unfashionable Theatre

Despite all his awards, it must be said that Ronald Harwood has never been the critics' darling, and some of his works received damning reviews. The reviews of *Mahler's Conversion* (2001) were "so savage that [Harwood] was plunged into depression and writer's block such as he had never known" (Fergusson, "Maggie Fergusson Remembers," 6). *Quartet* (1999), his play about aging opera singers, was initially dismissed, but in 2011 it was chosen by Dustin Hoffman as his directorial debut, starring prestigious actors including Tom Courtenay, Billy Connolly, Pauline Collins, and Maggie Smith (Itzkoff, 3).

One of the earlier reviews of *Quartet* as a play illustrated the critical misunderstanding that often appears in reviews of Harwood's works, with the critic dismissing it as sentimental and not only old-fashioned but out of fashion: "Anyone still hankering for those deadly 1950s country-house dramas, before Godot failed to arrive or Osborne looked back in anger, may find Ronald Harwood's *Quartet* is just their blast from the past" (De Jongh). The suggestion that Harwood was unaffected by the changes in the performing arts since 1953, the year *Waiting for Godot* appeared, is not only erroneous but fails to recognize what I define as Harwood's tragic vision. Admittedly, *Quartet* is more traditional than some contemporary dramas, but it does not fall below their standards. Rather, it presents an alternative aesthetic that this critic refused to engage with, caused by a serious disconnect between critic and artist.

The subtitle of Harwood's 1971 Wolfit biography, *Sir Donald Wolfit: His Life and Work in the Unfashionable Theatre*, illustrates Harwood's awareness of the potential for disjunction between art and critics. Even at this early stage in his career Harwood identified his mentor and himself as outliers, defining "unfashionable theatre" broadly as "that section of the theatrical profession, actors in particular, who are regarded by their fellow men with a mixture of grudging admiration, disdain, and often amusement" (xvi–xvii). Examples of fashionable types, according to Harwood, included John Gielgud, Laurence Olivier, Ralph Richardson, and Paul Scofield, all people Harwood sometimes admired and sometimes had the good fortune to work with in one way or another. Other unfashionable types included people Harwood admired and worked with over the years, performers such as Barry Sullivan, Baliol Holloway, and Anew McMaster who ran a theatre troupe that included both Harwood and his friend Harold Pinter.

The fashionable types are certainly popular, but not necessarily the most traditional. The unfashionable, on the other hand, may be popular as well, but they are also notoriously sentimental, stagey—perhaps just a bit too much. Both have their place in the theatre, as Harwood demonstrates in *Sir Donald Wolfit*, but the critical community tends to dismiss one and lionize the other: "The actor who stands outside the established côterie is remembered, if at all, more for his faults than for his virtues . . . what causes them immeasurable suffering during their lifetime is that they so often observe their more fashionable colleagues being forgiven the sins for which they themselves have been damned" (Harwood, *Wolfit*, xviii). It is no revelation that reputation, rumor, class, and pedigree, not necessarily talent, often establish success in the entertainment industry, and Harwood's works frequently encountered this reality: the difference Harwood articulates as affecting actors of Wolfit's day were often perceived in his plays as well.

The era in which Harwood entered the British theatre was a challenging one for artists of Harwood's skills and interests. In addition to the lack of government funding, in the late 1940s and early 1950s, British theatre had a number of great achievements, but impressive stage writing was not among them. Jean Chothia, who studies the early modern period from 1890 to 1940, notes that British theatre following World War II

> was one of the few places where the clock seemed not just to have stopped but to have gone backwards . . . . [W]ith censorship still very much in place and no public subsidy to encourage new or experimental work, London theatre was scarcely touched by the theatrical revolutions which were taking place in Europe under the impact of developing ideas about staging, the movement away from fourth-wall realism, of Strindberg's chamber plays, and of revolutionary politics. (88–89)

In his *British Theatre 1950–70*, published in 1974, Arnold Hinchliffe offered useful, near contemporaneous observations about the theatre of the period. Particularly relevant to Harwood and his cohort was his description of the years from 1950 to 1956 as "a period of great acting when stars like [Laurence] Olivier, [Sybil] Thorndike, [Ralph] Richardson, John Gielgud, [Peggy] Ashcroft, [Michael] Redgrave, and Edith Evans chose the right part, played heroic roles, and created memorable if ephemeral occasions" (20).

Harwood noted in his unpublished autobiography the comforting aspects of postwar British theatre:

> [T]he West End was dominated by H.M. Tennent, Ltd. and its Managing Director, Hugh "Binkie" Beaumont who presented all the leading actors of the day among whom John Gielgud, Edith Evans, Ralph Richardson, Margaret Leighton, Laurence Olivier, more or less guaranteed the House full boards-out on most nights. Binkie's Theatre was the theatre of Good Taste, beautifully designed and costumed, productions to please but not alarm. (91)

Exhausted from the two World Wars, audiences got what they needed from the British playwriting—relief and escape through the comforts of tradition.

That changed, of course, with the 1955 London production of Samuel Beckett's *Waiting for Godot* and with what Hinchliffe calls the "annus mirabilis," when John Osborne's *Look Back in Anger* and Bertolt Brecht's Berliner Ensemble arrived in London. Most theatre historians see these events as creating a division in the British theatre between the theatre of the absurd and the epic or political theatre.[3]

This divide left little room for Harwood and his unfashionables, who in the late 1950s were still performing Shakespeare. Harwood was neither a political dramatist nor an absurdist, but neither was he the Noel Coward of the Beaumont era. He loathed Brecht for his theatre, politics, and misogyny, and while he admired the work of his friend Harold Pinter, Harwood was not himself an absurdist. Harwood's plays, although they included politics and political themes and subjects, did not propagandize or moralize; but instead, the playwright challenged both his characters and his audiences to consider and respond to complex ethical situations.

The Tragic Vision

Shakespeare influenced Harwood's work tremendously. Not only did he study and love Shakespeare as a youth, but he also worked with Sir Donald Wolfit and his unfashionables who, as he notes in his foreword to *The Dresser*, "worshipped Shakespeare, believed in the theatre as cultural and educative force, and saw themselves as public servants . . . . [T]heir gifts enhanced the art of acting; they nursed and kept alive a classical repertoire which is the envy of the world, and created a magnificent tradition which is the foundation of our present-day theatrical inheritance" (*The Dresser*, 1983, 66–67). These experiences helped form Harwood's tragic vision, giving him a perspective that influenced all his works, the novels and films as well as the plays.

The range of commentary in the 2014 *PMLA* special issue on tragedy as a genre demonstrates that perceptions of the form continue to be complicated and subject to debate. Helene P. Foley and Jean E. Howard, who coordinated the issue, note that it is "the subject of endless commentary"

(631) and that the essays they curated do not "share a single definition of tragedy nor speak with one voice about its efficacy" (618). Some causes for the disagreements stem from changes in culture. George Steiner argues that tragedy cannot exist without the Greek context of gods and heroes, and as Foley and Howard show, today's common use of the term "tragedy" blurs its definition and the situations it is used to define. Referring to the bombing of Hiroshima as a tragedy obfuscates the responsibility of "particular agents" and political agendas (618).

Looking to Aristotle's *Poetics* does help create common ground, particularly his clarifying vocabulary describing and differentiating among *hamartia* (flaw), *peripeteia* (reversal), *anagnorisis* (recognition), and *catharsis* (hero) (22–27). The definitions generate further complexity and move the reader away from the stage and into greater abstraction. I am not arguing here that Harwood adhered to a rigid Aristotelian or any other formal definition of tragedy, nor do I wish to argue that he created tragedies in either dramatic or nondramatic works. He did, however, operate with tragedy in mind.

Francis Fergusson's work is useful here. He begins his discussion of tragedy with Aristotle's simple definition: tragedy is "the imitation of an action," a description he finds both insightful and obfuscating (4). In contrast to the new critics' emphasis on language and linguistic elements, Fergusson emphasizes the ritual foundation and rhythm of tragedy. Fergusson points to the history of Greek drama and its cultural context, concluding that tragic structure parallels ritual and that as viewers we experience the "this tragic rhythm of action which is the substance or spiritual content of the play, and the clue to its extraordinarily comprehensive form" (18). Fergusson's focus on ritual and patterns frees the tragic from the hyper-rational and a slavish adherence to theoretical models or rules. Harwood's tragic vision is similarly a habit of mind, a structure or dynamic that informs all of his writing, not just his plays; it provides a structure or dynamic that was forged through his work with Shakespeare and the Donald Wolfit Theatre Company.

In broad terms, the tragedy camps divide themselves into those, such as Aristotle and Friedrich Hegel, advocating for tragedy's universal appeal and those, like George Steiner and Terry Eagleton who, from very different perspectives, posit that each generation defines tragedy in its own way. Steiner goes much further, arguing that the genre is dead and that contemporary au-

Introduction | 17

diences can appreciate tragedy only as an antiquated relic. Rita Felski counters, saying Steiner's thesis

> may clarify why traditional tragedies are no longer being written, but it cannot explain why they are still being read, watched, performed, revised, and invoked. . . . From the standpoint of a strong historicism, tragedy could only be of antiquarian interest, a musty cultural relic as remote from the concerns of modernity as humors or phlogiston. That this does not seem to be the case suggests that we need to acknowledge generic continuity as well as generic change. (14)

Felski advocates a double vision, recognizing both the universal and specific characteristics of tragedies.

In many ways, Harwood's work accomplishes this double vision. His characters are haunted individuals faced with moral dilemmas and obstacles situated during specific historical periods. But the plays presuppose a universal human spirit, something that more contemporary tragic theorists, such as Elin Diamond in her "Churchill's Tragic Materialism or Imagining a Posthuman Tragedy," complicate (751). This does not make Harwood simplistic or a moralist, and his works certainly resist easy answers. But his works presuppose a human spirit or a human condition that unites us, perhaps by a moral presupposition. Without prescribing action, Harwood creates situations for readers and audiences to consider. The open-ended conclusions prompt ethical reflections, which may lead us to choose courses of action or at least think about alternative courses of action.

In this way, Harwood's heroes embody this human spirit in a way that Hegel describes as "romantic," requiring moral choices, not morality tales:

> [H]eroes of ancient classical tragedy encounter situations in which, if they firmly decide in favor of one ethical pathos that alone suits their own finished character, they must necessarily come into conflict with the equally justified ethical power confronts them. . . . Romantic characters, on the other hand, stand from the outset in a wealth of more accidental circumstances and conditions, within which one could act this way or that, so that the conflict that, to be sure, is occasioned by external preconditions, is essentially grounded in *character*. The individuals in their

passion obey their own character, not that it is substantially justified, but simply because they are what they are. . . . The greatest master . . . in the depiction of full individuals and characters are the English, and among them, in turn, Shakespeare excels all others and is almost beyond reach. (Hegel, qtd. in Kaufmann, 280–81)

In other words, the classical hero encounters an external, impossible situation. The romantic experiences internal conflict as well as external challenge. For Hegel, the character of the hero, as hero, must stand alone against the threat, but this pathological independence, the very characteristic that makes these characters heroic, is also their downfall. Again, quoting Hegel, "Shakespeare, above all, furnishes, as against this presentation of vacillating and bifurcated characters, the most beautiful examples of figures who are firm and consistent, and who, precisely by so resolutely clinging to themselves and their aims, destroy themselves" (qtd. in Kaufmann, 284).

Maintaining a pathological independence is not always an error. As Mark Roche explains, "the individual can be morally right, and the state retrograde, such that an individual may be more aligned with the universal, the state more with the false particularity that must ultimately give way. . . . Many tragic heroes stand for truths that are too new to have a majority behind them; after the hero's sacrifice the situation will change" (Roche, 13).

This misunderstood hero, perhaps a variation on Harwood's concept of unfashionable, is the hallmark of all of Harwood's work. His protagonists are unique; they are often artists who struggle to create. They are "special," geniuses, Titans among the rest of humanity who face remarkable foes or obstacles and who, ultimately, act and suffer. They are tragic heroes. Broadly speaking, such characters have fallen out of favor. Intellectual, philosophical, and social changes in the understanding of the hero mirror the changes that produced the absurdist and political theatre Harwood eschewed. For many, the "great man" and the "grand narrative" have been complicated by our new understanding of language and signification, the unconscious, diversity, race, gender, and politics. The individual meets with success or failure as a result of social forces, community patterns, and systemic political energies.

While Harwood addressed contemporary problems and inequities, he resisted the tendency to make each of his characters the same because he is suspicious of uniformity: it can too easily turn into authoritarianism. Harwood instead celebrates each hero's unique ability to resist sameness, whether the goose-step of the Nazis or the oppression of the postwar communist regimes. In Harwood's view, by cooperating in the obliteration of both the individual's potential for success and the individual's potential for failure, the contemporary world unwittingly participates in tyranny. He explored this in "Pop Voice":

> All tyrannies have one essential goal in common, and that is to crush the individual and especially the dissenter, more often than not the artist, to silence the voice that criticizes. . . . Totalitarianism holds that the more self-assertion, the greater the damage to the general good. . . . For the most part, the individual artist who sets the standards against which all others have to be judged, who discovers and maps out the cultural peaks of the social landscape. From the towering dramatists of Ancient Greece to their inheritors, the inspired, solitary voice has always been the unquestioned medium through which literature was expressed and then judged. The more the writer conformed, the less influential his writing. But when the writer's work opposed society, that work was the more highly influential. ("Pop Virus," 1)

Harwood recognizes the need for a hero—but not just any hero. He creates a tragic hero, which reflects his "double vision" of the tragic. Sir Donald Wolfit is a perfect example. On the one hand, he was a remarkable, driven, and successful theatre-manager, performing Shakespeare during the Nazi bombings of London and otherwise resisting the Nazi ideology, which he believed would eliminate art and culture. On the other hand, he, too, was a tyrant. His vision, his uniqueness, demanded compliance. But for Harwood, in the end, the battle against the Nazis, the battle for truth, trumped Wolfit's overbearing methods. Heroes act. They do not negotiate. And to some extent, they do not support a democratic method. Because they perceive a solution so clearly, a solution that their community has not seen or even considered, they are forced to move forward alone—living as unfashionable outliers.

Democracy and postmodernism can make tragedy seem common. As Eagleton observes, "Tragic heroes and heroines are now to be found loitering on every street corner, as each individual's fate becomes in principle as precious as every other's . . . one might well complain that if tragedy demands no more of human beings than to be human, then it demands too little of them" (95). Harwood felt as did Arthur Miller, who wrote in his essay "Tragedy and the Common Man" that "the tragic right is a condition of life . . . a condition in which the human personality is able to flower and realize itself" (Miller, 9). In other words, both Miller and Harwood see the tragic and the opportunity to suffer as not only a condition of human existence but as a necessity to spur growth and development.

While the tragic offers the opportunity, not all rise to the occasion. But tragedy may inspire audiences to consider their own heroic options. Robert Heilman, in 1968, the year during which students worldwide protested against the institutions symbolized by traditional genres such as tragedy, offered a compelling argument for greater understanding of the tragic. In response to popular culture's tendency to label every misfortune "tragic," Heilman sought to explain the difference between tragedy and disaster. Disaster involves complete victimization, while tragedy is a situation

> in which the always divided human being faces basic conflicts, perhaps rationally insoluble, between obligations, and among obligations and passions. In his strength he makes choices, electing a task with its inseparable penalties, seeking a greatness or power that he cannot have, or espousing an evil that he cannot resist; in his sentiency he hears an imperative that in prudence he might ignore; in confusion or willfulness or violence or pride he gratifies an impulse he cannot control. He undergoes the consequences of his choice, and in suffering achieves a new or a renewed awareness of his action and himself and the order of life. (19)

Heilman here emphasizes not only the culpability of the tragic hero but also the educational and perhaps ethical component to tragedy. He warns against blurring the line between tragedy and disaster. Disaster is easy but ". . . axiomatically perilous. The peril appears in characteristic intellectual, emotional, and moral errors—self-exculpation, self-pity, and the substitution of quantitative for qualitative standards. (The intellectual, the emotional, and the moral interpenetrate, of course, and are not wholly distinguishable; they are aspects of one simplistic way of interpreting experience)" (24).

What is interesting to note here, too, is the focus on the divided self, a popular representation of identity among postmodern philosophers. In Heilman's and Hegel's definitions of tragedy, the divided self does not prohibit moral judgment or educational outcomes; tragedy actually requires the divided self: "[P]aradoxically it is whole because it is divided. In tragedy, the implied end is not simply survival, or successful competition, or triumph, not simply saving one's life or reforming the lives of others, but insight into oneself and the understanding of moral reality" (Heilman, 100). This insight requires a critical view of the self.

According to John D. Barbour, tragedy also requires a critical understanding of virtue.

> Tragedy can help us take a critical perspective on our moral absolutes, which all too often justify our inflicting suffering on other persons. Yet if tragedy helps us to imagine the potential liabilities and dangers in particular ideals of virtue, it also forces us to recognize that a person's deepest moral beliefs are indispensable not because they are always successful in action but because even in failure they remain commanding as ideals or requirements for the self. Tragedy requires a recognition of the fallibility of particular moral ideals and aspirations; it involves, as well, the most powerful, because profoundly self-critical, reaffirmation of the ultimate value and significance for human life of particular forms of moral virtue. (25)

Harwood's focus on tragedy was clearly influenced by his interest in drama as a child, his obsession with Laurence Olivier's *Hamlet*, and his appreciation for Arthur Miller's *Death of a Salesman*. But through his work with Sir Donald Wolfit, who specialized in Shakespearean productions, particularly *Lear*, Harwood experienced a particular tragic structure on a daily basis for five formative years. What resulted for Harwood was a tragic vision, a perspective that may not fulfill the criteria for tragic drama but one that influenced all his writings, both dramatic and nondramatic.

For Harwood, tragedy required a flawed hero placed in a difficult situation by forces beyond his control. The hero addresses the adversity, but he makes mistakes along the way, and in the tragic universe, these mistakes may bring recognition or punishment. In the end, tragedy invites people to identify now with this character, now with that, seeing the same situation in different perspectives and thinking about the relative merits of each. In this process, human sympathies are enlarged and extended to unlikely characters; we are led to question what in ordinary life we took for granted; we are made more critical, more skeptical, and more humane. (Hardison, 351)

Though a single understanding of the tragic stance in art may be impossible, in Harwood's world, suffering often leads to understanding, knowledge, and, at times, wisdom, but it always foregrounds the value of the individual. In 1961, George Steiner wrote that the tragic genre was dead. In an essay nearly fifty years later, he supports his original claim, but he also, ironically and unintentionally, provides a succinct and beautiful description of the tragic hero we, according to him, are no longer capable of creating:

eminent human beings . . . stand out like lightning rods whom Olympian bolts irradiate and scorch. When they exercise dominion over matters of state, when they seek to bend history to their will, as do Shakespeare's or Sophocles' protagonists, that in life itself which is envious of man "answers back, 'fatally.'" The Promethean impulse in us is at once ineradicable and doomed. (38)

This study of Harwood's works shows that the Promethean impulse and those "eminent human beings" remain. In an increasingly mechanized, dehumanized, and digitized world, Ronald Harwood's characters—flawed, tempted, and weak as they may be—illustrate greatness: greatness of promise, greatness of will, greatness of suffering, greatness of passion, and greatness of compassion. In some ways, his heroes operate like Hegel's vision of the hero, representing an individual colliding with the absolute:

we fear the power of an ethical substance that has been violated as a result of the collision, and we sympathize with the tragic hero who, despite having transgressed the absolute, also in a sense upholds the absolute. Thus, Hegelian tragedy has an emotional element: we are torn between the values and destiny of each position; we identify with the character's action but sense the inevitable power of the absolute, which destroys the hero's one-sidedness. (Roche, 14)

In Harwood's work, the collision demands a reassessment of both viewpoints, leading to more significant experiences and greater understanding of the human condition. As Arthur Miller wrote, "tragedy requires a nicer balance between what is possible and what is impossible. And it is curious, although edifying, that the plays we revere, century after century, are the tragedies. In them, and in them alone, lies the belief—optimistic, if you will, in the perfectibility of man" ("Tragedy," 7). The depiction of suffering becomes instructive. The result is not didactic, but still, the outcome offers "substance or spiritual content" (Fergusson, 18). As O. B. Hardison, Jr. explains in his discussion of Aristotle's idea of catharsis: "[T]he prototype of tragedy is religious ritual; and the prototype of catharsis is a theophany, or joyous sense of rebirth and communion, that follows the sacrifice and rebirth of the god" (119). Harwood's works offer no solutions to many of the situations his characters encounter; instead, he creates, through his tragic vision, a moral palimpsest for us to decipher, consider, and perhaps unravel.

In a moving reflection at the time of her father's death, Deborah Harwood, perhaps better than Aristotle, Hegel, Miller, and all the tragic theorists, explains Harwood's reasons for writing, the motives behind his tragic perspective, inspiring us to continue reading, producing, and experiencing his work:

> He was a brilliant dad. He was hysterical, and he was wonderful with our friends. There are wonderful messages pouring in from people from our childhood. You just realize how many people he touched. He was so kind. He was so generous. He believed in human beings. He believed there was always something there in everyone, no matter who they were, no matter where they were from.

In these words, Deborah offers an important insight into Harwood's work that we will see repeatedly manifest. He and his characters are outsiders, immigrants to whatever world they inhabit, but from that perspective, they create art, no matter what obstacles they face. Art may have a lot to answer for, but it also has much to offer. So, let us begin to read Harwood's work, experience his tragic vision, and embrace the unfashionables.

CHAPTER ONE
SIR DONALD WOLFIT

"To strive, to seek, and not to yield":
Sir Donald Wolfit's Theatre and Influence

IN LIFE AND LEGACY, SIR DONALD WOLFIT MADE A POWERFUL IMPRESSION. Ronald Harwood, who worked with Wolfit from 1953 to 1958, memorialized the theatrical colossus in his award-winning play *The Dresser* (1980; 1983 film), as well as in his biography *Sir Donald Wolfit: His Life and Work in the Unfashionable Theatre* (1971). Although the biography was published in 1971, nearly a decade after Harwood's first novel, understanding Harwood's work requires understanding Wolfit's influence on him.

The biography also shows the course of Harwood's development as a writer and his tragic vision, for he uses a tragic structure to tell Wolfit's tale. Even the circumstances leading up to Harwood's task resemble a tragic hero's fated context. Upon Wolfit's death in 1968, Harwood attended the reading of Wolfit's will. Much to Harwood's surprise, he was assigned to write Wolfit's biography, for which he would receive "the sum of FIFTY POUNDS" (xi), which today would be about £744 or US$1,000. While not a significant sum, it shows that Wolfit recognized Harwood's skills as a writer, but Harwood, though honored by the gesture, felt panic over the responsibility. The two men had remained friendly, but they had not worked together in years, and while they had discussed the possibility of Harwood writing the biography, nothing official had been planned. Wolfit, in typical actor-manager form, settled the matter from the grave, making Harwood an offer he could not refuse. As Harwood later wrote in his introduction to the biography, "I owe much to Wolfit: he was, by far, the most important influence on my early adult life. The decision, then, to write this book was not forced on me by a clause in a will; I had no choice in the matter" (*Wolfit*, xiv).

Harwood wasted no time before describing Wolfit as a tragic hero: "I have never encountered anyone with Wolfit's size of personality, or anyone more unashamedly individual. I am able to remember well the awe in which I first held him, the terror I experienced in his presence both on and off stage" (xiv). Consistent with other tragic heroes, these qualities often failed to endear Wolfit to others and seemed to generate theatrical chaos:

> No actor of his generation was surrounded by more controversy than Wolfit. Every aspect of his life and work was subject to dispute. Some dismissed him contemptuously; others thought of him as a joke, yet others claimed that no one who held the stage in the last fifty years possessed, in such abundance, the qualities befitting a great actor. The argument did not only rage over his talent but also over his personality: he was hated and loved, disliked and admired, shunned and welcomed. (*Wolfit*, xv)

Such is the flawed hero of tragedy. As Harwood illustrates throughout the biography, Wolfit could not have withstood the rigors of touring the United Kingdom or performing in London as the Nazis bombed the city without his ego, his determination, and his, at times, annoying personality.

Harwood himself exhibited such characteristics in his pursuit of acting, but in the presence of this theatrical powerhouse, he realized he could not reach the performance level of Wolfit:

> When I first met him [Wolfit], I was consumed by ambition to be an actor; in seeing Wolfit night after night performing the great roles in his repertoire, by being present when he prepared for a performance or afterwards when he relaxed, I began to realise my own inadequacies: how paltry my talent, how misplaced my ambition, how half-hearted my determination. (xiv)

Though Harwood did not become an actor, it is clear that his affiliation with Wolfit inaugurated his writing habits and trajectory. Both men pursued their art monomaniacally, and through Wolfit Harwood made contacts that would establish his writing career and support it throughout his life. Llewellyn Rees, the Wolfit theatre group's administrator, helped Harwood find jobs after Wolfit retired, and he encouraged Harwood to submit the manuscript of his first novel, *George Washington September, Sir!* (U.S., 1961, and in the U.K. as *All the Same Shadows*, also in 1961), to a publisher he knew (Robinson, 73). While Harwood and Harold Pinter knew one another from their work at RADA, they also auditioned and were cast in the Wolfit troupe when they left the school. Harwood met John Osborne at the audition, too, and they remained friends, even though Wolfit rejected Osborne.

The company was a virtual time machine offering the performers the opportunity to experience a theatrical tradition that dated back to David Garrick and Henry Irving. As one of the last actor-managers of British theatre, Wolfit belonged to an illustrious group of theatre personages. As freelance journalist and theatre director Chris Wilkinson described this history on the Guardian Theatre blog,

> it used to be quite natural for performers to run their own companies. The tradition dates back to the mid-eighteenth century when Colley Cibber ran a company in Drury Lane . . . almost every actor of note, from David Garrick to Henry Irving . . . did the same thing, with the practice culminating in Laurence Olivier, who was the first director of the Chichester Festival Theatre and who went on to found the National Theatre. ("Whatever Happened")

Actor-managers reached the pinnacle of their power and influence during the Victorian era when touring companies dominated the British Isles. Drama was their religion and the works of classical theatre their gods. They worshipped the genius of the individual artist, particularly Shakespeare. They believed in human brilliance as much as they believed in human frailty. Most importantly, they believed in the moral and educational power of the theatre. The theatre was entertaining, but, for these early performers, it offered order in place of chaos and justice in the face of cruelty. Wolfit and Harwood shared these values, but they also saw the theatre as an alternative to the Nazi barbarism they witnessed.

Wolfit's fervor, however, often led critics to describe his theatre, methods, and performance style as old-fashioned, simple, stagey, and even anti-intellectual. Harwood's Wolfit biography showed that these characterizations were unfair, representing a divide he defined as being between the "fashionable" and the "unfashionable" theatre. Harwood listed as examples of fashionable actors Henry Irving, John Gielgud, and Laurence Olivier, and as unfashionable actors Wolfit, Baliol Holloway, Anew McMaster, and Wilfred Lawson (xviii).

Following the war, this distinction became more clearly defined. The postwar world introduced social, cultural, religious, and theatrical changes that challenged tradition, authority, convention, and cultural assumptions. The unfashionables tended to err on the side of tradition, while the fashionables erred on the side of experimentation. For both camps, these leanings affected their acting styles and play choices. It is impossible to imagine Wolfit performing in Harold Pinter's *No Man's Land* or Samuel Beckett's *Catastrophe* as John Gielgud did. The differences between the two camps include class and education, with the Oliviers and Gielguds brandishing elite theatrical and educational pedigrees and the Wolfits and McMasters wielding street-smart experiences.

By aligning Wolfit with these theatrical underdogs, Harwood established the dramatic environment of the biography—Wolfit against the popular theatre. With the theatrical context defined and the battle lines marked, he saw his hero as facing not only opposition and obstacles outside himself but as battling demons within. Ultimately, the conflict created the potential for tragic outcomes and glory.

Harwood's opening discussion of Wolfit's ancestry invokes traditional heroic murky mists. Beginning with the family surname during Shakespearean times, Harwood illustrates the dizzying permutations of the "Wolfit" appellation. Out of this linguistic whirlwind comes the name Woolfitt in the eighteenth century, but two hundred years later, it becomes Wolfit, because the "actor thought it looked crisper" (3). Harwood uses etymological gymnastics to establish Wolfit as thoroughly, unquestionably, and unreservedly British. The process also links Wolfit and Harwood, both men having sacrificed their family names on the altar of theatre.

With lineage and identity assured, Harwood moves on to Wolfit's childhood, which was fairly uneventful. Following his father's advice, Wolfit became a teacher at St. George's in Eastbourne. While there, he visited London and saw, among other shows, *Chu Chin Chow*, the most popular musical of 1920. Wolfit described it as "simply splendid" (35), while theatre scholar Jean Chothia has called it "inconsequential" (88) and used it to demonstrate the rather lamentable state of theatre following World War I. This was, however, the theatrical scene of Wolfit's youth. The preference may indicate Wolfit's early attraction to the theatre, no matter what kind, or it may simply highlight Wolfit's sentimentality. Whatever the case, the play initiated Wolfit's rebellion against the constraints of classroom teaching.

Shakespeare's biography provides Harwood with the template for describing Wolfit's final defection from teaching. Thinking of theatre but encamped and bored at St. George's, Wolfit began staging theatricals, but it was not until June of 1920 that his theatrical career began when he attended Charles Doran's Shakespearean performances. According to Harwood, Wolfit saw the performers and within days left St. George's to join Doran's company, which included much new talent, notably Ralph Richardson.

The story works on many levels. First, what better way to commemorate a Shakespearean than by characterizing his decision to work in the theatre in terms of Shakespeare's own similar decision? Second, the story serves as an endorsement for touring theatre companies like Wolfit's. Simply put, he was "like Shakespeare."

The Doran connection, too, links Wolfit and Harwood to the actor-manager tradition, as Harwood explains:

> Actor-management had a long and honourable tradition in the English theatre, but its greatest flowering was during the reign of Queen Victoria. Don [Wolfit] missed being born into that reign by fifteen months, but as a personality he belonged very deeply to that age, for it was to those standards, to those traditions, that he consciously adhered . . . . [Actor-managers] financed, chose and organised a theatrical company which was dedicated to performing plays in which the actor-manager had the best part. Paternalism was at the heart of the actor-management system. (*Wolfit*, 40–41)

The system had its advantages. Quoting actor George Benson, Harwood explains the code actor-managers lived by: "We go up and down the length and breadth of the land . . . that the country may never go without an opportunity of seeing Shakespeare played by a company dedicated to his service"

(*Wolfit*, 43). As Harwood saw it, for Wolfit, Doran, Benson, Irving, and the other great actor-managers, theatre was not a job—it was a calling.

But like the tragic heroes they performed, these actor-managers had their share of weaknesses. The entire system was authoritarian. Their understanding of their higher calling often led to egomania. Fueled by national, cultural, and personal pride, Wolfit would violate rules of etiquette, breech theatrical expectations, push himself and his company beyond the limits of physical endurance, and have little to no understanding of racial, gender, and ethnic diversity. When he found out that Harwood was Jewish, he immediately concluded that he was also good with money and put him in charge of finances.

The rigors of touring, which looked a lot like an Elizabethan royal progress, heightened the need for a strong leader. Wolfit and his travelers had to pay for their own makeup, tights, and shoes. Lodgings were in short supply. Wolfit and others used private homes run by that special breed, now almost extinct, the theatrical landlady, who provided bed, breakfast, lunch, tea, and dinner after the performance in return for astonishingly little payment. When touring actors learned which towns they would be visiting, the first thing they did was write to their landladies, reserving accommodation. A touring actor's digs list was a valuable, closely guarded document (49).

After working with Doran, Wolfit met Eleanor Elder, an equally impressive and indefatigable force in British culture during the 1920s who fostered Wolfit's belief in art as a social good. Like Benson and Wolfit, she was on a mission. She founded the Arts League of Service in 1919, the purpose of which, true to its name, was "to bring the Arts into everyday life" (76). Wolfit only worked for her for a year, but the connection between art and service, culture and community, was ingrained in Wolfit and, by association, in Harwood.

Wolfit then went into repertory theatre and married his first wife. Wolfit would marry three times, finally finding Rosalind Iden, a woman suited to his temper and tastes. Harwood reports these romances briefly and concisely, perhaps because he is writing about Wolfit's era, which did not relish salacious personal details, perhaps because these relationships are not crucial to the hero, who always stands alone. Harwood does take a moment to discuss the question of casual romances, and his observations reflect his solitary representation of the hero:

[I]f he ever did entertain casual affairs, and there is no evidence either way, it is certain they would have had to exist on an emotional plane in order for him to justify them. He loved fiercely and passionately . . . but what made this side of his life fraught with difficulties and pain was that his highly-charged feelings were extremely volatile and changeable. (85)

In 1928, Wolfit finally gained some recognition in London, landing a job at the Old Vic, run by the legendary Lilian Baylis, another important woman in theatre who "ruled her enterprise like a benevolent Head of State" (94). At the Old Vic, Wolfit encountered the fashionable theatre, best represented by John Gielgud, a performer who, unlike Wolfit, had had every advantage— a theatrical family, upper-class benefits, and education. Wolfit, a working-class, self-trained actor-manager could not work with such a group, and he left the Old Vic in 1931. This pattern would repeat itself throughout Wolfit's life. But class and educational differences aside, he needed to be at the helm. Collaborative ventures required compromise, something he was unwilling to do.

From 1931 to 1936, Wolfit worked, saved money, and dreamed of starting his own company. From 1936 to 1937, he was a member of the Stratford-Upon-Avon season and performed respectably as Hamlet. One critic likened him to Richard Burbage, who created a Hamlet of "passion, power, intense and lively humanity" (126). The Hamlets of Wolfit's, not Burbage's, day were not men of action, however, so Wolfit's "active" interpretation seemed, according to Harwood,

> at times anachronistic to his own generation . . . because his gifts, his style were drawn from a cruder past, and thus appeared irrelevant to a pseudo-refined present. Pseudo, because refinement in no way reflected the reality of the times; on the contrary, it was Wolfit's generation that was the product of the most horrendous war in human affairs, and was soon to plunge into the midst of a yet more terrible holocaust. (126)

Harwood's defense here clearly places Wolfit within the realm of unfashionable theatre, but it also illustrates the double standard frequently applied to Wolfit. Wolfit reflected his era through his interpretation of character, but he was dismissed and sometimes ridiculed by the critics of his time who saw themselves differently, who did not realize that Wolfit was portraying his and their generation.

While Wolfit may not have been one of the fashionables, Harwood repeatedly highlights his connection to theatre royalty to emphasize Wolfit's lineage and importance. As Wolfit is about to create his own company, Harwood carefully notes a connection to Randle Ayrton, the former stage manager of the Benson company.[1] Harwood claims that Randal Ayrton's Lear, reportedly one of the best of the day, influenced Wolfit's. Ayrton encouraged Wolfit to "don the purple," to go into management, and he gave him a prop that he used in his productions of *Lear*: a whip. The prop was said to have belonged to Oscar Asche, the writer and director of Wolfit's first theatrical love, *Chu Chin Chow*, who was inspired by Henry Irving's performances. Harwood uses these connections to show that Wolfit may have been unfashionable, but he had impeccable theatrical credentials and associations.

Under this auspicious aegis, Wolfit began his career as an actor-manager in 1937. Harwood commemorates the moment with a panoramic view of the company's past, present, and future:

> Armed with that talisman [the whip], and with the extraordinary energy and vast talents of its leading man, the Donald Wolfit Shakespeare Company came into being. Its principal player would be the recipient of high praise; the company, of repeated critical savagery. They would become the butt of the West End wags, of second-rate revues and third-rate comedians; actors, good or bad, would heap the company with scorn; even drama students would smirk in a superior way at the thought of them, for indeed anyone who wanted a quick and easy laugh would only have to mention the company's name. No matter if they trudged from one end of Britain to the other, or played in London with the bombs falling about their heads, or aboard troopships in the Mediterranean or across the vast North American Continent, they would be regarded as theatrical outcasts. Almost from its very inception, the Donald Wolfit Shakespeare Company became the Unfashionable Theatre. (*Wolfit*, 130)

Harwood rescues Wolfit and his company from the "slings and arrows of outrageous" bad reviews and treatment by repeatedly reminding us of the company's single-minded purpose: to bring art to the masses, to people who would typically never see a *Lear* or a *Hamlet*.

Even when Harwood admits that some of the criticism lodged against Wolfit and his company is valid, he protects Wolfit's acting tradition and the legacy to which it belongs by admitting that the weaknesses were the result of Wolfit, the actor-manager, not Wolfit, the performer. Wolfit's acting was strong and praised, particularly by James Agate, who thought he was the "greatest actor he had seen since Irving" (*Wolfit*, 167). As a manager, however, Wolfit made mistakes in play choice, treated cast members badly, lost his temper, fought with the wrong people, and had a terrible sense of stage design and visuals.

Perhaps by virtue of his ego and monomaniacal commitment to theatre, Wolfit led his company as a general leads his troops into battle, no idle metaphor in the early years of the Donald Wolfit Shakespeare Company. Wolfit toured until 1940 when he returned to London due to the war. Only one other theatre at the time offered any entertainment: the Windmill, which presented "non-stop revue" (145). True to his mission and vision, Wolfit rented the Strand and began offering Shakespeare excerpts, and on the second day, the theatre was bombed but still operable. According to Harwood, this was the company's finest hour, and Wolfit triumphed:

> He gloried in the discomfort; he rejoiced in the danger, for this was the theatre put to use he understood and which inspired him. He was serving the community in an hour of great national emergency in the only way he knew: by acting and by acting Shakespeare. It was the Arts League of Service . . . all over again, but now with manifest purpose for all to appreciate. Never could Wolfit's definition of the theatre's true function be more clearly demonstrated. . . . (146)

World War II and the bombings of England allowed Wolfit to show the world that he and the theatre, both his theatre specifically and theatre in general, had a purpose. Performance served a higher good. Proving this to the world motivated Wolfit and moved him to accomplish the impossible. In the end, Wolfit even managed a full production of *Merry Wives of Windsor* during the bombings, prompting the newspaper headline, "Shakespeare Beats Hitler" (148).

At his moment of triumph, Wolfit had heard that the Stratford Memorial theatre had visited the British army in the field. Wolfit offered his services, only to be turned away by the "director of entertainments" because the troops just did not care for Shakespeare. In a passionate defense of the bard, Wolfit reminded the director that "to pander to popular taste in the matter of our national drama is unworthy" (147). Harwood wrote that Wolfit argued that drama "made an immeasurable contribution to the quality of human life" (147) and that denying the Allies access, even if those soldiers were ignorant, was akin to treason.

Finally, in 1944, when matters were particularly desperate, the British army relented, partly thanks to Wolfit's persistence. Wolfit and company traveled to Paris to perform for Allied troops. As Harwood gleefully understates, "one soldier, Field Marshal Montgomery" praised Wolfit, whom he had seen before, saying "This is what I have said the men have wanted for a long time" (188). And even a young American, Wayne C. Booth, who would later become famed as a literary critic, noted that "in the desert of my life then, it [Wolfit's theatre] was a great moment of release" (188).

Here was Britain's hero performing miracles disguised as a tragic hero, notably King Lear. From 1938 to 1943, Wolfit played "all but one of the major Shakespearean roles," and between 1942 and 1944, he played Lear "forty-two times before he was seen in it in London" (157–58). On April 12, 1944, Wolfit was again in London, and this time again London was under attack. Amid the battle, Wolfit decided to do *Lear*. The moment glistened for most, particularly for critic Agate, who wrote with reference to the political battles surrounding the formation of the National Theatre, "If I were Government I would let any bricks-and-mortar National Theater stew in its own juice, and send Mr. Wolfit round the country with a sufficient subsidy to enable him to make first-rate additions to his company, and a posse of dramatic critics to see that he did so" (qtd. in Harwood, *Wolfit*, 166). Agate's review established Wolfit as an alternative to fashionable theatre, illustrating his tragic strength and persistence and highlighting his power as an actor.

Wolfit's triumphs, however, were short-lived, and the very strengths that brought him to his theatrical pinnacle would also cause his decline. External forces were at work, and the final chapters of the biography take on an elegiac quality. Theatre was changing. While the older generation could overcome their weaknesses "by the immensity of their projected passions"

(*Wolfit*, 169), Binkie Beaumont offered a theatre of distraction, not a vocation.

Like Tennyson's Ulysses, Wolfit continued "to strive, to seek, and not to yield," and he even landed a dream job. In 1951, the Old Vic was rudderless after its leaders quit over disagreements with Llewellyn Rees, the theatre's administrator. Rees, who knew the departures were imminent, had Tyrone Guthrie waiting in the wings. Guthrie hired Wolfit. It was the job of a lifetime. No more touring. Prestige. Consistent work. Security. But again, like Tennyson's Ulysses, Wolfit found it dull to pause. Harwood explains:

> As an actor-manager Wolfit embodied the ruthless virtuoso performer who viewed acting as a combat. . . . But when, at the Old Vic, Wolfit's fellow actors fought back, the virtuoso was compelled to show his strength . . . . [B]ut he did not realise that in the modern preference for *ensemble* playing, which is another way of describing the director's theatre, the tradition had outlived its usefulness. The age of the great virtuoso performance was at its end; in the future, leading players would have to make it seem that they were part of a team. (218)

Ostensibly due to schedule disagreements, perceived snubs, and other "demons," Wolfit "departed from the Old Vic and never returned" (217).

Wolfit was a theatrical warhorse, so once again he began his own company, hiring Llewellyn Rees to serve as his administrator. The 1953 season opened "in a blaze of glory" (223). Critics were amazed by Wolfit's *Oedipus* and other offerings. His success was his best revenge on the Old Vic. But it did not last. Wolfit could not keep up the pace and retired with a knighthood in 1957.

Retirement did not mean the end of Wolfit's acting career or of his touring. He and Rosalind traveled nearly 29,000 miles between 1959 and 1960, hitting cities as diverse as Oklahoma City, Bombay, and Beirut (259). The rest of the decade did not bring as much work, however, and many of Wolfit's contemporaries were either dying or falling on hard times (269). During a performance of *The Barretts of Wimpole Street* in 1967, he fell ill and never returned to the stage. He died on February 17, 1968.

Despite Wolfit's years in the theatre, few spoke at Wolfit's memorial: "[T]he isolated nature of his career followed him to his grave" (*Wolfit*, 275).

For tragic heroes, life is lonely at the top and at the bottom. Harwood concludes the biography with an image of Rosalind and of the British theatre without its last actor-manager, without Wolfit's powerful, virtuoso presence. For Harwood, Wolfit embodied the nature of a hero: a relentlessly independent individual and artist. Harwood explains this when he memorializes Wolfit early in his biography:

> If a balance sheet of Wolfit's Shakespeare company is to be drawn then it will show a rich surplus: service to the community and to the English classic repertoire stand high on the list of assets, but most important of all was the opportunity playgoers had, from 1937 to 1953, of seeing a great actor in great roles, an actor in whom some ancient fire burned. His contribution to the art of acting was of immense importance to the theatre, not only because he illuminated human passion and folly, but also because he deliberately upheld the traditions of the past which, as a function, is as essential to the mystery of renewal as any wild or daring innovation; for finally, there is no way of judging the present or the future but by the past. (226–27)

Harwood, too, was connected to this past through not only his intense devotion to and participation in the life of Sir Donald Wolfit but also to his commitment to a life in the arts. Throughout the Wolfit biography, Harwood memorializes not just an individual but an era and the traditions and beliefs that motivated both Wolfit and that era to persevere despite tremendous odds. For Wolfit and his theatre, the arts offer solace, education, moral instruction, and entertainment and serve as a repository of cultural heritage. The arts are essential, not a luxury. These are the ancient fires, and after reading about Wolfit and analyzing Harwood's works, it is clear that they still burn. Living life in and by art may be difficult, painful, financially unrewarding, and at times humiliating, but, for Wolfit and for Harwood, the suffering brings rewards, both in tragedy and in life.

CHAPTER TWO
THE NOVELS

Books have to be read.... [I]t is the only way of discovering what they contain.... The reader must sit down and struggle with the writer.
—E. M. Forster, *Aspects of the Novel*

HYPERVENTILATION, INSPIRATION, BLIND LUCK, TIME, AND THE KINDNESS OF in-laws led to the creation of Ronald Harwood's first novel, published in 1961 both in the United States as *George Washington September, Sir!* and in England as *All the Same Shadows*. His Wolfit years were behind him, and the work at Lyric Hammersmith was completed, and Harwood had married Natasha Riehle, with whom he was expecting his first child. The couple were, unfortunately, on the dole, but they had a flat thanks to Natasha's father. Harwood later recalled that his only job prospects were "either building the Hammersmith flyover or joining a traveling circus—suggestions put to him by officials at the Labour Exchange" (Robinson, 69). Harwood was spared both fates when he received a typewriter from Natasha's father for his twenty-fifth birthday: "Natasha thought I was just teaching myself the mechanics of the keyboard, but in fact, before long, I had started to type a story, written in the first person of George Washington September, a Zulu houseboy in Cape Town" (Robinson, 70).

Harwood realized his vocation as a writer as he worked: "I had tapped into some deep source within myself, a source of which I had never been remotely aware" (71). Enter the hyperventilating. Harwood did not know what to do next, so he put the novel in a drawer and began work on what was to become a television play, *The Barber of Stamford Hill*. Why? Because, he said, he "wanted to go on writing" (77).

Fortunately, a theatre friend, Llewellyn Rees, a former administrator for the Old Vic and for Wolfit's Shakespeare Company, came to dinner one night and asked Harwood about his activities. Harwood admitted that he had a novel and part of a television script, and Rees offered to show it around. The rest, as they say, is history. The novel was picked up. Moreover, the television script reconnected Harwood with Casper Wrede, a director Harwood had worked with elsewhere and would later work with on the 1970 film adaptation of Aleksandr Solzhenitsyn's *One Day in the Life of Ivan Denisovich*.

Given Harwood's earlier and extensive experiences in the theatre, it may seem odd that he did not pursue playwriting at this time. Harwood, however, felt alienated from the London theatre. In a speech on adaptation requested by Susan Segal, Harwood noted "the new plays, the Royal Court plays, were, it seemed to me, all obsessed with class and resentment" ("Adaptation," 19). Harwood was for several reasons especially critical of Bertolt Brecht, whose theories and productions had been introduced to London in 1956. As he notes in *All the World's a Stage*, while Brecht was "the loudest and most gifted voice of the political theatre," he had failed to protect his mistress when she was arrested by the Soviets (302). But more importantly, the two playwrights' visions were diametrically opposed: Harwood wanted audiences to feel, while Brecht wanted audiences to think. In the end, Harwood dismisses Brecht: "I only have to think of Mother Courage and, if I can't sleep at night, I'm off" (qtd. in Harris, "Ronald Harwood Obituary"). At the opposite end of the spectrum were the absurdists. And though Harwood and Harold Pinter were lifelong friends, Harwood did not embrace the absurdists' artistic style, even though it eschewed the political, at least initially. (Later, many absurdists, especially Pinter, changed their attitudes and embraced politics in both their plays and public lives.)

Artistically, critics complicated the separation of the traditional and the contemporary. For example, Jan Kott's *Shakespeare Our Contemporary* highlighted the characteristics shared by authors such as Shakespeare and Beckett. During Harwood's time, however, the division was more pronounced, and he identified with the more traditional theatre embodied in the work of his mentor, Sir Donald Wolfit.

At the time, then, Harwood felt himself an outsider—an unfashionable—in the theatre world. He felt that he could not participate in the absurdist theatre, explaining that these works represented humanity as "an accident of random circumstance, living on a dung heap" ("A Personal View"). Current theatrical criticism challenges and complicates such interpretations of absurdism and existentialism, but Harwood's assessment reflected the prevailing understanding of these new works in literature, arts, and philosophy.[1]

These artistic and commercial contexts influenced Harwood's initial decision to write novels. David Kurnick's fascinating study *Empty Houses: Theatrical Failure and the Novel*, however, corrects a common misconception about the genres of play and novel. He notes that novel-writing playwrights are common: "the list of important novelists writing for the theatre is long, stretching at least from Aphra Behn to Samuel Beckett" (2). Arguing against the conventional wisdom that cast the novel as a response to the theatre's failure, Kurnick shows that the traditional interpretation of generic development, particularly from theatre to novel, has been too simplistic.

Kurnick demonstrates that conventional literary history explains the rise of the novel as a move from the culture of collectivity embodied in theatre to a culture of individuality and interiority expressed in the novel. He debunks this interpretation and illustrates that the move from theatre to the novel is neither clear-cut nor a representation of the cultural desire for solitude: "The theatrical energy encoded—genetically, as it were—in the novel of interiority continually point beyond the enclosures represented by the family, the home, individual psychology, and sexual identity" (4). Admittedly I am simplifying Kurnick's subtleties, but *Empty Houses* demonstrates that the novel does not preclude a desire for the communal, nor does it show the fall of the dramatic. Kurnick's perspective is constructive when approaching the Harwood canon. Because Harwood had early successes in the novel, it might be tempting to assume that he abandoned his dramatic sensibilities. But as we shall see, his novels rely on his theatrical experience, particularly his tragic vision, a vision that not only permeates all his work but was refined in his novels and later perfected in his plays.

In some ways, the persistence of the tragic distinguishes Harwood further from his fellow modernist writers who wanted to break with tradition entirely. It may be stretching it a bit, but Harwood's impulse to remain connected with the past, including various works of art and literature that may at the time have gone out of fashion, positions him closer to a postmodern author than a modern one. Whatever the case, Harwood's novels are an essential component of his future work in theatre and film, and ignoring them diminishes our understanding of the depth of the later works.

The E. M. Forster epigraph to this chapter highlights the inherently dramatic nature of reading—the reader struggles with the writer. A community between the two is formed. Harwood's community included many modern British writers such as Evelyn Waugh, Graham Greene, E. M. Forster, and Somerset Maugham.

Graham Greene's *The Power and the Glory* (1940) was particularly important and is worth discussing briefly. The story is about an unnamed, derelict, alcoholic "whisky priest" in Mexico who will do almost anything for a drink, breaks his vow of celibacy, and fathers a child. Despite his sinfulness, he continues to minister to the faithful. The government in Mexico at the time of the novel, however, wanted to obliterate the influence of the Roman Catholic Church and ordered its agents to hunt down all priests who were still practicing. In the context of the novel, only one—the whisky priest—remained. As the priest tries to escape this looming death sentence, he offers the faithful the sacraments, sometimes risking his life. Finally he is caught, but before his death, a sympathetic lieutenant asks another man, a lapsed priest who has forgone all Catholic rituals and married a Mexican woman, to perform—just once—the last rites for the whisky priest. This ritual would have offered the whisky priest absolution, but the former priest refuses, and the protagonist dies with his sins on his soul.

It might come as some surprise that the story appealed to the Jewish Harwood, but it reflects Harwood's tragic vision and the attitude toward art held by both his family and Wolfit. Though the novel does not include the *anagnorisis*, the awakening of the tragic figure, we see the aftereffects of the fall, in a structure similar to that of Sophocles's *Oedipus at Colonus*. As flawed as he is, the whisky priest embodied nobility and continued to minister to and inspire his flock despite his sinfulness and failures. As E. M. Forster explains in *Aspects of the Novel* (1927), "novels, even when they are about wicked people, can solace us; they suggest a more comprehensible and thus a more manageable human race, they give us the illusion of perspicacity and of power" (64). As did the actor-managers and the culture-makers of

Harwood's South Africa and London, Forster proclaimed the restorative and redemptive power of art and suffering that Harwood embraced.

Like Forster, Harwood resists propagandizing: "all literature must concern itself with a vision of human identity. It must ask the questions who are we, where are we, and why are we? It does not necessarily have to answer those questions, but, it seems to me, they must be asked" ("A Personal View"). While this perspective may seem old-fashioned, Harwood's work presumes a universal, shared human experience, a recognition of the tragic energy that runs through our lives no matter our historical moment, ethnicity, gender, or individual preferences. For Harwood, art has a lot to answer for. However, it also has a lot to teach us about ourselves and our relationship to others, particularly those we would like to marginalize or ostracize as "others" or, to use Harwood's words, unfashionables.

All the Same Shadows / George Washington September, Sir!

Harwood's 1961 novel *George Washington September, Sir!* offers the most fully developed expression in Harwood's novels of his tragic vision. Through the life and struggles of first-person narrator George Washington September (modeled on a handsome young Zulu man who worked in Harwood's childhood home in Sea Point, South Africa), the novel illustrates and indicts apartheid. Officially initiated in 1948, apartheid did not end until the early to mid 1990s, thanks to the leadership of Nelson Mandela and F. W. de Klerk, who were jointly awarded the Nobel Peace Prize in 1993 for their work to end the racist legislation.

The Sharpeville massacre inspired Harwood to write the novel. On March 21, 1960, the newly formed Pan-Africanist Congress (PAC), an offshoot of Nelson Mandela's African National Congress (ANC), "launched a campaign against the pass laws" that required Black South Africans to obtain and carry special passports at all times and limited their movement to ensure segregation. The story behind the massacre, as recounted by Leonard Thompson, began when "[l]arge numbers of Africans assembled at police stations without passes inviting arrest in the hope of clogging the machinery of justice. At the police station at Sharpeville, near Johannesburg, the police opened fire, killing 67 Africans and wounding 186, most of whom were shot in the back" (*History of South Africa*, 210). Further disturbances continued throughout the country, leading to the declaration of a state of emergency. In addition to 11,279 Africans, about 200 whites and Indians, another 6,800 were arrested and hundreds more were beaten (Thompson, 210). Later, intensifying protests led to Mandela's imprisonment in 1962, heightening international attention on the issue of apartheid in South Africa. Harwood, too, continued to address South African racism in such later works as the novel *Articles of Faith* (1973); the screenplay written for HBO's *Mandela* (1987); Harwood's own play, *Another Time* (1989), which opened at the new Steppenwolf Theatre; and his screenplay for the 1995 film version of *Cry, the Beloved Country*, the first film shot in South Africa after the end of apartheid.

In addition to the inhumanity of the Sharpeville massacre, Harwood may have been inspired to write *George Washington September, Sir!* by the international Jewish response. South African Jews not only remained silent on apartheid, they supported the status quo. They may have seen the similarities between the treatment of European Jews and the non-white South African population, but they also understood their precarious relationship to the Afrikaner community. Like the Afrikaners, they initially claimed the race question was too complicated to solve quickly or easily. Despite their attempts at neutrality regarding the race question, when Israel voted against South Africa's apartheid laws throughout the 1950s, South African Jews experienced significant pressure from the Afrikaners, and anti-Semitism increased.

Harwood does not chastise the Jewish community, but the novel indicts apartheid and those who do not actively resist systemic oppression. Harwood also makes the risky decision to tell the story from the perspective of George Washington September, a young Black man. Such a choice invites criticism. How could a white man, living in England, depict the experience of a South African non-white? Admittedly, some moments in the novel would probably be written differently today, given the growing understanding of race and systemic racism, but at the time, speaking out against apartheid and speaking for the silenced non-whites in South Africa and elsewhere was not only admirable, it was necessary. Harwood's use of tragic structure results in a fully developed protagonist, one who is neither stereotypically good nor simplistically evil, but instead a human being with strengths and weaknesses, a depiction that ran counter to popular beliefs among whites worldwide, not just in South Africa.

The novel opens by establishing the apartheid reality. A white woman accuses George of touching her skirt. White police officers come to her aid, rough up George, and send him on his way only after the woman decides not to press charges. With the racial stereotypes established, Harwood counters with the innocent George's assessment of the situation: "If it's one thing I don't like, it's hair on a lady like that. So one thing's for sure: I would never touch a skirt of a lady who had hair on her lip. Especially a white lady" (10). He is also most concerned about the condition of his clothing and how he will appear to the Finbergs, the Jewish family he works for. His earnestness and somewhat comic response win our sympathies and highlight the Kafkaesque world of apartheid.

Jannie, a local criminal, offers to help George with his clothing and invites him to his home to change. Jannie, however, compromises him by spiking his drink, introducing him to a beautiful Zulu girl, Nancy, and subsequently taking pornographic pictures of George and Nancy to sell on the lucrative Zulu porn market, which targets both white and Black consumers. George somehow returns to the Finbergs, ignorant of the night's activities and the photos, and talks to Abel, the Finberg's nineteen-year-old son. The two have a good and easy friendship. George appreciates Abel's encouragement to write and reflect. George comments about Abel that he "is making me all the time write down things I think because he says I'll be a better educated native boy when I get educated about myself" (32).

The scene is fraught with political land mines. It could easily support a colonial viewpoint: Abel, the white, knows what is best for George, the Black. Harwood, however, creates equality between the two men, although their friendly relationship would not be permitted outside the home. The scene suggests a means of assisting non-whites in South Africa—through education. By juxtaposing scenes between George and Jannie and George and Abel, Harwood avoids simplistic racial representations. Some Blacks oppress Blacks, and some whites support them. In all cases, the moral choices our hero faces are complicated.

Initially, George chooses unwisely. Driven by an insatiable desire to see Nancy again, George returns to Jannie's house, where he learns about the pictures. Shocked but also aroused by the photos of Nancy and himself, George declines the offer for more work, but he keeps a photo and accepts the money Jannie gives him for the previous night's "work." Dehumanized by porn and by Jannie's treatment of him, George does not reform his behavior initially; instead, he reproduces it by using other women selfishly and abusively. The repetition illustrates the insidious effects of systemic racism and oppression, which George internalizes, treating Black women like objects, as the white men do.

Abel's response to finding the pornographic material interrupts the cycle of victimization. Abel urges George to follow his conscience, his "inner voice." In response, George articulates the realities of his life: "But I want to tell you I got no voice inside me telling me those photos are bad. Sometimes that voice tells me other things are bad but not those photos" (106). For George, some transgressions are more grievous than soft-core porn photos—transgressions that make the objectification of Blacks for white consumption possible.

This conversation awakens George to the dehumanization of apartheid. Harwood avoids condescension by aligning South Africa's struggles over apartheid with George's search for answers for his own life. As George searches, so, too, does the country. A new white English minister arrives and encourages whites and Blacks to attend services together. George does not participate because "it's difficult to believe in Christ because of Christians. . . . They tell you things, these people, like love everybody. But they don't love everybody. No, sir. So who you going to listen to?" (115–18).

George turns to his Uncle Kalanga, who has renounced religion and white culture. As George puts it, "he is saying if they just let us be natives, we'd be okay and they'd have no trouble at all" (127). Uncle Kalanga is the only character who calls George by his Zulu name, Tabula. Both the author and George agree with Kalanga's ideas, but not with his methods, which include violent responses to the police and the white community.

Finding both Kalanga's revolution and the Christian religion unsatisfying, George betrays his uncle by sleeping with Nancy. He discovers that Jannie and Nancy set him up from the moment the police hassled him. Filled with anger, George nearly kills the two but returns to the church of the new English minister, only to find that he and the congregation have been imprisoned, establishing apartheid's omnipotence and omnipresence. George continues to seek an answer, and on his journey out of town, like Paul on the road to Damascus, George finds a means of resistance:

> You don't have to kill them to show them you're equal. You can just love Jesus with them. Man, they don't like that. No, sir. But I'm telling you something. It shows we're equal, hey? This is the way you got to do it.

> This is the way you can show them we're equal. Just kneel down and love God with them. That's the weapon, you understand. That's the gun. That's the rifle. You can't help smiling. I'm telling you. (206).

The novel ends with George's arrest and awakening.

In his review of the novel, Robert Pick of the *New York Times* describes Harwood as a "skillful writer" and the story as "a tragedy born in the fear that rules his country." The tragic pattern is clear: a sympathetic but flawed character faces a moral challenge and changes for the better. His journey ennobles him. For George, like many tragic heroes, the truth is brutal, humiliating, crushing, and horrible. It does set him free, however, not necessarily to live in paradise but to attempt to change his flawed country. As Arthur Miller explains:

> Tragedy arises when we are in the presence of a man who has missed accomplishing his joy. But the joy must be there, the promise of the right way of life must be there. Otherwise pathos reigns, and an endless, meaningless, and essentially untrue picture of man is created—man helpless ... man wholly lost in a universe which by its very nature is too hostile to be mastered. In a word, tragedy is the most accurately balanced portrayal of the human being in his struggle for happiness ... the most perfect means we have of showing us who and what we are, and what he must be—or should strive to become. ("Nature of Tragedy," 11)

In a political maneuver that transcends propagandizing, Harwood created a tragic hero in George, an uneducated Zulu, in order to show the greatness in all: Black, white, South African, English. Though he offers no dramatic political solution, Harwood shows readers an outlet, an alternative that may not be realized in the novel, but that is certainly suggested. George has changed, and this novel attempts to change his country.

Harwood understood that his experience in writing the novel brought him to a deeper understanding of South Africa's systemic racism as well as of his vocation as a writer.

> On the morning that I began the last section, the denouement, I had a sudden and unexpected realisation. The adventures I had put my hero

through were, it transpired in a final spasm, all part of a plot engineered by the South African police. I had no idea of this before I began; I discovered it at the last moment in the process of writing. My hero's victimisation encapsulated, without my being conscious of it, the viciousness of the totalitarian state South Africa had become. The moment this was revealed to me, I began to hyperventilate. Natasha was out shopping. Alone in the flat, I started to pace up and down trying to catch my breath. When at last I regained control and sat again at the typewriter, I knew with wonderful certainty that I had tapped into some deep source within myself, a source that I had never been remotely aware. ("Memoir," 181)

The Guilt Merchants

Following the success of his first novel, Harwood received offers to write plays and television scripts, notably *The Barber of Stamford Hill* (1960 television play; 1961 film) and *Private Potter* (1961), which starred Tom Courtenay, who would become a Harwood favorite. He also worked on films such as *A High Wind in Jamaica* (1965), with Anthony Quinn and James Coburn, and *Arrivederci, Baby!* (1966), with Tony Curtis and Zsa Zsa Gabor. Most were successful, but Harwood continued to write novels because, as Robinson notes, Harwood wanted to become "a respected literary figure" (Robinson, 87). *The Guilt Merchants*, set in a fictional South American village, is "loosely based on the story of Adolph Eichmann" (Robinson, 87) and introduces a subject that will dominate much of Harwood's later work: the Holocaust.

Harwood's novel examines the issues of crime, punishment, retribution, and revenge raised by the Eichmann trial, as well as the repercussions of establishing a Jewish homeland in Israel, through his depiction of a Nazi-hunter's tragic journey. Adolf Eichmann was a Nazi war criminal who conceived genocide as the "final solution" for European Jews and others, leading to the deaths of six million Jews and five million prisoners of war. After escaping the Allies in 1945, he hid for years in Germany before moving to Argentina in 1950 using false papers. In 1960, Mossad, Israel's intelligence agency captured him, and he was tried and hanged in Israel in 1962.

Despite his clear guilt, negative responses worldwide to the Eichmann trial and verdict inspired Holocaust misinterpretations and even denials.

Eichmann's death penalty was condemned by some as barbaric or ineffectual. In Israel, however, the verdict had widespread support and was seen not only as "the embodiment of human justice," but also as evidence that Israel had overcome "the fate of Diaspora Jewry—only in their sovereign state were the Jewish people able to capture Eichmann, put him on trial before Israeli judges in full accordance with the law, and execute him" (Mikel-Arieli, 94). South African Nationalists faced a complex situation in terms of allegiances. To condemn the Holocaust and anti-Semitism could be interpreted as indirect support of anti-apartheid movements. So, they "mobilized the world struggle against anti-Semitism for its own ends by representing anti-Semitism and what it perceived as communist anti-apartheid sentiments as two dangerous phenomena to be condemned" (Mike-Arieli, 99). The situation perpetuated many South African Jews' silence regarding apartheid.

The Guilt Merchants is set in this complex moral and political context and several years before the Six-Day War, where Harwood examines the issues of crime, punishment, retribution, and revenge raised by the Eichmann trial and also complicates the repercussions of establishing a Jewish homeland in Israel through his depiction of a Nazi-hunter's tragic journey.

Known as the "wandering Jews," Sidnitz, who has worked as a Nazi hunter for sixteen years, hopes to capture Brullach, an infamous Nazi responsible for killing at least 1,500 Jews a day, and take him to Israel for trial. The task brings him to El Pueblo, Argentina, and the home of Cordonez and his wife Anna, both of whom are Jewish, she a recent convert. They are convinced that Brullach is being held in a shack owned by Anido. Anido is Jewish and so observant that it embarrasses Cordonez, who says that his behavior brings too much attention to their Jewishness in the predominantly Catholic town. There are so few Jews in the town that they have to take Anido's wife's body to another town for religious services and burial because there are not enough Jews to create the minyan necessary for such observances. Further, Anido's son, who is gay, has received no Jewish training and momentarily thinks about converting to Catholicism because the young man he desires is Catholic.

What Sidnitz and the townspeople discover is that Anido, part Jewish, is the killer Brullach, who has been keeping this secret from the town for many years. Sidnitz uncovers the truth by breaking into his private quarters, a shack removed from his home and filled with pro-Nazi memorabilia and recorded speeches that he has been listening to over the years and which prompted Cordonez to assume that Sidnitz was hiding a Nazi in the shack. Of course, there is no other Nazi except Anido/Brullach, a self-hating Jew who idolized Hitler's Germany: "I killed the Jews. . . . I hate them. . . . It's their blood that poisons me. . . . We are Germans. . . . They are our enemies" (*Guilt Merchants*, 181). Enamored with the Reich, Anido/Brullach expurgates his self-hatred on innocent Jews.

Anido/Brullach, however, has some kind of conscience or at least a kind budgetary understanding of the afterlife. He knows that his actions have consequences. He experiences, if not guilt, then fear of retribution, so he seeks conversion to Catholicism, which offers the promise of forgiveness and grace no matter the offense. But even the priest, who does not know about Anido's identity, recognizes that Anido's motives are more selfish than spiritual. He does not seek forgiveness, only an existential "get out of jail free card" that he thinks Catholicism offers.

However, Anido is not the only one guilty of past sins, and the novel illustrates that we are all, if not guilty, then complicit at least. Harwood complicates the establishment of a Jewish homeland in Israel here. Sidnitz recalls that the need for justice prompted his desire to become a Nazi-hunter. However, his military service in the Middle East only brought further injustice. He says, "what we were doing to them had been done to us a thousand times and there is a terrible vengeance in that. . . . We were the dispossessed dispossessing" (177).

But it is not just Sidnitz who is also guilty. When he confronts Anido/Brullach with his crimes, Anido/Brullach reminds Sidnitz of the sins Jews have committed throughout history. In this way, the novel complicates the easy and simplistic quest for retribution and revenge. We are all "guilt merchants" seeking justification for our actions and revenge on those who harm us.

Cordonez, however, breaks this deadlock of ambivalence in the victimization game, and poses the reality of punishment in this complex situation. He asks Anido/Brullach: "Where can you go? You destroy yourself. From the four corners of the earth Jews will come and spit on you! . . . You're doomed. . . . You're cursed! Cursed in the name of God" (187). Since Anido/Brullach carries his own punishment, as we have seen through his pathetic life in the small town, his offenses do not require trials or human justice—his life is enough punishment.

Sidnitz concludes similarly and undergoes a tragic transformation. He became a Nazi-hunter to exact punishments, but he also perpetuated injustices. Refusing to be a "guilt merchant" any longer, he leaves the small town and Brullach. With natural retribution in place, the novel veers toward a completely secular ending. But in the last scenes, Anido/Brullach's son asks Sidnitz to help him become a proper Jew. Rather than escaping his legacy, the son embraces the faith and heritage his father loathed. Sidnitz promises to contact a rabbi from the adjoining town to help with religious instruction.

While justice and retribution occur differently than expected, and Sidnitz no longer sees situations in morally dichotomous ways, the novel leaves room for religion and faith. The novel suggests, however, that we may need to readjust our understanding. In the end, as Sidnitz enters the adjoining town, leaving the land of the guilt merchants, the taxi driver says to him, "Come on, señor. You're in the land of the living" (188).

Though the novel was a success, Harwood's editor, Tom Maschler, was not as impressed by this work as Harwood had hoped. He recommended that Harwood focus on novels about the "Jewish soul," not because he was Jewish but "as someone who loves that kind of writing" (Robinson, 89). Robinson reports that Harwood was furious and did not write a novel for another five years because, Robinson surmises, the editor devalued Harwood. But given Harwood's sometimes ambivalent relationship to his Jewish heritage, particularly early in his career, the anecdote might reflect his unwillingness to be slated as a "Jewish author," rather than a "great author," a perspective that would change as he continued to write and find his strengths as a writer and his commitment to writing about the Holocaust.

Harwood turned his attention to working on films such as *A High Wind in Jamaica* and *Arrivederci, Baby!* (Robinson, 89). The redirection paid off in several ways. *The Guilt Merchants* caught the attention of Elizabeth Taylor and Richard Burton who bought the film rights, giving Harwood enough money to focus on his other literary pursuits (Robinson, 104).

The Girl in Melanie Klein

Ronald Harwood's *The Girl in Melanie Klein* (1969) does not exhibit the tragic patterns evidenced in his other novels; instead, it uses the popular mental illness genre and comedy to explore the generally tragic subject matter of mental illness. As cultural and sexual mores changed during the sixties, so did the treatment for mental illness. The era marked a shift from institutionalization to new drug treatment therapies. Many artists used mental illness to critique a society gone mad, not its citizens. Unlike works such as *Snake Pit* (1948), which depicted mental illness as torment and its treatment hospitals even worse, for example, works such as Ken Kesey's *One Flew Over the Cuckoo's Nest* (1962) and the film *The King of Hearts* (1966) depicted insanity as a reasonable response to a dysfunctional world. So, too, in Harwood's *Klein*.

Harwood calls his sanitarium the "Nest," perhaps as a nod to the Kesey novel, but also perhaps to highlight a plot built like a set of Russian nesting dolls. If there is a hero, it is Hugo, whose attempts to get his writing career off the ground sound remarkably like Harwood's. He, like Harwood, is learning to type by writing, but in Hugo's case an autobiography, not a novel. As Hugo describes his life and talents, he mentions his brief career as an actor, which can only be described as Harwoodesque:

> Having thus discovered my talent for speaking on stage I decide to become an actor: small parts at first and at last, too, I'm afraid: tours and repertory and summer seasons in the rain. I am still convinced that, given the right opportunities, I could have been a great, worldwide success. But I was too versatile, too gifted, too—dare I say it?—too clever to be an actor. I had the lyricism of Gielgud, the naturalism of du Maurier, the power of Wolfit, the appearance of Henry Ainley and the gaiety of Ralph Lynn but I never played a part bigger than Oswald in *King Lear*. (*Girl in Melanie Klein*, 38)

Hugo's compatriots are Wassler, who thinks he is Hugo's "wing commander" and follows Hugo's orders precisely, and Nora, who thinks she is Queen Elizabeth. Conflict ensues when the three, who have been benignly neglected for years, have to deal with a new director, aptly named Dr. Lipschitz. Lipschitz has a distinguished professional record and is determined to treat his patients. Harwood increases the conflict by bringing in a new patient, Niobe, as well, a catatonic schizophrenic.

According to the inmates, one of Lipschitz's most unreasonable changes to the institution is to number the patient rooms. Wassler confronts the director: "[W]e refuse to use numbers when referring to our rooms. I am not in number 4, I am in Ernest Jones. And Hugo is in Karl Abraham and Nora in Anna Freud!" Then casually he turned to Niobe. "Don't worry, my dear, you're not in number 6, you're in Melanie Klein" (35). Hence, the title. Dr. Lipschitz may be trained in new psychiatric methods, but he knows nothing about Melanie Klein, so he does some research. The work comes in handy when he experiences impotence during his affair with a nurse. Unable to have sex, they argue about Klein just to pass the time.

While the doctor is distracted, the inmates break into his office and they discover that he is not the director, but a patient. His mentor, the legitimate doctor Gerald Ogilvie Davis (initials G-O-D), has sent Lipschitz to the Nest to recover from a nervous breakdown. With this mystery successfully solved, the inmates turn their attention to Niobe, who has been institutionalized for unnamed reasons they are determined to unearth. The inmates escape by stealing G-O-D's car, but they are caught and recommitted to different, more secure institutions.

Harwood ends the novel neatly and comically. Niobe, who has been flirting with Hugo throughout the novel, decides to end the romance and become a nun; G-O-D is knighted for his work, and so becomes Sir G-O-D; and Hugo continues typing. Harwood's novel concludes "qs89nw-27/8=hhhsgtzry-uivsb(h&55dfknan end" (182). A clear departure from Harwood's usual tragic perspective, the novel nonetheless takes a comic romp through tragic territory, the precarious division between reason and madness.

Articles of Faith

Following the amusing *Klein*, Harwood wrote the epic novel *Articles of Faith* (1973), which charts the histories of two South African families, the Dutch Hennings and the British Thompsons. Scandals bracket the novel, one in 1794 and the other in the early 1970s, and both involve white men from important families who conduct romantic relationships with non-white women. The novel is expansive and ambitious, and it includes much detail about non-white communities and their struggles.

At the time Harwood wrote *Articles of Faith*, apartheid was at its peak. Cities were segregated, with non-whites having been moved to "homelands" where they had few resources and no power, and resistance was squelched whenever possible. Classrooms, textbooks, and universities presented only white history. Harwood's historical novel offered an alternative viewpoint to the then accepted history of his home country. Written prior to the Soweto uprising of 1976 but anticipating the growing interest in a more accurate and inclusive South African history that began in "the mid-1970s" (Worden, 1), Harwood's novel presents the non-white situation sympathetically and, in some detail, while "Afrikaner nationalist writers tended to laud the achievements of the trekkers and their descendants, while English-speaking historians placed emphasis on the role of the British government and settlers. Indigenous South Africans played only a background role in these versions of the past" (Worden, 2). In this way, *Articles of Faith* served as a means of apartheid resistance, exposing the reality of racial oppression in South Africa from its very beginnings. Its expansiveness underscores the persistence and systemic nature of racism and, at the end of the novel, anti-Semitism.

The novel's premise is the real challenge for Harwood and his tragic vision. While many characters in the narrative represent tragic heroism in traditional ways, such as rebelling against the status quo, immoral laws, or physical violence, the unnamed narrator presents an unusual tragic hero: an archivist and writer. As he learns the truth about his family, he, like George Washington September, learns the truth about his country. One of the results of this narrative strategy is that it places the novel's readers in the same position as the narrator. Through reading, not necessarily through physical prowess, the narrator does not merely witness events, he experiences the tragic. He discovers his country's rootedness in oppression and how it was perpetuated and integrated into every aspect of South African life. With this revelation, he faces a decision, transforms, and decides to fight his country's current iteration of racial oppression. He will be neither a victim nor a perpetrator, but a true Harwood outsider.

The novel inspires audiences as they also read about and discover the realities of South African history and systemic racism, a project that was not only necessary in the apartheid era but, as Worden argues, remains necessary today:

> The ending of apartheid has not yet produced a new version of national history akin to those that emerged in many post-colonial countries. Although Black Consciousness intellectuals . . . called for the re-writing

of South African history from an Africanist perspective, this has only taken place to a limited extent. . . . A key reason for this is that the post-apartheid government consciously sought to be reconciliatory and include rather than to promote an exclusively Africanist version of the South African past. (4)

The novel opens in the 1970s with its narrator and hero, the bastard son of a Jewish lawyer and a rebellious woman from an influential family. Thus already an outsider, the narrator is also a criminal, having been charged with violating the Immortality Act, enacted in 1950 at the beginning of the apartheid era, which made illegal marriages and sexual relationships between whites and non-whites, including Indian, African, and Black. But as the narrator's family lawyer informs him, it was not that he slept with the Bantu woman that resulted in charges; it is that he sent her love letters, even quoting Shakespeare, to express his love.

The novel's representation of writing is ironic here. First, his letter is, in fact, what brings the charges. As is made painfully clear through numerous excruciating rape scenes, South African white men, from the moment they landed in South Africa, had sex with, sexually abused, and raped non-white women all the time, so much so that they created a new mixed race, "Coloureds," who, as the novel later points out, were considered "untaught, ill-used, neglected," and treated even worse than enslaved people (*Articles of Faith*, 182).

The narrator here treats the Bantu woman like a white woman, romancing and finally loving her like a human being, not an object. The novel makes it clear that it is easier to dispatch unwanted children from such liaisons than to eliminate written evidence of emotional connection between the races. Until the narrator's family finds the note, or the prosecutor releases it, the narrator is under arrest, not for having sex with a non-white but for having the audacity to treat her as an equal.

But the power of writing works both ways. As a result of this charge, the narrator is placed under house arrest, leading him to find the family's documents—written evidence of systemic racism and of his family's secrets. Writing led to his incarceration, but it also leads to his discovery of the truth as he writes the novel we are reading, documenting his findings, discoveries, and revelations.

Harwood and his hero highlight the critical nature of the archivist's work and of understanding ancestry, not by invoking white Western heroes and their mythic journeys but by highlighting African heroes:

> In the religion of the Abantu there is a belief that the dead go on living underground just as they had done here on earth. The place they inhabit is called Kuzimu in Swahili, and you may reach it by following a porcupine or mole. In Uganda it happened to Mpobe, the hunter, and to the Zulu, Ucama, and also to one of the Wairamba. (*Articles of Faith*, 4)

Like these heroes, the unnamed narrator "is gathering together the strands of which he himself is made" (10). By beginning the novel in this way, Harwood highlights his determination to tell a different South African history.

Set during a period of colonial expansion and indigenous dislocation, as well as the final years of the multinational corporation, the Dutch East India Company, the Henning story starts several years before, in 1794, in the Cape of Good Hope, South Africa, a company town ruled by white Christians, most of whom are greedy and corrupt and all of whom perceive the indigenous populations as substandard threats who need to be corralled, killed, or abused.

Johannes Henning, like the narrator, has fallen in love with a Khoikhoi woman, Alala, and fathered a son, Adam. He is charged with "blasphemy, incitement to riot, and other grievous offenses" (26). To highlight the "unnatural nature" of the crime, reports of nude dances on an altar and Satanic rituals embroider the case. As a result, he is found guilty of violating the company policies and banished to Amsterdam, but he sickens and dies at sea.

Like the narrator, Henning, is an outsider. As a young man, he had decided to be a preacher, but while working with another pastor, he impulsively sleeps with his daughter, who forces him into a loveless marriage that produces two children, Daniel and Sybille. Inspired by a young preacher who preaches that everyone should be taught the Gospel, even non-whites, Henning decides to go to South Africa with his family. There, he becomes tempted by complacency. Isolated from his family, who remain at the Cape, he finds acceptance and celebrity in a small town. Seduced by busyness and his desire for acceptance, which is gladly given as long as he focuses on the colonists, not the non-whites, Henning succumbs to what he describes as the "blind eye" disease: "It is a creeping paralysis of the spirit, which, once attacked, seems to bask in its own inertia. There is no cure, except the conscious of will, and that can be hard to come by" (86). After a brief encounter with renegades and a few alarming interactions with enslaved people being starved to death by their owners, Henning realizes that he has lost his way. He recommits to his original purpose: ministering to all people, not just whites.

The novel, however, challenges this decision. It is not enough to minister to non-whites; freedom and equity are also necessary. Henning's relationship to Alala illustrates the reality of integrated relationships, but it is not enough, and even it is unsuccessful.

The novel does not end with Henning's death at sea, however. Harwood instead suggests that the flicker of belief in equality established by Henning may have continued with his daughter, Sybille, who, understanding the reality of his marriage, sympathizes with his situation. Before he leaves, her father asks her to search for her half-brother, Adam, and she agrees.

Sybille's journey, also heroic, leads her into the non-white world of South Africa, where she learns alternative healing techniques and overcomes the South African "blindness." While she expands her understanding of humanity, saying, "God listens in any language," she also casts herself in the role of outsider by voicing such sentiments among the whites. Harwood here even takes the opportunity to ridicule his own obsession with the British, shared with many South Africans at the time, particularly in the Jewish community, noting how Sybille felt the "chasm between herself and the [white] others who were of the opinion that God being an Englishman had difficulty understanding even Dutch, let along Xhosa" (*Articles of Faith*, 201).

During her travels, she meets Michael Thompson and not only heals his illness but introduces him to whites who believe in racial equality. During the period covered in this section of the novel, South Africa gains independence. Michael's daughter, Victoria, moves the story into the twentieth century, bringing the two families together by marrying David Henning, the son of Daniel, who had become a slave trader and "scallywag" (346). His money, however, enabled David to become a "scion of Cape aristocracy" (346). Their well-educated daughter, Anna, resists the traditional roles laid out for women, and eventually she has an affair with Leonard Levine, a young Jewish lawyer with communist leanings. He is tried for his communist beliefs in an attempt to destroy him and keep him from making a living true to his progressive beliefs. The case is corrupted by inequities on many levels—white versus non-white, Jew versus non-Jew—and it eventually breaks Levine down. He denies fathering Anna's child, the narrator; marries another woman; and sets up his law practice. Anna dies years before her son's incarceration. Once again, Harwood demonstrates that when systemic oppression exists, there can be no justice at the individual level. The unjust system poisons the entire culture. Trying to help his son, Levine tells him to leave South Africa, because he will always be an outsider:

> You don't fit here. You are neither a Christian nor a Jew, neither Dutch nor English. You know what it's like to be apart. The vitality of our society depends on adherence to one group or another. Even the Bantu hate the Indians, and the Indians hate the Coloureds, and the Coloureds hate the Bantu. We live in separate pockets and you belong in none. That's not your fault. You did not ask to be born that way. (483)

Not only does the speech solidify the narrator's position as outsider, but it is clear that Levine, overcome by the trial and the machinations of an anti-Semitic community, has compromised himself, he "has allowed his aspirations to be swamped by his ambitions" (483).

If we miss the symbolic power of Levine, a communist turned compromiser, Harwood makes it clear that this is a particularly Jewish trait and strategy. After a sweeping history of Judaism, Harwood concludes that because the Jews were always persecuted, they discovered "[t]heir unique gift, the ability to ponder and worship the mystery of God's nature without for a single moment neglecting the ways of man . . . . [T]he Jewish talent to straddle heaven and earth, to balance with such apparent ease the tightrope between Jehovah and Mammon, was to cause them as much sorrow as it did joy" (367). Embodying this philosophy and highlighting the need for a comfortable life, Levine leaves his son to reflect upon this choice and opportunity.

While *Kirkus Reviews* praised the novel as a "generational story" with well-defined characters, the review faulted Harwood's homiletic style and stolid tone. The novel's conclusion, however, challenges the easy solutions the *Kirkus* posits. Harwood has persuasively presented a negative view of apartheid, but he leaves to his characters the responsibility to respond to it. Beaten down by the system, Levine chooses complicity. Newly informed about the atrocities committed by his family and country, his son does not embody the role of a conquering political hero. He chooses instead to find his faith not in religion, one of the major perpetrators of inequities in his country, but in the possibility of change. As he explains to his father, referencing Levine's trial and loss:

> I, like you, am not the stuff martyrs are made of. And I do not for a moment believe that by remaining here I will make one jot of difference to anything, nor do I believe I will affect any other human being. . . . But I choose to remain for my own sake, an act, as I have said, of atonement. To alter the collective will, to bring about change, needs a faith stronger than Christ's. I will work for my own conversion. (486)

Such a conclusion is far from simplistic.

By keeping the narrator anonymous, he remains a cipher, suggesting one means of resisting the extreme divisions tearing the country and its people apart. The empty set, far from being weak, is powerful in its openness. Unfettered by "articles of faith," the unnamed narrator is free to consider, respond to, and create alternatives never considered by the two entrenched and opposing views. The novel concludes by offering a new kind of tragic hero, one who does not have the answers but instead awaits them, suggesting that a race of nobodies, a race affiliated with neither the white nor the non-white side, might be best suited to solve the divisions in South Africa and the world.

Genoa Ferry

With *Genoa Ferry* (1977), Harwood continues his investigation on the efficacy of religion and faith to address the problems he raises and, once again, leaves the questions he raises unanswered. The novel also challenges simplistic binary divisions of people and politics. Harwood's experiment in genre was described by Newgate Callendar in his 1977 *New York Times* review as "part murder mystery . . . part travelogue . . . partly a novel of ideas," and concluding it was an "unusually gripping piece" (15). Since the novel's events take place near the time that Menachim Begin became prime minister of Israel, Anwar el-Sadat began breaking with other Arab nations, and Israel was recognized as an official state, reading *Genoa Ferry* in the post–9/11 era not only elicits uncanny resonances but also offers a global perspective on the Middle East at this time.

The novel includes one of Harwood's outsider heroes on a journey toward self-discovery that leads, if not him, then his readers, to a greater understanding of global politics, intrigue, and faith. His hero ultimately makes the right choice, but he is unsure why and so continues to search, leaving us to question the novel's various conclusions.

Set in Libya, *Ferry* begins with a murder. Fisher, who has traveled to meet his estranged half-brother, Gerald, to make amends and reestablish their relationship, discovers that Gerald committed suicide the day before by driving his car into the sea. The trouble is, Gerald did not drive. And so the journey through the exotic, unnamed city begins, with Fisher becoming an unlikely and unwilling investigator and ultimately the story's hero.

Within the fabric of a noir thriller, Harwood embroiders the tragic. Fisher is a flawed hero. He has had an affair with an underage student at his school and lost his job. He ostensibly contacts Gerald to reconcile, and perhaps as a kind of penance for his personal mistakes, but as we learn, he is actually only there to borrow money.

He encounters a mysterious North African Muslim town where moral ambiguity reigns, like Casablanca or Thebes. Muslims, Christians, Japanese, and mystics practice their rituals, but the rules of the game change as fiercely as the *ghibli*, the area's hot summer winds.

Fisher enters this moral morass and quickly becomes entangled in a terrorist plot and a sexual relationship with a young man who is eventually killed for his political affiliations, not his sexuality. In the novel, sexual behavior causes no problems among the terrorists or the authorities. Locals offer to help Fisher meet even more men for sex: "Here . . . we would never deport a man [for homosexual sexual behavior]. Half the male population would have to live elsewhere. . . . But for drinking alcohol we may deport a man" (*Genoa Ferry*, 122). Women, at least British women, live similarly. Paola, the British ambassador's wife, has had affairs with Gerald and many other men, all of whom abused her, as did Gerald. At the end of the novel she has a nervous breakdown brought on by this mistreatment.

As Fisher investigates his half-brother's death, he learns that Gerald had aligned himself with a group of Muslim terrorists planning to bomb Fisher's London school if the British government does not release two of its members from prison. The terrorists are hoping that the British will reject the offer, so that they can pay them back in blood for years of mistreatment.

Clearly, Gerald is a traitor, but he also betrays his brother by volunteering his services to the terrorists, assuring them that Fisher will be a perfect patsy who will transport the bomb into England and identifying Fisher's school as a suitable target. The motives behind this Cain and Abel relationship stem from their parents. Gerald and his mother were revolutionaries, while Fisher's father was a staunch British patriot who always stood for "the King's speech on Christmas Day" (200), and Fisher followed his political leanings.

As Fisher struggles to find the truth about Gerald and the revolutionaries, he makes personal realizations, concluding that "Gerald has always stood for chaos and death, and I stand for something else" (148). But what that something is remains initially unclear. When one of the terrorists asks, "Are you a God man?" Fisher questions himself, thinking "he should have the courage to answer—but what?" (150).

Though he cannot answer the existential questions, he has no qualms about trying to stop the bomb plot. He attempts to warn the Embassy about the terrorists, but they dismiss him, and the Muslims quickly take him hostage to prevent any other attempts at thwarting their plans. Betrayed, alone, frightened, and disillusioned, Fisher reflects:

> He wished he could pray. How pleasant, he thought, to subscribe to the infallible order of things. How more courageous he would be now if he was able to rely on the well-trodden path of doctrine, worship, entreaty, reward, and punishment. His cowardice, he acknowledged, sprang from his lack of trust in his own resources.... Why was it so hard to stand up and confess that I am something more than a scavenger microbe fouling the Earth? And he understood dimly that he never fully entered another's life only because he had never entered his own. (210)

Fallen from grace, destined to wander, and faced with a moral decision, Fisher does not discover a simple moral code. Instead, he realizes that he has not been a participant in his own life. This realization inspires him to do what he can to stop the bombing.

In a dramatic conclusion, he escapes the terrorists and heads to London via the Genoa Ferry. The terrorists abandon their plans because they cannot move forward "until we find out what's happened to Fisher" (217). With that open-ended conclusion, Harwood's unlikely hero simultaneously completes and continues his search. And like many tragedies, the solutions to the moral questions raised in the novel remain unanswered and highlight the inadequacy of all the religious traditions represented in the Middle Eastern city to respond to moral dilemmas.

César and Augusta

At the end of *The Genoa Ferry*, as Fisher oscillates between reflection and self-pity, a blind pianist plays a Beethoven sonata (*Genoa Ferry*, 204). The music moves the previously disaffected Fisher to action. The role of the sonata is one of Harwood's first references to the transformative power of music, a theme that will continue throughout his career. In *César and Augusta*, which takes the struggles of César Franck for its focus, music no longer plays a supporting role: it is the novel's subject. The subject is unsurprising, given Harwood's passion for and knowledge of music. During a 2010 interview, however, Harwood also explained that music is an effective and dramatic trope for artistic creation. Scenes of writers at their desks do not provide the drama, intrigue, and potential for spectacle that music does. Seeing a writer receive bad reviews is nothing compared to a composer whose works inspire thundering applause or raucous catcalls.

Kirkus Reviews hailed Harwood's first foray into using music as a theme as a "bohemian day-outing to Fontainebleau by the Paris composers" and described it "as vivid as a Manet painting," but faults its almost clichéd theme, romantic betrayal in the face of artistic ambition ("*César and Augusta*," Kirkus). While romance and desire propel the plot, there is more to this novel than romance. By examining the novel through Harwood's tragic perspective, we see a tragic hero, blinded by his monomaniacal pursuit of music, succeed at a significant cost. Franck is talented, selfish, and weak, but he creates a masterpiece. The novel does not excuse his behavior but presents it as one of the potential pitfalls of artistic creation: the inability of love, particularly domestic love, to coexist with the pursuit of art.

The novel begins by depicting Franck as a washed-out composer and musician. This is, of course, communicated by his competitor in love and music, Camille Saint-Saëns. Saint-Saëns desires a new singer, Augusta Holmes, who wants to learn to compose. Saint-Saëns recommends Franck through underhanded compliments: "He . . . is a failure as a composer (awful sanctimonious religious works, awful) . . . but he is a first-class teacher of composition" (Harwood, *César and Augusta*, 4).

And to a certain extent, the assessment is accurate. At the play's opening, Franck's difficult life seemed to be coming to a mediocre end. According to Laurence Davies's *César Franck and His Circle*, Franck's life was fraught with difficulties. Born in Belgium in 1882, he and his brother were groomed to work as musicians to support their domineering father who dreamed that his sons would succeed by acquiring wealthy private patrons. Patronage, however, was going out of fashion, and so, thanks in part to his father's aspirations, the historical Franck was out of touch with his cultural context: "[Franck's] entry into the sycophantic world of private patronage coincided so exactly with that world's decline" (Davies, 37). Franck's personality, too, was ill-suited to currying favor, much to his wife's consternation.

While Davies's biography hints at marital difficulties, Harwood's novel makes them explicit. Franck's decision to marry Félicité, rather than her cousin Claire, and the couple's differing temperaments, resulted in a loveless union. The stress becomes so great that it affects Franck's ability to compose. He wakes every morning not with music in his head but with silence.

Harwood's Franck channels his disappointment and frustrations into teaching. He gains an exceptional reputation, so much so that his competitor compliments him, and his students are known as "his circle." Many go on to write brilliant compositions of their own and later repay him through their admiration and support; among them, in real life and in fiction, were Vincent d'Indy, Ernest Chausson, Louis Vierne, and Henri Duparc.

In Harwood's novel, Franck refuses to accept Augusta Holmes as a student because she is a woman, so she disguises herself as a man, performs, wins a spot at the Franck table, and then reveals herself to Franck, who falls in love with her. Her charisma tempts all. Even those composers who think she is mad agree that "where Augusta is, there is life" (96).

Bewitched, Franck imagines "Augusta naked. Augusta, naked, followed him into his study, down the boulevard . . . . Augusta naked pressed her awesome breasts against his lips even as he prayed for peace and quiet in

Sainte-Clothilde. Augusta, naked, haunted him by day and night" (*César and Augusta*, 107). With superb comic timing, Harwood has Franck's son give him a copy of Kant's *Critique of Pure Reason*, and both Franck, and perhaps Harwood, conclude, "[T]here is no pure reason in the inner world: no matter how well ordered the brain, thoughts themselves were subject to a higher law" (107). For Franck in the novel, this law is the law of Holmes and of art. Love and creation do not follow logic, social mores, or conventions—at least for a while.

The reference to Kant's book also highlights the two opposing views on the nature of art that Franck and Holmes embody. Franck and his circle believe in "pure music," that higher law Kant refers to. Much like Wolfit, the other actor-managers, and Harwood, they believe that art transcends differences and communicates to our shared humanity, reflecting the great highs and lows of the human condition. The actual Holmés (she had changed the family spelling), who was born in Paris, perhaps of Irish heritage, suffered prejudice for both her ethnicity and her gender; but for Harwood she represents those who believe that art expresses individual culture or experience. Her work would not reflect the universal; rather through it she sought to create an art form that reflected her as a woman and an outsider. Franck and Holmés represented opposite poles in their era's culture wars.

Harwood's novel emphasizes the manner in which Franck integrated both the universal and the specific in his famous interdisciplinary Piano Quintet. He attributes Franck's success to his interactions with Augusta, which prompted him to experiment with his musical compositions. In the Harwood novel, as well as life, the piece reflects Franck's desire for Augusta, creating a musical copulation obvious to all listeners. A scandal erupted during its original performance. Saint-Saëns, who saw the piece as a threat to his relationship with Augusta, stormed off the stage, refusing to shake Franck's hand and leaving behind the score that Franck had dedicated to him. Félicité Franck intuited the music's inspiration, telling Franck, "[Y]ou have committed adultery in public, Franck. You've brought disgrace on us with that obscene, depraved work" (*César and Augusta*, 261). She demands they leave Paris to break up the relationship with Augusta and escape the ridicule and gossip that followed this erotic composition. Years later, the real-life Félicité concluded, "His organ pieces are everything that is admirable but that quintet! Ugh!" (Bartel). Marked by its emotional and erotic power, the piece, according to the critics, signals a shift in Franck's work and is considered one of his best.

Though Harwood's dedication of the novel to his wife, Natasha, claims that the work is a love story, it is not the usual kind. There is no happily ever after, and as the details reveal themselves, Franck's motives become clear. He is passionate about music. All else is secondary or a means to his musical ends. He may have desired Holmes, but she also served a purpose—to reignite his passion for music.

In a twist, the temptress Augusta becomes another woman done wrong. Following the concert, Augusta proposes that Franck leave his wife and work with her. But Franck, who has seemed the victim of a loveless marriage and an overbearing father, asserts his agency and refuses. He ostensibly abandons her because of his family commitments or from cowardice. But as the novel ends it is clear that it is all about the music. Prior to Augusta, Franck woke to silence; after their work together, he awakens to "ear-splitting" sounds and music, "creation was the pleasure, not the love. To survive was all. He felt somehow whole. He regretted, but only in passing, the pain he would cause. His music came first.... Augusta. She had divined the spring. She had served her purpose" (266).

Franck's romantic journey is an artistic and surprisingly cold-hearted one. When allowed to renew his talent, inspired by Augusta's sexuality, he proceeds with the egotistical ferocity of a tragic hero. He conquers his musical doldrums and reestablishes himself as a musical powerhouse. In his wake, however, he leaves behind lovers, family, and even his own non-artistic desires. The real and fictional Augusta, like Dido, is left to wander through a dismal musical afterlife. She has a success, "Ode Triumphal," but Harwood presents her at the novel's end as aged, alcoholic, and impoverished. (The real Augusta Holmés, however, lived a more satisfactory personal and professional life.) In a final ironic twist, Harwood depicts Augusta's encounter with Saint-Saëns at Franck's funeral, where he gives her the quintet manuscript that Franck gave to him the night of the infamous first performance. Taking the score, she hears the music and feels "loved" (277). In his first examination of art and artistic creation, Harwood neither idealizes nor excuses the weaknesses of art or its artist-outsiders but instead illustrates the power of both. Art requires sacrifices, selfishly devours time, family, and self, but it can also offer rewarding and beautiful masterpieces.

Home

In his dedication of *Home* (1993), his personal version of *War and Peace*, to Lady Antonia Fraser and her husband, Harold Pinter, Harwood implores the couple to "do the decent thing and take full responsibility for having encouraged me." Inspired by a visit to Moscow in 1983 for a production of his hit *The Dresser*, Harwood began investigating his and his wife's shared Russian roots. While Natasha's family descended from the aristocracy, notably Catherine the Great, Harwood's Jewish family were persecuted peasants trying to find safe haven in an anti-Semitic world. As the novel progresses, the fictional versions of Natasha and Harwood, named Natalya and Harrison Wilde because of Harwood's love for Oscar Wilde, find one another, offering if not a happy ending, at least a "kind of justice" in a world seemingly set on separating them and people like them. Here, the movement of the families and of time itself follow a tragic trajectory.

In the prologue, the Wildes, who are visiting Russia because of Harrison's play, are about to enter Natalya's ancestral home, from which her mother's family was forcibly removed during the Russian Revolution. Some locals not only remember the family but inform her that their peasant family gave refuge to her aristocratic family. One neighbor, who is Jewish, says to Harrison, "In this country is not possible a Jew to marry aristocrat.... Yes, glorious irony, Jew like you make this day possible. I tell you, my friend, today is a kind of justice" (7). Harrison reflects on this observation: "What anguished decisions had to be made, brutal orders obeyed, sufferings endured, catastrophes experienced to allow her, a descendant of Catherine the Great, and him the descendant of wandering Jews, to make this journey together" (8).

The novel presents those decisions in subsequent chapters, alternating between the two families. We open with Harrison's Jewish ancestors, the Wildnowitzs, who are trying to escape the Russian pogroms in 1911. One family member, Laban, a professional mourner, a *nakhtwatcher*, proposes that they stage the death of one of his brother's three sons, Isaiah, who will later become Harrison's father. The death allows them to escape Russia with the ruse that they were going to bury the body elsewhere, but Harrison notes that it was the horse manure in the cart that made the plan successful. It smelled so bad that the guards let them go. "They're going to die anyway," says one guard presciently (21). Natalya's family, in contrast, experiences further promotion in their already prestigious and wealthy positions. Of course, the Russian Revolution changes that.

While Harrison's relatives successfully leave Russia, they have difficulty finding work in Warsaw, where refugees compete for jobs. Some decide to try Germany, while Harrison's family chooses South Africa. In her research on Harwood's family, Danielle Lockwood suggests that the decision was part of an advertising campaign made by Donald Currie, "the shipping magnate," who "eased the passage of immigrants from the Pale to South Africa" (*Without the Past*, 12). There was also the promise of work. The decision to travel to South Africa was auspicious; those who chose to stay in Europe perished during the Holocaust.

Laban, based on one of Harwood's uncles, remained in Europe, thoroughly enjoying his life there, but he later perishes in the Holocaust. This memory haunted Harwood, who found out as a young child what had happened to Laban when watching a newsreel on the death camps. In the novel, Harwood uses the fate of one man to illustrate how much was lost. In addition to his job as a mourner, Laban is a poet, philosopher, and unrepentant womanizer who even seduces grieving widows while performing his role during funerals. He offers Isaiah advice that resonates throughout the novel and illustrates Harwood's keen, dry, and wicked sense of humor. On their wandering life, he tells his nephew, "Remember especially that where a man lives inside himself is the most important address in the world" (*Home*, 155). Other commandments are both wise and funny. He tells Isaiah to keep certain Jewish customs, but warns him, "[D]on't get too involved with God. . . . Think of Him as a rich elderly relative you visit once, twice a year in the hope you'll inherit" (18). He warns him that the goyim advocate loving neighbors a bit too much, but he advocates an "eighty-twenty split" (18). Other maxims include being "decent to parents, but honour you must keep for other things" (19). What should a man honor? According to Laban, who has spent his nights with the dead, "mysteries and unknowable secrets" of the world, art, and culture. As for women, "this is tricky ground. . . . And remember these words: carnal, erotic, passionate, lustful, titillation, lewdness. Please God, one day you'll find out what they mean" (20).

Unfortunately, Laban's codes do not protect him from Hitler. While in Warsaw, Laban meets the love of his life, Europa, a madam in a house of ill-repute, and it is because of her he does not travel to South Africa with his family. The family loses touch with him, and only later, when Isaiah and his young son watch dated newsreels, do they discover he was one of the casualties of the concentration camps. Overwhelmed with grief, Isaiah remembers another piece of advice from Laban, one that helps him overcome his grief and move forward: "Remember that we can change our lives. Fate can be fought. . . . Life is not a curse it is a blessing. So, if life becomes cursed transform it. This can be done" (410). And to a certain extent, the family does so through its time in South Africa.

But one cannot ignore the irony of Laban's situation. Isaiah asks, "Why did he submit to an insane conviction of insanity?" (411). As Harwood depicted systemic racism's effects in his earlier novels, here, too, the culture of systemic anti-Semitism leads to inexplicable behavior, mimicking the absurdity of the totalitarian system. In *Articles of Faith*, apartheid was the focus, but here and elsewhere, Harwood examines the Nazi's systemic oppression.

Given Natalya's family's experiences with communism, her father, Stephan, a non-Jew who sympathizes with the Jewish plight in Western Europe, shares Isaiah's perspective on totalitarianism. During a discussion comparing the Nazis with the communists, Stephan argues that both should be opposed because "one should oppose any system that destroys individual freedom" (388). In a humorous commentary, Harwood notes Stephan's reasonable views "in no time at all" made his friends describe him as "simple-minded" (389). Totalitarian regimes dismiss reason. The revolution, however, allowed Stephan to marry a former aristocrat.

Juxtaposed to Stephan's successful marriage is Isaiah's. Both married above their class, but Isaiah's union was disastrous. Based on Harwood's own parents, these characters stay together out of custom and for the sake of their only child, Harrison. After his father's death, Harrison leaves South Africa to study acting in London. And like Harwood, who changed his name from Horowitz, Harrison changes his name from Wildnowitz to Wilde (429) when he begins his acting career. He meets Natalya, and they fall in love, marry, and have a family.

Publisher's Weekly faulted the book for its expansiveness, calling it "a whirlwind of events, but it's an unmanageable one, with no focus, little strength, and a vast array of characters merging into a colorless mass." Admittedly the novel is ambitious, and the breadth limits the number of details. However, this broad look at the period from 1911 to 1983, nearly the entire twentieth century, offers an impressive overview of Europe and its struggles. Harwood had already offered more details in his plays, such as *A Family* and *Another Time*. But in the epilogue, Harrison contemplates the people, places, and events that not only created Natalya and him but also the forces that brought them together. Was it time, fate, sheer human will, or determination? These are the questions that propel the novel. There may be no hard and fast answers, but the questions represent life at all times, everywhere: the loss, pain, sorrow, joy, life, and death. Given the scale of the project, *Home* has no single tragic hero or occurrence; instead, the novel exposes the tragic purpose that underlies human struggle. The breadth of the project may mute Harwood's tragic vision, but the elegiac strain remains, as does the tragic optimism Harwood employs. At the end of the novel, Harrison and Natalya take some earth from Sobliki, the ancestral family home, to Natalya's mother, the last member of the family born on Russian soil. This gesture serves both to remind us not only of the historical events, as traced in the novel and as lived in the real world, but also to recall us to our own mortality. We are dust, and to dust we shall return. The marriage story, however, suggests a purpose to these events. We may not influence our circumstances, but we have the power of choice: to persist, to behave nobly, and to love boldly.

CHAPTER THREE

THE PLAYS

I hold that the Theatre is absolutely necessary to civilized society.
—Ronald Harwood, "Notes on Theatre"

TRYING TO CHARACTERIZE THE RONALD HARWOOD DRAMATIC CANON IS LIKE herding cats. On the one hand, because he has written so many plays on so many topics, it is both challenging to articulate an overarching statement about his works and unfair to do so because such an enterprise homogenizes the detail of the individual plays. On the other hand, including a detailed discussion of every one of Harwood's major plays would take volumes. Since this is the first significant and comprehensive analysis of his work, my purpose is to highlight Harwood's contributions to encourage further discussion, production, and analysis of his impressive literary output. So I will choose among the many possibilities based on this book's purpose—to introduce Harwood's work and vision to audiences—as well as my own preferences. I will thus limit the number of plays and films discussed, but also attempt to offer guidance to facilitate a greater understanding and appreciation for Harwood's work and dramatic power.

My rationale for limiting the plays is subjective but also practical. First, some plays are not readily available, so those, such as *March Hares* (1964) and *Country Matters* (1969), or his musical *The Good Companions* (1974), are not included. Second, when Harwood returned to theatrical writing in earnest during the 1970s, he did not stop: "Plays are my great love. In the theatre you can have a long debate, on the screen you have to move on"

(Thompson and Sylvester). From that moment on, Harwood used stage plays to develop his original work because "it's a struggle to get a film made. If you write an original screenplay, you have to get a director on board, there's the whole business of raising money. It would be too daunting" (Gritten, 42). Harwood wrote many plays, some of which were not as powerful as those included here or they repeat themes better represented in other plays. Specifically, *Tramway Road* (1984), *Ivanov* (from Chekov, 1989), *Reflected Glory* (1992), and *Equally Divided* (1998) are not included. Instead, only Harwood's most successful plays—or those that should have been successful—are represented here.

Though categorizing Harwood's work is challenging, the subjects of his plays tend to adhere to four major subjects: art, family, apartheid, and the Holocaust. Harwood's plays embody the tragic vision articulated in his biography of Donald Wolfit and in most of his novels.

All contain an unfashionable character who faces challenges and responds to them, often failing, but in doing so either behaves nobly or inspires others to do so. True to tragedy, Harwood claims that no matter what the situation, his works contain individuals "facing up to themselves" (Gidez, "Ronald Harwood," 245). Generally, there are no clear solutions to the dilemmas Harwood weaves. His theatrical Gordian knots are tight, leaving audiences with ambivalent closing scenes to ponder long after the play has ended.

Harwood's own experiences in life and the London theatre fueled his fascination with the ambivalent and inspired him to identify with "unfashionables." When he first arrived in the late 1950s and early 1960s, he did not respond to or create art in the way the fashionable political and absurd theatre movements did. He notes in his introduction to his second volume of plays, "In every way I feel myself to be outside the mainstream of the contemporary theatre. I am, however, often accused of writing well-made plays or West End plays. I take this as a compliment" (*Ronald Harwood: Plays 2*, vii). In later years, he thought his moderate political leanings kept him from success in the London theatre. In a 2016 interview, Harwood admitted that he "loved Osborne," but could not stand his "left-wingery" (qtd. in Nathan). He joked that in the early days, even his good friend Harold Pinter may have been experimenting with drama, but he did not even know the name of the standing prime minister. The joke, of course, alludes to Pinter's shift from an apolitical, experimental artist to a political dramatist and writer in the 1980s. Friendly jabs aside, Harwood was convinced that his politics inhibited his theatrical success, particularly noting the National Theatre's refusal to produce any of his plays based on what they considered his old-fashioned politics (Jacobs).

Like many of his characters, Harwood chose the unfashionable path in his art and politics. He created a political stir when he disapproved of the casting of Glenda Jackson as King Lear. Harwood's defense was the text. Shakespeare wrote it for a man, and the text should be respected. He, like Pinter, believed that the playwright must be a "guardian of the work" (Fullerton). Harwood took this even further by amending his will to prohibit women from playing male roles in his plays, perhaps thinking that Jackson might have her eye on his most famous character, Sir, from *The Dresser* (Nathan). Harwood's stance is consistent with his lifelong defense of the text through his work with International PEN and during writers' strikes, but his adamant refusal to include female performers in male roles is particularly surprising and seems misguided given that he wrote a play, *After the Lions*, about Sarah Bernhardt, a woman who played Hamlet very successfully.

Harwood courted further controversy and unfashionable status through his defense of smoking, something he continued until his death. Many of his plays and screenplays contain barbs against "this ghastly business of telling us how to live." And when an "American academic" wrote a letter asking that no smoking be included in the screenplay for *Oliver Twist*, Harwood "tore it up in a fury" and revised the script to include smoking (Alberge).

Harwood's friends also caused a stir. Richard Fullerton's 2018 interview quotes Harwood for its title: "I only know people in trouble!" His work with Roman Polanski on *The Pianist* may have won him an Oscar, but his loyalty to the film director alienated some. And when he tried to tell a sympathetic story about Harvey Weinstein, who offered to help his dying wife with exceptional experimental health care, he was asked not to tell the story because Weinstein's name was publicity poison. Harwood concluded, "You have to be so politically correct that you don't even say one good thing about anybody who's in trouble" (qtd. in Fullerton).

Whatever one may think about Harwood's stances, in his plays he resists moralizing. He maintained that he "keeps an even hand . . . the job of the writer is not to write propaganda" (Nathan). In other words, placing himself in the role of the audience, he said, "I don't want to be preached at . . . I want to make up my own mind" (qtd. in Jacobs). This attitude informs his personal views as well. He tended to see the good in the sinner, and the rotten in the saint. And he certainly did not want to be preached to regarding his personal habits, such as smoking, eating, and drinking.

In his introduction to *A Night at the Theatre* (1982), a collection of essays he edited, he argued that the theatre has been changed by an academic and, though he did not say it directly, a political approach to theatre. He noted that plays were studied for their messages alone, their themes. Worse, people write "tedious essays" about them (8). He lamented that critics, particularly, have lost their ability to reproduce the production for their readers and discuss the emotional, even subconscious power of performances. The moral of the story is all.

While Harwood eschewed propagandizing or moralizing, his plays do not prohibit analysis. His concept of catharsis was based in critical thinking, or better, critical feeling. His dramatic output illustrates that though he may not be polemical, he tackled political situations, and his characters certainly engage in rational discussions of contemporary and compelling issues. Many such situations are irrational and absurd. But Harwood, as an outsider, presented the matter objectively and allowed audiences to reflect. By withholding solutions to particular dramatic problems, Harwood placed us on the outside. The plays become a mechanism for creating the unfashionable, and through that experience, audiences can consider alternative perspectives.

In the conclusion to his obituary for Harwood, Chris Harris writes, "although he had the regard of the Establishment he never felt part of it. 'I don't think of myself that way,' he said. 'I always think of myself as slightly outside. You can't be more outside than a Jewish immigrant from South Africa, can you?" ("Ronald Harwood Obituary"). And that may be the secret to his appeal: standing on the outside, Harwood created art that challenges us to experience the outsider's viewpoint and from there to consider new alternatives and experiences.

The Ordeal of Gilbert Pinfold

Harwood's first critical dramatic success was an adaptation of Evelyn Waugh's *The Ordeal of Gilbert Pinfold*, which was produced in Manchester in 1977, and then in London in 1979. Based on Evelyn Waugh's breakdown in 1954 and his 1957 novel on the subject, the play charts writer Gilbert Pinfold's break from reality. Harwood's attraction to Waugh is understandable. Waugh was one of the great unfashionables of the day. His early success as a satirist dwindled, and Waugh took unpopular political stands and distanced himself from the Britain's cultural center, London: "For much of his life, Waugh played the role of crank, a man proudly in step with his own time, an arch reactionary and pugnacious opponent of anything 'modern.' Decamping to the English countryside in the late '30s, he set up as a reactionary rural squire whose sensibility was built almost exclusively on a foundation of antipathies" (Price). He was the perfect outlier: "a cutting observer who resided at once inside and outside the mad swirl of drunken chatter, all-night parties, and cynical vanities of a fallen world" (Price).

Buy why did Harwood choose *Pinfold*? Harwood said the play gave him an opportunity to experiment. It "was the first time I was able to free my imagination from the tyranny of the proscenium arch and from the political correctness of the 1960s" (*Ronald Harwood: Plays 2*, viii). The comment highlights the irony of British theatre at this time: while the political theatre pushed the boundaries in terms of content, they tended to retain the traditional theatrical form and even architecture. Absurdists stretched the limits in both directions, so Harwood navigated between the two extremes, offering traditional narratives in experimental spaces like the Royal Exchange Theatre in Manchester. It was a theatre in the round, founded by some of Harwood's colleagues, such as Casper Wrede and Michael Elliott, and included productions by Joe Orton and performers such as Albert Finney and Tom Courtenay, who would work for Harwood throughout his career.

Performance space aside, Harwood may also have identified with Waugh's Pinfold, an exhausted middle-aged artist, and used the play to explore his relationship to art and commerce. Harwood, who had established himself as a novelist, biographer, short story writer, television series writer, screenwriter, and script doctor, may consciously or not have chosen to inaugurate his playwriting career with a play about writing and a writer's life.

Waugh's Pinfold serves as the perfect outsider. Overcome with exhaustion, Pinfold decides to take a restorative cruise and some medications. The name of the ship, the S.S. *Caliban* highlights not only the nightmares to come but also references another artist at the end of his rope and talents, Prospero from Shakespeare's *The Tempest*.

Troubles begin when Pinfold overmedicates himself and drinks too much. He becomes delusional, and the imaginative powers that make him a writer here serve only to heighten his fears and anxieties. The voices and delusions include anti-Semitic and homophobic commentary, which Harwood defends as a side-effect of Pinfold's overdosing. Once he returns home, gets off the meds, and reconciles with his family, Pinfold decides to examine his delusions to gain insight into his psyche. In the end, the mental breakdown, complete with biases, brings him to wellness. James Lynch notes of the novel, "Pinfold emerges victorious from his ordeal first by maintaining his belief that the 'voices' were real—real to him at any rate—and then by establishing control over his imagination through writing his own *Ordeal*" (543).

Harwood's explicit references to Shakespeare—*The Tempest* and *King Lear*—resonate with Harwood's tragic vision expressed in his play. Pinfold, like Lear or Wolfit, a flawed and exhausted character, encounters his limitations and personal demons. He emerges wiser, though not perfect, for he does not acknowledge the impact his wife had on his return to sanity, but returns to his work changed, offering us an experience that will help us with our demons: "I've endured a great ordeal and, unaided, emerged the victor" (258), says Harwood's Pinfold. It is a brutally honest and humorous look at a writer's descent into irrationality that demonstrates that truth, art, and creativity may appear amidst chaos and disorder. But most significantly, the play highlights the dual nature of art. While his writing exhausts Pinfold, it also rejuvenates him. He returns to it after his experiences to process and share these experiences. Writing overcame him, but in the end, it offers, if not answers, at least a direction.

A Family

Based on a true story about one of Harwood's relatives, *A Family* (1993) is the first of many Harwood dramas to explore familial dysfunction like Eugene O'Neill and Sam Shepard. Among these were *Tramway Road* (1993), documenting the effects of apartheid on a family, and its members' reaction when they discover someone they know and love has been reclassified as "Black"; *Reflected Glory* (1992), Harwood's response to his sister's criticism of his use of personal material in *Another Time* (1989); and *Equally Divided* (1999), addressing the question of inheritance, particularly when one sibling bears the burden of parental care without the financial benefits.

A Family, first performed on May 11, 1978, starring theatrical heavyweights Paul Scofield and Harry Andrews, addresses toxic relationships in the context of World War II. Ivan and Emma represent the prewar values of sacrifice and family. Freddie, their only son, has an unnamed illness, caused both by war-induced post-traumatic stress disorder, then commonly termed "shell shock," and by the weight of a festering secret revealed only at the end of the play that he and his father share. Ivan and Emma's daughters struggle with their own families and marriages, notably teenage Paula, who suffers from depression and threatens suicide.

The play suggests an Oedipal conflict between Ivan, the patriarch, and Freddie, his son, attested by references to *King Lear* and *Hamlet*, but in some ways, the play has no tragic hero. Both father and son are too weak or interdependent to function as individuals. Instead, the family itself is flawed, but driven as a heroic entity by its search for meaning. For patriarch Ivan, the answer is simple: family. For Emma, it is Ivan and her children. But for their children, the answers are not so simple. One daughter is happily married but perhaps not entirely satisfied; another struggles with a gambling addict for a husband. Granddaughter Paula suffers from depression and suicidal tendencies. She explains that her parents no longer talk to one another and use her to communicate, just as Harwood's parents used him as a child. The pressure is incredible, and Paula's attempts to escape catalyze much of the dramatic action. Freddie appears to offer some stability to the family, but he, too, struggles with his post-traumatic stress syndrome, leading him, like Pinfold, to self- and overmedicate. As the play progresses, we learn the truth about Freddie's trials.

In an episode taken from a true story involving members of Harwood's family, Freddie's plane was shot down during the war and he was taken prisoner and went missing. Overcome with worry, Emma goes gray overnight. The family hears that some men may have escaped to San Angelo, Italy. In a decision that looks like it came out of a Hollywood movie script,

Ivan joins the Allies, jumps out of an airplane, and finds his son on June 8, a day the family has celebrated every year since Freddie and Ivan's return from the war.

The trouble is, Freddie did not want to be rescued. He had found an Italian lover, Ardella, but his father will not let him remain in Italy or marry a Catholic woman whom he thinks is only after his son's citizenship. Ivan forces Freddie to return with him. Of course, Freddie returns a changed man; as Emma observes: "Who knows what happens to young men who fight wars? Who knows what they see, what they suffer?" (*Collected Plays*, 12). And, Harwood seems to add, who knows what they suffer after they return?

With family chaos established, Harwood illustrates the various responses to such situations. For Ivan, order controls chaos, and he is adamant about honoring holidays, gender norms, and domestic rules and conventions. But Harwood does not depict Ivan as a monster. Ivan explains the importance of the rituals. He says love is not the stuff of "woman's magazines." It is:

> ... a muscle, love is a hammer, love is a parachute jump from 12,000 feet at age forty-five. Love is an *effort*. You think it's easy for me to be hard on that child? You think I'm so stupid I don't know she must feel pain to act in the way she does? Of course, I know these things. But I am telling you this is a *community* of love .... You allow one member to believe that the individual is more important than the community and you bring down the Temple. It's up to Paula to return to the circle but that means there must be a circle for her to return to, which means the circle must be unbroken. (*Collected Plays*, 29)

Later Ivan challenges his children and grandchildren's privilege and petty behavior:

> ... you [Paula] must get it into your skull that you are not the only person to walk on this planet, that the world wasn't created for your personal pleasure a second after you were born. You are not solitary and self-contained. There are others in the world. ... You were born with the possibility to live fully, to inherit the riches of thought, expression and freedom. You have the possibility of culture, books ... poetry, the

Theatre, music. . . . And there was only one obligation upon you: that you cared for and protected your inheritance, that, in time, they may be passed on enriched by your presence on this earth. Now, if you don't want that, if you cannot comprehend that simple beauty, go into a nunnery. I personally will purchase the veil for you. But do not spit in the face of those who have made these things possible. (44–45)

For Ivan and his generation, community is essential; sacrifice and duty assumed; and love is an act of will.

Through Ivan's action, Harwood inverts the opening scenes of *Lear*. Ivan is Harwood's first exploration into the dual nature of totalitarianism here on the domestic front. Ivan's values are noble, even heroic, but the play demonstrates the shadow side of these aspirations, truths perpetuated during the war and that led to the Allies' victory. Personal desires and needs had to be ignored for the greater good, to further the war effort, but they constructed a kind of positive form of totalitarian rule. Yes, they promoted the advancement of democratic principles, but they also diminished individual desires and principles. Of course, Ivan's actions cannot compare to Hitler's, but both override the individual, seeing the sacrifice as the expense incurred to reach a common goal. From Ivan's perspective, the family is intact, but as we see throughout the play, his assessment is delusional. Freddie is unhappy; the other couples struggle; and his granddaughter rebels. Through Ivan's action, Harwood inverts the opening scenes of *Lear*; rather than dividing the kingdom to create unity in the future, Ivan forces unity, and that leads to division.

Blighted unions characterize the entire clan. Gambling addiction, indifference, and impotence threaten the daughters' marriages. There is something wrong with this family, an "illness," as Ivan calls it, but the group cannot discover a cure. Referencing *Lear*, Freddie, perhaps the one most damaged by the enforced familial intimacy, articulates his ambivalence to his and his father's overbearing personality and familial vision when he states: "We need an act of healing; we'll get an act of war" (39).

But what is the solution? The play does not end so superficially. Freddie and Paula represent opposing views of the freedom that appears to be the solution to Ivan's dictatorial ways. Ivan's weaknesses are clear, and even he realizes his error and asks Freddie for "a blessing" (61). In this way, Ivan could be a modern Lear, finally coming to a tragic realization regarding Freddie's rescue. Freddie and Paula offer opposing views on freedom within the familiar context. Freddie is a dutiful son, who participates in the funeral ritual for his father. Paula does not attend the service, but she appears later beside Freddie at the grave. Freddie praises her freedom: "You have freedom to feel what you like. I envy you. I only know that I grieve. I mourn, I . . ." (62). While Freddie may admire Paula's perspective, the play, finally, does not. Freddie's grief is real and reflects the complex nature of love, family, war, and peace. Paula's freedom is enviable, but not entirely satisfying.

Harwood leaves us with a tableau of familial perspectives, from isolation to rejection. The play does not endorse any perspective on this continuum. Instead, it shows the strengths and weaknesses of all, perhaps in an attempt to have us reconsider attitudes toward self-sacrifice and self-fulfillment. And while we do have the fall of the flawed patriarch who embodies noble ideals and who risks his own life to save another, Ivan is not the tragic hero of this play. There are too many perspectives and too many alternative views about family and individuality. Instead, the family itself, the divided unit, serves as the tragic figure in this play. Weaknesses and all, struggles and all, faced with the vagaries of fortune, the family, like many tragic heroes, soldiers on.

The Dresser

Based on his experience as a dresser for Sir Donald Wolfit from 1953 to 1959, Harwood's *The Dresser* (1980), its subsequent film version (1983), and its television version (2015) depict the life of an aging actor-manager, Sir, and his dresser, Norman. Set during World War II, the play depicts the many challenges such acting troupes faced: lack of men for male roles, diminished supplies, and treacherous traveling and production conditions. The play highlights the claustrophobic and dingy atmosphere of life backstage in these small theatres, while the film version extends the mise-en-scène and misery to include scenes of bombed towns, empty food stalls, and displaced people. In keeping with the evangelical zeal of other actor-managers and their troupes, Sir and Norman hope to offer consolation by way of the theatre, particularly through the art of William Shakespeare and other classic dramatists.

The Dresser is one of Harwood's masterpieces. As Dominic Cavendish reminded audiences in 2020, the 1983 play "was hailed by the critics, adored by the public and lauded by the profession." He also notes that Tom Courtenay, who originated the role of Norman, suggested "it will be performed for as long as actors and theatres continue to exist." And he quotes Harwood as saying, "I don't think there's been a night since it first opened that it hasn't been performed somewhere in the world" (Cavendish, "Why the Dresser"). The original stage production was nominated for a Tony; the film version was nominated for an Oscar; and the teleplay attracted two of the most prominent performers in theatre and film, Ian McKellen and Anthony Hopkins.

Ironically, and true to Harwood's reputation among theatre insiders, John Gielgud discouraged Harwood after he had completed the play, saying "Backstage plays never do well" (Cavendish). And despite awards, popularity, and longevity, some spectators still do not appreciate or understand the play. Richard Gilman backhandedly praises the play as a "good old-fashioned drama of character, one that makes no pretense of imaginative discovery, that turns over thoroughly familiar psychological ground" (26). Frank Rich, regarding the original New York production with Paul Rogers and Tom Courtenay as particularly good, concludes that the ending is "sentimental melodrama, not tragedy" (7). And while *Variety* says that the film version is "indisputably one of the best films ever made about theatre" ("The Dresser"), film critic Vincent Canby faults the conceit that likens Sir to Lear and Norman to the fool by saying it "works at first, but then ... gives out. Mr. Finney's Sir is a vain, irascible, funny, fascinating actory turn, but he is not an especially tragic figure, and Mr. Courtenay's Norman is a sharp-tongued, loyal, heart-breakingly limited, backstage queen, a middle-aged man who moves from deceptively unthreatening camp mannerisms to serious ferocity in a single speech" (19).

Despite the star-power of its cast, the 2015 teleplay also received lukewarm reviews. Peter Sobczynski writes that the play "is never quite as deep or profound about either the stage or the human condition as it clearly thinks itself to be." Neil Genzlinger, while dazzled by McKellen and Hopkins, betrays his lack of understanding when he suggests that the play needs more historical imagery and detail, concluding it should be a series, like *Downton Abbey*.

Regarding this particular television production, even Harwood had his reservations and created quite a stir when he said that he was "happyish" about the final outcome. To calm the storm, and in typical Harwood fashion, he clarified his remarks with further obfuscation:

> What I was keen on was it being revived in the theatre. And with Anthony Hopkins and Ian McKellen I thought that would be good. But it didn't happen that way, and then they put pressure on me, and I thought 'Oh screw it.' . . . I am honoured to have watched my friends, Anthony Hopkins and Ian McKellen, deliver a masterclass in acting in Richard Eyre's majestic production of *The Dresser*, a play of mine that I hold dear for a number of personal and professional reasons. (qtd. in Plunkett)

In other words, great performances, but not his play. Part of the problem was the direction. Directed by Richard Eyre, the teleplay is a filmed piece of theatre, with little attention to camera work and mise-en-scène. The 1983 film, directed by filmmaker Peter Yates, assisted by Harwood, creates a screenplay that offers a successful film version of a stage play that makes the most of both mediums.

Regardless of the critics and the disappointing televised production, the play and the film remain favorites. As Harwood bragged, "this is what gives me great pleasure. . . . The plays of the Fifties and Sixties that were thought to be masterpieces are not played any more. . . . But *The Dresser* goes on and on" (qtd. in Nathan). The major roles for aging performers certainly account for some of its popularity, but as we examine the play through the perspective of Harwood's concept of tragedy, its power moves beyond an entertaining "backstage" piece or star vehicle. It offers a poignant and moving response to Nazi barbarism and totalitarianism in general—art.

The work illustrates the passion that fueled Wolfit and other such theatre personages throughout history by charting the everyday life of an aging actor-manager and his troupe. Sir is the leader of this theatrical pack and the tragic hero of this play, egotistical, authoritative, a womanizer, albeit a low-key one, given today's revelations. Norman, his effeminate dresser, ensures he is ready for the stage, orchestrating everything from makeup application to bathing to conflict management among the many who seek Sir's attention or throne. On the day that will become his final performance,

Sir is frail. He has had a breakdown in town, been sent to the hospital, and appears utterly unprepared for the evening's performance of, appropriately, *King Lear*. Sir fulfills his duty to the theatre gods. However, he dies trying, leaving Norman to mourn not only Sir's death but the fact that Sir has not even mentioned him in the opening pages of his unfinished biography, unimaginatively titled *"My Life."* While Sir's dedication and sacrifice are admirable, his treatment of Norman illustrates what it is like to live with a tragic hero. To the victor go the spoils, but not to his dresser.

Although clearly modeling the play on the relationship between Lear and the fool in Shakespeare's work, Harwood revised the opening. As in *A Family*, the patriarch does not divide and retire but instead remains, with equally tragic ends. Letting go and withholding bring about the same results in these tragic contexts. And as in other tragedies, the gods, Shakespeare, art itself—something greater—moves Sir's life and work. Throughout the play and film versions, he cries out to the heavens, "How much further do you want me to go?" (*Collected Plays*, 72).

Of course, while Sir sacrifices, he also reaps narcissistic pleasure from his starring role in everything from the plays to the company management to the directorial decisions. Harwood highlights this tendency by adding a scene to the 1983 film during which Sir abusively critiques performances by fellow actors while they are bowing to the audience, thereby diminishing their experience of the audience's appreciation. He, however, takes center stage, even during the curtain speech, one which Harwood admitted he took directly from Wolfit: "Donald could exhibit the grand manner; the curtain speech . . . is very much like his grandiloquence; people used to come in at the end of plays just for Wolfit's curtain calls" (Blau). In all versions, Sir's power may be tried, but it is always assumed.

Such a characterization pitted against the play's totalitarian context of the Nazi bombings of England highlights the tenuous difference between leadership and tyranny. Yes, Sir is abusive, but without such a personality, the troupe would not move through the challenges of theatrical touring. Harwood counts himself lucky "to have caught the end of what was really a great period," during which "troupes went to every corner of the country. Some were great actors and some were awful. . . . They were important because they kept alive the repertoire" (Blau), but he does not idealize the real challenges of touring or the star system. They were autocrats, but without such leadership, they never would have brought the plays to audiences throughout the United Kingdom.

Harwood punctuates this point in an additional scene in the film. Late for a train to their next gig, the troupe panics. Despite Norman's best efforts to bribe the conductors to postpone the train's departure, they will miss their connection. Sir, trailing behind Norman, commands, "Stop that train," in a booming voice that silences the entire train station. No ensemble or collaborative approach here. This is time for action; the troupe needs a leader, not a negotiator.

Sir's continued success at moving the ragtag group reinforces his power and this method of theatrical direction. At the end of the play, a scene between Oxenby and Sir reinforces this perspective. Upset that Sir will not read his play, the actor makes the issue explicit, saying, "I look forward to a new order. I want a company without tyrants" (132). Norman asks, "Who'd be in charge?" Oxenby responds, "I would." The moment highlights the hypocrisy of the theatrical revolutions that occurred when Harwood came to London. Comically, the revolutionary performer desires the power he wants to overthrow.

Physical and psychological decline, however, bring Sir, like Lear, to his knees. Prompted by the New York production of *The Dresser*, Michiko Kakutani noted the various iterations of *Lear* throughout the ages and concluded that the challenge of the play is

> to find a balance in performance between age and physical strength, to portray an old man in decline who has the power to shout down a storm—this remains one problem with Lear that no change in philosophical interpretation or staging style can circumvent. And this, in the end, is perhaps what finally makes Lear, as Sir says in *The Dresser*, "the severest test known to an actor," as well as "the greatest tragedy in our language."

Harwood's play, like Shakespeare's, manages the tension. Sir may command a train, but his mental health is diminishing. Sir may be hospitalized for exhaustion, but the show must go on, so he leaves the hospital despite the doctor's orders. Sir may challenge and bully some performers, but he cowers when meeting Oxenby, the pretentious new actor. Sir, however, has wit enough to dismiss the upstart performer's play by saying he writes for "critics, not people" (99), an approach anathema to both Sir and Harwood.

Unlike Lear, though, Sir has not forgotten his responsibilities to the less fortunate. Abandoned by most, Lear realizes, tragically, that he has neglected his duties and admonishes himself, other rulers, and the audience: "Take physic, pomp, / Expose thyself to feel what wretches feel, / That thou mayst shake the superflux to them, / And show the heavens more just" (*King Lear*, 3.4.33–36).

Sir has a clear sense of his duties and obligations throughout—he must bring art to his community. Early on, the play poses the question of theatre's effectiveness: Can it make a difference? During a scene in which Sir's partner, Her Ladyship, tries to keep him from performing Lear, she justifies the decision saying, "He's ill. There's no crime in being ill, and it's not high treason, not a capital offence, not desertion in the face of the enemy. He's not himself. He can't work. Will the world stop turning? Will the Nazis overrun England? One Lear more or less in the world won't make any difference" (*Collected Plays*, 76).

Harwood's experiences with Wolfit prompt him to answer in the affirmative: yes, art makes a difference. In his biography of Wolfit, Harwood proved the actor's performances made such a difference. He notes that the *Daily Record and Mail* "roared: SHAKESPEARE BEATS HITLER" and praised Wolfit's work (*Wolfit*, 147–48). Inspired by the belief "that drama, on the highest plane, made an immeasurable contribution to the quality of human life" (*Wolfit*, 147), Wolfit performed, persisted, and triumphed.

The Dresser reinforces this perspective throughout. In response to Her Ladyship's question, Norman distills the Wolfit creed, saying, "Sir always believes it will" (76). Sir's final curtain speech defends his work, as well as art's necessity for those who need a utilitarian reason for such entertainments:

> We live in dangerous times. Our civilization is under threat from the forces of darkness, and we, humble actors, do all in our power to fight as soldiers on the side of right in the great battle. Our most cherished ambition is to keep the best alive of our drama, to serve the greatest poet-dramatist who has ever lived, and we are animated by nothing else than to educate the nation in his works by taking his plays to every corner of our beloved island. (128)

The speech is as applicable today as it was in 1980. While Sir's performances may seem old-fashioned and unfashionable, his motivation is noble, and his quest heroic. He has a calling, a higher purpose, and he answers to no one but art, personified in Shakespeare.

Following the heath scene during his final production of *Lear*, Sir returns to his dressing room, thinking his acting that night has perhaps brought him into the Shakespearean realm. Norman praises the performance, saying audiences are calling him Michelangelo and Blake. Her Ladyship and Oxenby scoff at Norman's flatteries, dismissing them as his standard comments after every performance. But on this particular evening, the night of Sir's last performance, something has occurred:

> I thought I caught sight of him. Or saw myself as he sees me. . . . I was suddenly detached from myself. My thoughts flew. . . . Go on, you bastard, I seemed to be saying or hearing. Go on, you've more to give, don't hold back more, more, more. And I was watching Lear. The agony was in the moment of acting created. (116)

Sir has attained his goal, to see as Shakespeare sees. His dedication to art, with all its sacrifices, has been fulfilled.

In contrast to such lofty goals and experiences, the play presents the realities of life and touring. While Sir serves art, he is also blind to human relationships, notably his own with the two women in his life: Her Ladyship and Madge. Both women devote themselves to Sir with little reward. Refusing to divorce his wife, who remains unseen, Sir demands that Her Ladyship be satisfied with a marriage "by troupe." Madge reconciles her desires for Sir by stage managing, a job that allows her to be near Sir, but he treats her as a servant, throwing a few complimentary crumbs her way.

While the women represent Sir's blindness, Norman represents the biggest lacuna in Sir's monomania. The ubiquitous Norman handles the most intimate details of Sir's life. The film accentuates this point during the opening scene by presenting the theatrical "stuff" necessary to create stage magic: makeup, mirrors, hot tea, and the bath, for example. Norman facilitates Sir's greatness because he loves Sir. Without Norman, Sir could not create his art.

While Norman has been portrayed effeminately, Harwood argues that he is "not necessarily a homosexual" (Blau). And while some have argued that there is some homosexual tension between the two, it seems that the play resists such conclusions, perhaps going out of its way to highlight Sir's heterosexuality and Norman's asexuality to offer an alternative to binary gender divisions, as well as offering an alternative to the war that rages outside the theatre—love.

Ensconced in the womb-like atmosphere of the dressing room, Norman and Sir create a relationship so close that it looks like a long-term marriage: they argue constantly, quip, joke, forgive, and enjoy one another's company in the way that only people who live with one another daily can experience and appreciate. The ordinary details fuel their affection, and Sir and Norman take it for granted. Sir needs Norman, and Norman needs Sir, but neither one of them sees how important they are to the other until Sir's death, when Norman realizes not only that Sir did not appreciate him and his work but that he himself did not appreciate what Sir meant to him. Norman refused to face facts regarding Sir's health. As he tells Her Ladyship, "I've never done that [face facts] in my life . . . and I don't see why I should start now" (78). Madge accuses him of having a disease, "hopefulness" (78). He presumes, as we all do, that his situation is immutable.

Norman may not serve art in the way Sir does, but he serves Sir, and the play validates his work. But it also suggests that while the service to art is noble and necessary, it is not the only way to contribute to the world's well-being. Norman's friends' stories offer some examples. While trying to invigorate Sir at the beginning of the play, Norman mentions that one of his acquaintances had been suffering from exhaustion and depression. An unknown "they" want to put this friend away, but one day he received a telegram with an offer of work. It is a small part, but the offer transforms him: "An offer of work. Meant someone had thought of him, and that's ever a comfort" (83).

Caught up in his monomania and self-pity, Sir says, "I'm sick of your friends. Motley crew they are. Pathetic, lonely, despairing" (133). Hurt, Norman says:

[N]ever, never despairing. Well. Perhaps. Sometimes. At night. Or at Christmas when you can't get a panto [pantomime]. But not once inside the building. Never. Pathetic maybe, but not ungrateful. Too mindful of one's luck, as the saying goes. No Duke is more privileged. Here's beauty. Here's spring and summer. Here pain is bearable. And never lonely. Not here. For he today that sheds his blood with me. Soft, no doubt. Sensitive. That's my nature. Easily hurt, but that's a virtue. I'm not here for reasons of my own either. No one could accuse me of base motives. I've got what I want and I don't need anyone to know it. Inadequate, yes. But never, never despairing. (133–134)

The shift from third to first person illustrates that Norman's friends are not, in truth, "friends" at all; the stories are about himself, a lonesome man who found meaning, purpose, and friendship through his work with Sir.

Through both men, Harwood celebrates the unfashionable and, ironically, the power afforded by such a position. Sir wields tremendous creative freedom as an outsider, and Norman finds meaning in his life. But most importantly, Norman, who initially rages against Sir's callousness, concludes, "This is not a place for death. I had a friend—" (137). Through this underling, this "dresser," and his determined, unfashionable performer, Harwood explores the brilliance of the ordinary. Great tragedy occurs within the confines of a small dressing room, showing us that there is power and purpose in the ordinary. The ordinary can become extraordinary, and art can stop Hitler.

After the Lions

Harwood faced criticism in 2016 when he not only said that women should not play male roles but also changed his will regarding the casting of his plays, Sir in particular (Ward). His position was surprising, since following the success of *The Dresser*, he wrote a play offering a tour de force performance for a tour de force female character, Sarah Bernhardt, who had played Hamlet. *After the Lions* (1995) takes place at one of the lowest moments of Sarah Bernhardt's career. She had fallen during a performance, and her leg was not healing, making it impossible for her to return to the stage, which she desperately wanted to do, so she sought an amputation, which many doctors refused to do. Harwood envisioned the two plays as companion pieces, and perhaps after this discussion, more productions of *Lions* will be paired with *The Dresser*.

As with many of Harwood's plays, *Lions* was not well-received. Michael Coveney, for example, faults the density of the "writing and the acting," and makes a terrible pun saying, "the whole occasion, as unfortunately befits the tale of a one-legged monster, is limp" ("'After the Lions.'"). While other reviewers did not dismiss it entirely, their praises were mixed. Paul McGillick describes the play as "colourful, funny, and often moving. . . . It is about how an especially gifted actress brought meaning into her life through self-dramatisation" ("Evelyn Does Sarah Proud"). Described by Evelyn Krape, who performed Bernhardt in the Australian production, as an "actor's dream," the play "forgets the Bernhardt legend and looks instead at a woman of extraordinary spirit fighting old age and obscurity" (Krape, qtd. in Freeman). And in a piece on Dorothy Tutin, who played Bernhardt in the original production and was now playing a role in Pinter's *Party Time* (1991), Michael Arditti indicated that *Lions* was an "unfortunate choice" for her; Tutin, however, defended the play as "fascinating."

I hope to demonstrate that the play merits further productions and consideration, especially in light of interest in Bernhardt shown, for example, in exhibitions of works by Alphonse Mucha, who memorialized her brand and that of other art nouveau cultural figures and artifacts. The play is unique, too, in that Harwood suggests several endings, giving the director an interpretive challenge.

Harwood admits that several biographies were crucial to the creation of this play, which represents an experimental synthesis of several techniques and themes that characterize his work: adaptation and meta-artistic dramas that explore art's power and price to society and the artist. As in *Pinfold*, it focuses upon a relatively obscure and mysterious moment in the life of a great, internationally acclaimed artist. In *After the Lions*, Bernhardt struggles against the status quo, embodied in the play by two minor characters, Pitou, her secretary, and Madam de Gournay, her companion and maid, who serve as a chorus of conformity. Like Sir, Bernhardt sacrifices everything to her art, but she is also aware of the price she pays, uttering, "Art has a lot to answer for" (292).

The play opens during World War I, with Bernhardt considering the amputation of her damaged leg and discussing the possibility with Major Denuce, a military doctor noted for his success with wartime amputations and one of the few doctors willing to do such a procedure. Sarah faces risks, not to mention the discomfort of a prosthesis, because she is older than most of the young men the doctor has operated on in battle. While the doctor is willing to operate, he wonders what kind of roles a one-legged actress will land. Bernhardt assures him, "Second-rate actors may be beautiful, athletic, even look the part, but I can give you the very essence of a life on my own terms. I created the role of a sixteen-year-old boy . . . when I was fifty-six years old. I never had a more authentic triumph" (*After the Lions*, Ronald Harwood: *Plays 2*, 266). With hubris and Shakespearean reference intact, Bernhardt becomes the tragic over-reacher in this Harwood tragedy.

As in other Harwood works, the seriousness of the protagonist's situation and injury does not prevent absurdity, perhaps not the kind of Ionesco or Genet, but certainly close to the humor of Harold Pinter. Bernhardt did not break her leg in a tragic accident or performing a romantic part; it was the result of bad stage management—while playing Spoletta in *Tosca*, she threw herself over the castle walls. The trouble was that the hands had forgotten to put down the mattresses needed to break her fall. Harwood is not above sight gags. When leaving for the surgery, Pitou, this play's version of Sir's Norman, cuts up a newspaper and creates a "string of paper men and snips off the leg of one of them" (272). Later, a phonograph plays Bernhardt's *Tosca*, and in the next scene, we see her maid cutting up black stockings "just above the knee" (273).

But Sarah is, well, Sarah, above and beyond mere mortals. Divine. When she returns from her operation, she discovers that the prosthetic is not working correctly and becomes depressed and maniacal. Frustrated, her maid declares, "she's so—so ordinary." To which Pitou replies, "Yes, but the gods whisper in her ear and not ours" (288).

Sarah finds inspiration, almost as if to demonstrate her connection to those "gods," amid her despair. Remembering how the pope was carried around Rome, Bernhardt resolves to use a litter to visit the soldiers on the front and deliver a speech on amputations. She has marketed herself for years, and turns herself into a symbol of war's cost and the suffering it causes. Pitou, however, has reservations. He encourages her to return to Paris, where she will become a "monument. . . . Immortal." And, of course, immobile. Sarah's passion for performance prohibits her from acquiescing to such a suggestion. She says, "Infirmity is terrible for actors," while Pitou quips, "It's pretty bad for audiences too" (282).

At the front, they meet Dr. Denuce, who has been injured and is close to death. She tells him a story about art and life that revives him: "A man I once loved told me we are duty-bound to live. He was cruel and gave me pain. But the pain, he said, was a sign of life. Better to suffer than to die, he said. He was a playwright. His plays were full of death and despair. Art has a lot to answer for" (292). At the same time, art fuels her: "Take strength from me. See in me a body bereft but a spirit indestructible" (293). Her surgeon recovers, and the first act ends triumphantly. Sarah performs to "two thousand men stamping and calling" her name (293).

Sarah's performance at the front results in a job offer in the second act. Unfortunately, the offer is from a circus in the United States. The invitation assures her that she will receive the recognition she deserves: "She would, of course, appear in what is called the star spot, that is to say, after the lions and before the elephants" (301). Thus a lifetime of theatre, successes, and celebrity has resulted in humiliation. Pitou offers to write a play for her, but Bernhardt recognizes not only the changing culture but the diminishing interest in her form of art and entertainment. She accepts the job.

In the final scene, Sarah rehearses for her new role. Playing ringleader, Pitou announces her to their imaginary audience:

> Welcome to Sarah's Circus. Admission free, children and invalids half-price. . . . I am your guide into uncharted territory, that country where . . . the divine queen-goddess is determined to continue her life as though neither time nor surgeon's knife scarred her. . . . For, she belongs, lady and gentlemen, to the tribe who crawl from their dens at night, who prowl and strut and stalk their prey in darkness and like moths drawn to the bright, bright light. I mean, of course, the theatre tribe . . . . (312)

Bernhardt then appears as the stage is being constructed and attempts to reprise her role as Hamlet. She teeters on her leg and cannot remember her lines, "but she stands in a glorious pose" (313). Bernhardt sells it, saying she will "take affliction into my being and transform it into triumph" (304). Awestruck, the crew clap wildly. She is victorious.

The play, however, does not offer a triumphant ending with artistic passion overcoming all obstacles. Harwood offers directors two options. As Bernhardt delivers her final line, Pitou takes a photograph and either cries or laughs, a determination left to the director. Surely, placing Bernhardt in a circus is absurd and represents the indifferent nature of the art and entertainment industries. Bernhardt is nothing more than a commodity. At the same time, her "performance," failed though it may be and set amid stage construction, illustrates the divinity she proclaims, demands, and exudes. She, as she says earlier in the play, is part of a tribe; "artists are the torchbearers of civilization" (285).

Harwood concludes the play, giving the director and future productions the opportunity to decide their viewpoint on art, whether it offers brilliance or begets humiliation. Bernhardt's pose at the end and Pitou's positive response ironically creates the monument she wished to avoid in order to symbolize the triumph of art over commerce. Pitou's tearful response, on the other hand, suggests that her pose represents artistic prostitution, reflecting how her artistic passion crippled her. Both responses, however, validate Bernhardt's determined spirit and her and her losses. Both responses highlight Bernhardt as a tragic hero and the tragic nature of a life in the arts.

The Deliberate Death of a Polish Priest and *The Interpreters*

During the mid-1980s, the art world focused on the plight of artists and dissidents in Eastern Europe, particularly Václav Havel, the frequently imprisoned dissident and playwright who led the Velvet Revolution to win the Czech Republic independence in 1989 and who ultimately became president. Global art communities, particularly theatres, pressured the Soviets to release Havel. In 1984, the Avignon Theatre Festival focused on Havel's imprisonment and censoring. It included playwrights worldwide, with Samuel Beckett's especially noteworthy contribution: his first explicitly political play, *Catastrophe*. Perhaps also inspired by these events, Harwood's next two plays, *The Deliberate Death of a Polish Priest* (1985) and *The Interpreters* (1986), expose totalitarianism's effects on communities and relationships. The two could be companion pieces, with *Priest* illustrating the ramifications of oppression on the justice system and *Interpreters* exploring its effects on intimate relationships.

Based on the transcripts from the murder trial of Catholic priest Jerzy Popiełuszko, the play, closely adapted for television by Harwood and Kevin Billington, who also directed the stage production, exposes the hypocrisy of totalitarianism and ennobles the absent priest who supported the Solidarity movement in Poland. While Irving Wardle noted that Harwood misses some ironic moments in the actual trial, he praised Harwood's "intercutting testimony so as to combine retrospective narrative with documentary immediacy, and bringing on Popieluszko's driver (the only murder witness) as a spokesman to report background rumours and awkward questions" ("Theatre: Echo of Truth").

The first act focuses on the plan to kidnap and intimidate the priest. The men botch the job and the priest dies. A cover-up ensues but it, too, fails, as the body they deny exists washes up on shore. The second act exposes totalitarianism's insidiousness. The man responsible for the murder, Piotrowski, assumes that his superiors will reward him, but as the case gains more publicity, not only in Poland but abroad, his superiors realize they need a scapegoat. As soon as his accomplices realize that the authorities no longer protect him, they implicate Piotrowski and gain immunity for themselves.

It seems logical that the case would be over at this point. But this totalitarian regime must protect itself, so the process becomes more absurd. The judge argues that both sides are guilty: Jerzy Popieluszko, the priest, for inciting hatred against the state, and the murderers for killing him, with Piotrowski receiving the death penalty. The auxiliary prosecutor argues against both the characterization of the priest as guilty and the death penalty, a sentence Popieluszko would not support. The judge relents and reads the reduced sentences by listing the guilty parties. The list serves to highlight one of the major themes of the play. These men are not party elites. Instead, they are reasonably educated Poles not only afraid to resist the totalitarian regime but also tempted by the promise of promotion.

The driver, played by Brian Cox in both versions, asks: "Why did Piotrowski get twenty-five years?" And responds sardonically, "One for murdering Father Popieluszko and twenty-four for screwing up" (61). In the end, however, the play demonstrates that despite their best efforts and surreptitious means, truth prevails, even after the death of the priest and the trials. Harwood concludes the play with a voice-over of Popieluszko quoting Christ, suggesting the immortality of resistance in the face of totalitarianism: "Be not afraid of them that kill the body, and after that have no more that they can do" (61).

Moving away from the political and public arena, Harwood's *The Interpreters* (1985) explores totalitarianism's effects on individual psyches and its use or misuse of language. As John Peter noted in the *Sunday Times*, the play illustrates how we are all "interpreters trying to read the elusive, coded language of life" ("Mind Stays"). Peter and others praised the play, particularly Maggie Smith's performance as Nadia, but ironically, they neglected to address its political context.

The play is a failed love story. Two interpreters work together, fall in love, and begin misinterpreting their meetings, and in the end, their relationship. The Russian Viktor, played in the original production by Edward Fox, is using British translator Nadia to defect. Her superiors discover the error and the defection plot. Viktor, now revealed as an abusive playboy, denies his love for Nadia and returns to Russia. He is a product of his regime, and his oppression expresses itself in his personal life.

Nadia, whose grandmother has told her that the only "human virtue" is "the ability to tell truth" (*The Interpreters*, 35), realizes that not only has Viktor lied to her, but she has lied to herself. Viktor's failing was, "he couldn't tell lies from truth. . . . The result is he's lost all respect for truth" (61). Though Nadia loses her interpreting job, she has learned the truth about Viktor. She still loves him, however, and suffers despite her realization. The truth has not set her free, but as for many tragic heroes, it has inaugurated another journey. Nadia resolves: "I shall try to conduct my life decently. That's all I can do. That's all any of us can do" (63).

J. J. Farr

With *The Deliberate Murder of a Polish Priest*, Harwood explored one priest's effect not only on his Polish community but on the world. In *J. J. Farr* (1993), Harwood explores the effects of the priesthood on its priests. Where *Priest* inspires, *Farr* challenges; where *Priest* highlights religious leaders' strengths, *Farr* exposes their weaknesses. Both document the search for truth, one from the outside and one from the inside, with *Farr* also representing Harwood's most explicit investigation of faith and Catholicism.

Set in a rehabilitation center for priests with problems ranging from sexual misconduct to alcoholism to mental illness, the play presents a group of clerical misfits searching for a leader, whom they hope to find in Farr. They idolize his loss of faith and public challenges to Catholic church leaders, exposing their hypocrisy and greed. Lowrie is particularly enamored with Farr. He has lost his faith, as he says, "Basic stuff. Instead of feet, I saw hooves.... People, a herd. Music, an algebraic formula, poetry, the accident of alphabet" (*Collected Plays*, 178). He attempts suicide and, while recovering, reads Farr's heretical tomes and even writes an anti-theological book of his own, which preaches the word of Farr, beginning with the opening line: "[F]aith in the supernatural is a neurotic device to deaden fear of death" (149).

As the play opens, the men await Farr. He has been abducted by Muslim terrorists and held captive for five months. Given the year of the play, 1987, many assumed that the play was about Terry Waite, who had been taken earlier that year. But as Bernard Levin notes in his praiseworthy *Times* review, "the play displays a remarkable prescience; the eponymous hero is a former priest who has been kidnapped by Middle Eastern terrorists and kept hostage for months, being beaten and tortured in his captivity. Yet, Harwood had finished writing the play *before* Mr. Terry Waite was taken prisoner."

After viewing the play, audiences will see that Farr is more accurately characterized as Harwood's homage to Graham Greene's *The Power and the Glory* and constitutes an investigation into the nature of the priesthood and the Eucharist than as a fictional account of a specific hostage situation and specific Middle Eastern event. In both Greene's novel and Harwood's play, flawed priests—Greene calls his character the "the whisky priest"—denounce their faith and journey forward. In the end, however, dire circumstances require that they perform Catholic rituals. While their oppressors' nationalities differ, both priests are asked to perform rituals in a faith and/or religion they have abandoned.

In both cases, they are asked to offer the sacrifice of the Mass, which Catholicism teaches will literally transform wine into the blood and bread into the body of Christ through a process called transubstantiation. The issue for both Greene and Harwood is whether or not a flawed vessel, priests in both works, can create the divine. In both cases, they are successful. Both authors uphold the old adage, "once a priest, always a priest" (Harwood, *J. J. Farr*, 169). In *Farr*, as in Greene's novel, the investigation is taken a bit further. To provide the body and blood of Christ to a dying priest, Farr needs wine. The priest offers him the only liquid he has, a vial of his own urine, which Farr consecrates. As the terrorists torment the prisoners and threaten Farr and his precious liquid, he consumes the liquid, only halfheartedly believing that it is anything other than urine. But the liquid and situation change him; he has a spiritual experience, and he returns to his faith as a Catholic priest.

When Farr appears at the center for lost priests hoping to see their rebellious hero, they are surprised by his conversion. No longer the provocateur, they test him, arguing that he may be psychotic, traumatized, or delusional. They offer logical arguments, even using his own publications to persuade him to return to his atheism and anti-Catholic activism.

In the end, Harwood shows there is no accounting for faith. Faith just is. Even Farr's Muslim captors encouraged Christian hostages to pray and practice religious rituals. They punish Farr by branding him when he ridicules his fellow Christian captives and their prayers. He assumes that they branded him with a cross for punishment, but it is only when he returns, having had his spiritual awakening, that he realizes that the crescent moon branding him is the symbol of Islam (181).

The play further suggests that faith and the divine defy categorization. Farr found peace while imprisoned:

The terrorists worship time, the past and the future and so they persecute and make wars . . . [for me] there was no separateness of anything. . . . . And it was *in* me. In me. In my mouth, my gullet, my intestine, my bowels. And there were beautiful things, too. The making of beds and the cleaning of the cell and eating the dry, glutinous rice. It didn't matter what happened to me then. I was free. And it was in me. Outside me. Nameless. (177)

Farr leaves the center ready to stand on his own and his newly reclaimed faith: "in the world, with all its terror and pain and horror, there are scales tipped in the favor of harmony, beauty, love, goodness" (193). Through Farr's tragic and faith journey, the play underscores the hopefulness afforded to believers. Farr's weaknesses and belief in his and others' ability to participate in the spiritual and the mystical illustrates that the divine continues to work no matter how unworthy the priest or his followers are.

In all cases, certainty, rigid adherence to ritual and tradition is undermined. Farr succeeds because he is flexible and open to change. Lowrie, a determined atheist, is left in a hell of repetition. He cannot adjust, amend, or revise his views. Lowrie asks Farr to admit doubt, but he cannot do the same for his own beliefs and principles. In the end, the inexplicable is what we are left with. There is no explanation for faith, goodness, and the divine in the world. As Farr's final speech indicates, good prevails, sometimes for no intellectual reason, and Farr's departure at the end of the play indicates that he, as damaged as he is, can advance goodness in some way.

Bernard Levin praised Harwood's work here, saying the play is "his most complex, arousing and advanced yet . . . a search study of searching human beings." But the subject matter put off theatregoers who abide by the old cocktail party rule of avoiding any discussion of politics and religion. Michael Billington agreed in his review, saying the play was too conceptual, which not only begs the question regarding the kind of audiences Billington perceives exist but also misses the tragic trajectory of the work ("When Guilt"). Levin defends the work, asking, "What is it about the most important thing in the world that terrifies so many people today, and particularly those who occupy what I have called the tin thrones of comment? Certainly, something to consider." Given scandals in the priesthood, Harwood's play seems particularly relevant. And given the uptick in anti-Semitism, the play might serve to show that a Jewish author can write about Roman Catholicism. This reality may prompt further discussions about the arbitrary divisions of religions and writers. Of course, another reason to produce the play is because it is compelling and interesting.

Another Time

While Michael Billington faulted *Farr* for being too conceptual, he praised *Another Time* (1989): when Harwood writes "from the pressure of personal experience (as here and in *The Dresser*) his work has a spontaneous life" ("When Guilt"). Other reviews were equally positive, with Michael Coveney calling it Harwood's "best work since *The Dresser*" ("Another Time"). Notably, the Steppenwolf Theatre in Chicago chose the play to open its new theatre space in 1991. Both London and Chicago productions starred Albert Finney, who brought star power and an understanding of Harwood's vision to the stage. It also won three Molières, the French national theatre award.

Despite these accolades, some faultfinders misunderstood the second act because they misread Harwood's vision and purpose in this play, namely, exploring art's power to transform both individuals and communities.

The play, the most autobiographical that Harwood wrote, centers on a child prodigy, Leonard, who leaves his South African home to pursue his career as a pianist in Europe. He lands in London, becomes an international success, and must now decide if he should return to South Africa for a celebration in his honor. The decision is difficult because while his family wants him to receive the South African honors he has earned, the international artistic community has banned all work in South Africa as a protest against apartheid, which he also wishes to support.

Harwood turns to two topics prominent in his novels: music and apartheid. As in *César and Augusta*, music plays an important part in the play, but more importantly, *Another Time* marks Harwood's first stage play to use music and musicians to symbolize art and artists in general. Harwood admits that he was always interested in music. As he notes in "I Know What I Like," a script he wrote for a 1980 radio program, "I can't remember a time in my life without music," and he says that it was Beethoven's Emperor Concerto that first affected him deeply and imprinted the importance of music on his life. Beethoven continued to be an important influence because "his music never hints of despair" (2). Harwood had even considered becoming a musician himself:

> That I was completely without talent did not seem to me an insuperable obstacle. I learned the piano, but I needed to practise for that, so I thought the best thing was to become a conductor. You obviously didn't need any skills at all: you simply stood before an orchestra with a white stick, and everyone looked at you, and a great volume of sound was produced. I began with knitting needles. (3)

Harwood's interest in conducting informs his later work *Taking Sides*, and his interest in the piano influenced his award-winning screenplay *The Pianist*.

As in the novels *All the Same Shadows* and *Articles of Faith*, Harwood returns to the subject of apartheid, perhaps inspired by the global demonstrations demanding the release of Nelson Mandela, to explore resistance strategies. The novels' protagonists remain in their countries, with both novels suggesting that their tragic heroes will persist, resist, and perhaps undermine the unjust political system. In *Another Time*, however, protagonist Leonard decides to remain in exile, with the play using his decision to explore art's efficacy, specifically theatre's power, to make political change.

Soon after the institutionalization of apartheid in South Africa, Athol Fugard's "open letter to playwrights" was included in a document published by UNESCO. Commenting on the construction of the Parthenon, "the new civic theatre of Johannesburg," he wrote, "This theatre was built with the labour of hundreds of non-Whites . . . but not one of these labourers, not one non-White actor, singer, or writer will be able to see a performance in the season of opera" (qtd. in *Apartheid*, 169). Thanks to the work of anti-apartheid activist Freda Troup Levson, forty-eight playwrights signed the boycott petition that was presented to the House of Commons in 1963 ("Playwrights Against Apartheid"). Their works were prohibited from production in "any theatre where discrimination is made among audiences on the grounds of colour" (qtd. in *Apartheid*, 48). John Arden's statement explains why withdrawing theatrical performances was particularly problematic:

> I think I would not do so if my works were novels or poetry: and indeed, I have never withdrawn my published plays from anywhere. But the theatre is nothing if not a public art, presented before an audience. If that audience is forcibly confined to one section of a community at the expense of another, the play performed is not public. Its very performance is a declaration of support for whatever laws or customs, or prejudices have prevented certain groups or individuals from attending. (qtd. in *Apartheid*, 169)

Later, however, Harwood and others, including Fugard, argued that the measures were counterproductive. Fugard asked for playwrights to reconsider: "Arthur Miller, Albee, Pinter, and others are keeping their own ideas out of South Africa—that's doing the censor's job . . . . I understand their motives, but by keeping their plays out, they're doing nothing to improve the quality of living here" (Howe, "Fugard Opposes"). In a 1965 interview, Fugard further articulated the problem:

I am in it here. . . . We have each to make a personal assessment of what is going to be most effective . . . speech under certain conditions or silence. I believe speech is of more value. Paton has made the other choice. We respect each other. Moreover, I think I have reached a stage where the horizon is tomorrow. . . . At the moment I think I can go on producing plays under segregation (even admitting some non-Whites to private readings). But eventually, I may have to take a stand like Paton's. We are in a corner. And all we can do is dodge here and push there. And under it all, there's a backwash of guilt. (qtd. in *Apartheid*, 157)

Harwood's archives include a letter Arnold Wesker wrote for *the Morning Star* agreeing with Fugard and pleading for "another way" (Harwood, "Apartheid").

In *Another Time*, Harwood returns to when Leonard, not only wracked with guilt over apartheid but also over his dysfunctional family relationships, faces the question: To boycott or not to boycott? The first act establishes protagonist Leonard Lands's dysfunctional family life in South Africa. As his musical talent develops, he yearns to leave for more training, ultimately landing in London, where he has a brilliant career but unsuccessful marriage.

Like Harwood's own dysfunctional family, Leonard's parents, Ike and Belle, no longer communicate directly to one another. If they do, Belle uses the opportunity to abuse Ike verbally. Paralyzed physically and emotionally following his mother's death, Ike, who was not a skilled breadwinner anyway, wallows in self-pity and pipe dreams. Belle, who must work to support the family, resents his behavior. Both not only use Leonard as a vehicle for communication, they also see him as their only hope, so his impending departure creates crises.

Belle's sister, Rose, encourages Belle to be optimistic. Her husband has been a disappointment, but she has borne an artist: "By some accident of evolution, by some random disposition of the species, this couple, thrown together at the bottom of the world, produce a child of extraordinary gifts. And believe me, Belle, it's compensation for all the pain and misery and heartache" (*Collected Plays*, 225).

For Rose, art, particularly the work of Shakespeare, offers solace and purpose. As she reminds Leonard, "But English. Oh, Leonard, what a language.

The Plays | 97

Take time to read, I beg you. You can keep your Russians . . . your French. . . . devour William Shakespeare, drink John Milton, taste Jane Austen, consume George Eliot, drown in Charles Dickens, glory in John Donne . . ." (221). While the play does not entirely endorse Rose's assessment of the British, it establishes the power of art and, through her, our need for it. As she explains to Belle and Ike, who are apprehensive about their son's departure, they have no choice. Leonard "has to leave. He has to go out into the world so that the world can admire this accident of birth, this comet, this star" (225).

But with this gift comes responsibility, and as Leonard contemplates his decision to boycott or return to South Africa, the play explores the various interpretations of boycotting. Uncle Leonard, for example, surmises Leonard's reasons for boycotting are the result of public relations, his reputation:

> He wants to be loved by the world. He wants to be thought well of. He wants not only to be on the right side, but also to be seen to be on the right side. . . . It's not enough for him to be a wonderful pianist, he has to be a public figure, sign petitions, march, support causes. (251)

His mother, with whom he has a tense relationship, believes that his choice to boycott is about her, to hurt her personally: "You have to make a stand. Against your own mother?" (257).

Even his own son, Jeremy, believes Leonard's decision is selfishly motivated: he thinks his father is trying to impress his ex-wife. This accusation brings the family interactions to a climax. Leonard slaps his son and says:

> Look, whatever I am, whatever I've become, the price was paid by me, not by Mom or Dad, or by any of us here, but by a great mass of people who had no say in the matter. I was able to flourish at their expense. And for that I feel deeply ashamed, deeply, deeply ashamed . . . canceling my concert in Cape Town is my only weapon. (267–68)

But there is the more public, universal power or effect of art, as Rose explains:

> [A]rt is an expression of what's best about each and every one of us . . . art is a solace, art is a benediction. . . . There is not a thought in my head, not

a feeling in my body that art hasn't, in one way or another, informed and fired. . . . You must hold your talent in very low esteem because it seems you believe deep down that not one note you play will change a single human heart. That's where I disagree with you. . . . I believe there's a chance that music might, might, just might, turn the whole world upside down, all right, not the whole world . . . but one individual world, that's a chance, in my opinion, you're meant to take. (269)

While Leonard dismisses Rose's perspective as old-fashioned, a time when change could occur through art's appearance, the play raises the possibility that the boycott is not the only means of political change. Art itself may be more effective, and, as Fugard's statements suggest, denying its expression may enable further oppression and censorship.

But, as in all of Harwood's plays, art and its power frequently take an incredible toll on the artist. Harwood experiments with casting to show its effects, like Caryl Churchill's *Cloud Nine* (1978). The actor who plays Leonard's father in the first act later plays Leonard in middle age in the second act, suggesting a kind of genetic predetermination or at least emphasizing the father-son connection that persists despite their physical separation and differences. Leonard's South African heritage provides discomfort, however, not a sense of place or self. He says, as Harwood said of himself at times, "I am an alien wherever I am" (272).

To some extent, Leonard's art alleviates some of his suffering and gives him a sense of identity: "What I am is how I play" (275). And as Belle and his son prepare to return to South Africa without him, and as he plays Rachmaninoff's *Elégie*, Opus 3, No. 1 (276), Belle realizes she must let her son go. Her decision may reflect Harwood's desires for his own relationship with his mother, but in the play, Belle's decision, by way of art, offers at least some resolution to the family dysfunction. Like Wolfit, Harwood himself, and many other Harwood heroes, Leonard is an outsider, but the art that both sustains and makes him suffer provides purpose and a sense of self despite his circumstances.

Poison Pen

After the success of *Another Time*, Harwood's *Poison Pen* (1995), which starred Tom Courtenay, opened to high expectations. Based on Cecil Gray's memoir of music critic Philip Heseltine, also known as the composer Peter Warlock, it is a psychological thriller that continues to explore the alienated self, gender, and the tensions between artist and critic. Like Oscar Wilde's *The Importance of Being Earnest*, *Poison Pen* presents a divided world and a divided character. When in Chelsea, Erik Wells identifies as a homosexual man who writes music criticism. In Kent, he is known as Peter Godwin, a composer who identifies as a heterosexual. Conflict ensues when the schizophrenic separation of personalities erodes. Wells accuses Godwin of losing his artistic edge, pandering to popular tastes, and plagiarism. Rupert Grace, a publishing representative, and Larry Rider, Wells's lover, discover the truth about Godwin/Wells. The confrontation results in Godwin/Wells's breakdown and ultimate suicide. The play ends with a voice-over of the BBC reporting that Wells is dead and Godwin is missing, oblivious to the fact that they are the same person.

The play explores the nature of creation and the complicated relationship between artist and critic, here embodied in one person. Wells/Godwin's schizophrenia, painful as it is, produces great art. Wells admits that he "never stood on my own feet. . . . But when I met Peter [Godwin], oh, that was an awakening. He was everything I was not. . . . After every day's work [of composing] he'd ask my opinion. . . . That was the loveliest time" (130). And Godwin confesses, "I relied on him. He questioned the notes I recorded" (140). When they begin separating, both art and artist suffer.

Critics praised Courtenay's performances, but many found fault with the convoluted play. Nick Kimberley of *The Independent* wrote, "the play was not well received by the critics, many of whom took exception to the way in which 'facts' had been distorted" ("Glimpse of God"). Harwood responded by saying, "we live in a journalistic age where people like it very hard and documentary. I don't. I'm much more interested in the creative process than in the composer per se" (Kimberley). The criticism reappeared regarding Harwood's later adaptations, and Harwood's response will remained the same. He is not merely copying an original; he is transforming one work into another work of art.

Robin Thornber criticized the play for its "unresolved debate on the Apollonian and Dionysian aspects of criticism and creativity, the yin and yang sides of everyone's head" ("Manchester/Poison Pen"). Jeffrey Wainwright was intrigued by the play's exploration of dualisms regarding art, gender, and identity, but he faulted the play's conclusion, with its use of mental illness as an explanation for the Wells/Godwin divide. Inconclusive endings are Harwood's forte, of course, part of his tragic vision and project, in that they highlight conflicts without resolving them. Wainwright's suggestion that the play ends with madness as a deus ex machina overlooks the subtle tension between madness and artistic creation. Here, insanity may create the art, but the art also creates madness. Even Harwood deemed the productions weak because of his weak direction (*Ronald Harwood: Plays 2*, x). Admittedly, the piece is challenging, but given the compelling questions it raises regarding art and criticism, as well as the opportunity for a tour de force performance for an actor in the dual roles, the play seems ready for a revival.

Taking Sides

Taking Sides is Harwood's second most well-known and well-received play (1989) and film (2001), helping to inspire Roman Polanski to work with Harwood on the Oscar-winning *The Pianist*. Most importantly, the play and film mark a turning point in Harwood's writing through its explicit representation of the Holocaust. Harwood's tragic vision, his focus on art's power, and his commitment to challenge—rather than placate—audiences through facile conclusions appear here, and he has found the subject that shows his skills to their best advantage.

Directed by Harold Pinter in London and well received in New York, the play takes place during the denazification process in Germany following World War II. Major Arnold, a crude American military man, has been tasked with interviewing the German conductor Wilhelm Furtwängler and determining whether he colluded with the Nazis. Already cleared by a tribunal in Berlin, Furtwängler enters the interrogation with an advantage. As the play progresses, however, Arnold demonstrates his keen investigative skills, and Furtwängler comes to appear complicit. As in *George Washington September, Sir!*, *The Guilt Merchants*, and *Another Time*, *Taking Sides* examines the efficacy of exile, participation, and art. And like Harwood's other works, *Taking Sides* resists easy answers. Even Harwood's motives for writing the play are bifurcated. He admits he wanted to write about Furtwängler to investigate the role of the artist in the totalitarian state (*Ronald Harwood: Plays 2*, xi) and explore the causes for the poor treatment the conductor received following the war (*Ronald Harwood: Plays 2*, 3).

As Harwood explores the various sides of art, war, and totalitarianism, he relies on the tragic structure we have seen in his other works. He admits that he wants to avoid "feel-good" endings and create a "genuine tragic experience" (Harwood, "Truth and Fiction," 11). That tragic experience is best defined by Rita Felski, who identifies tragic heroes by their "miscalculated confidence and its consequences" ("Introduction," 2) and the tragic structure itself by its refusal to offer "clear-cut solutions and absolute judgments" (7).

Here, however, Harwood splits the tragic hero in two. Furtwängler miscalculates and falls from grace but remains blind, denying his error. Arnold, initially presented as a philistine, exhibits the detective skills of Oedipus and unearths the truth about Furtwängler, but without finding tangible evidence, thereby leaving the audience to determine the veracity of both men's viewpoints.

The play is notable, too, for its more explicit representation of the Holocaust, marking a turning point in Harwood's writing. While World War II served as the backdrop for works such as *The Dresser*, here and in subsequent plays and films Harwood uses his Jewish heritage and culture more explicitly, often within a musical context.

The play version opens by establishing Arnold as an "ugly American." He sleeps through Beethoven's Fifth Symphony, and then explains to Emmi, his German anti-Nazi secretary, "Beethoven's Fifth Symphony bores me shitless" (*Ronald Harwood: Plays 2*, 8). The film more heavily underscores Arnold's lack of cultural knowledge. Arnold, an insurance adjustor before the war, has heard of Arturo Toscanini, but he has never heard of Furtwängler, so his culturally astute superior officer explains that he is like "Bob Hope and Betty Grable rolled into one" (*The Pianist and Taking Sides* [*Screenplays*], 123). Even Arnold's appreciation of the distinctly American art form jazz is not particularly nuanced. He compliments a saxophone player saying, "[N]ot bad. Not good, but not bad. Played one-night stands in Illinois and Michigan" (*Ronald Harwood: Plays 2*, 8). In contrast to the musical tastes of Germans, both Nazis and non-Nazis, Arnold looks like a "vulgarian." His musical assessment of the sax player appears in the context of an insurance scam story that Arnold tells to Emmi, which includes an anti-Semitic remark.

With Arnold's lack of cultural literacy established, the play leads us to underestimate him. As the play progresses, Arnold exhibits keen instincts, tenacity, and an incredible sense of justice, despite his cultural and ethnic insensitivity. In the film, his superiors praise his conscientiousness and determination (The Pianist and Taking Sides [Screenplays], 122). He has an uncanny memory and a technique he used to uncover insurance fraud: there is "always one question the guilty can't answer" (Ronald Harwood: Plays 2, 8). And while Arnold may not be a music critic, his love of jazz represents a threat to the totalitarian powers. As Michael Kater shows, "the Nazis hated jazz" (237). It represented a new, modern art form that threatened the Third Reich aesthetic.

Though flawed, Arnold, who is on a mission to find the truth about Furtwängler, is our tragic hero. In the opening scene, Arnold has interviewed twenty-eight orchestra members, and all tell the "baton story" as a means of defending their conductor, their "band leader" in Arnold's terms. Based on a real picture of Furtwängler and Hitler, the story is about a performance Hitler attended. At the end of the concert, Hitler comes to congratulate Furtwängler. Not wishing to offer a salute, the conductor merely shakes the Führer's hand and holds the baton in the other. Unimpressed, exasperated, and keenly aware of the self-serving nature of the narrative and narrators, Arnold concludes, "[W]hat they're trying to do is cover the band leader in roses in the hope they'll come up smelling just as sweet. But it's difficult to smell sweet after you've crawled through the raw sewage" (Ronald Harwood: Plays 2, 12).

More defenders enter the interrogation room, and Arnold remains unmoved. A non-Jewish woman forces her way into the office with lists of names of Jewish musicians Furtwängler helped to escape from Germany, her husband included. David, another of Arnold's assistants and a German Jew whose parents were killed by the Nazis, also defends and lionizes the maestro. When another orchestra member says that Furtwängler made anti-Semitic comments, David brushes the accusation aside: "Show me a non-Jew who hasn't made anti-Semitic remarks and I'll show you the gates of paradise" (Ronald Harwood: Plays 2, 49).

Arnold has a different perspective, which he illustrates with a story about his arrival in Berlin. As he and a driver made their way through the city, Arnold said "to think, a million of these people came out to welcome Adolf on the day he entered the city, millions of them, and now look at 'em." To which the driver responded, "Oh, not these people, major. These people were all at home hiding Jews in their attics" (25).

Arnold clearly has a keen sense of truth and falsity. Here, Arnold appears to have these characteristics naturally, perhaps honed by his work with insurance scams. In the film, however, Arnold goes through military indoctrination. American soldiers were literally trained not to trust Germans: "In a German town, if you bow to a pretty girl or pat a blond child, you bow to all that Hitler stood for. You bow to the reign of blood. You caress the ideology that meant death and destruction" (The Pianist and Taking Sides [Screenplays], 125). And while historically interesting, the play seems more effective without such explanations.

Arnold is a hero bound for truth, not a trained military interrogator. In his book on director István Szabó, John Cunningham compares Arnold to the Edward G. Robinson character in *Double Indemnity*, the insurance man who ferrets out murder and corruption (110). In this way, Arnold may be ignorant about art, may be uncivil, and may not be particularly astute when it comes to diversity, equity, and inclusion, but he is a noble man of conscience.

After the interviews, interruptions, and deliberate delays by Arnold, Furtwängler enters the room. He is a formidable foe, and he has the sympathies of Arnold's staff as well as of the nation of Germany. His defense is that art and politics do not interact: "[T]hey have nothing to do with one another" (*Ronald Harwood: Plays 2*, 29). He kept himself out of the political fray, he maintains, focusing only on artistic excellence. He argues that he remained in Germany to give people hope, to support "the maintenance of liberty, humanity, and justice" (51). Under the totalitarian regime, he thought he could offer hope: "I know that a single performance of a great masterpiece was a stronger and more vital negation of the spirit of Buchenwald and Auschwitz than words. Human beings are free wherever Wagner and Beethoven are played. Music transported them to regions where torturers and murderers could do them no harm" (63).

Like Rose in *Another Time*, Furtwängler believes in the efficacy of art.

David, whose parents were killed by the Nazis, even tells Furtwängler, "ever since I heard you, music has been central to my life. My chief comfort. And I've needed comfort" (35).

Such a defense may have worked during another time, and it is certainly appealing to those working in the arts, but Arnold looks for more practical motivations. Furtwängler admits that he may have been naive, but he does not admit any wrongdoing or accept any responsibility for working with the Nazis.

Arnold will have none of this "airy-fairy" explanation:

> I don't see a great artist.... I see a man, an ordinary guy, like a million other ordinary guys. And I ask myself, what keeps him in a situation in which he says he did everything in his power to resist except to get the hell out of it? What keeps him here... I look for ordinary reasons. (57)

Furtwängler claims that he resisted the Nazis through his writings, but Arnold dismisses this noble act because he did it for selfish reasons—ethnic cleansing decimated orchestras; many of their most talented escaped. He claims that he remained for the German people, but Arnold discovers that there is a competition between Furtwängler and a new conductor, Herbert Van Karajan: "Never mind art and politics and symbols and airy-fairy bullshit about liberty, humanity, and justice.... Youth was knocking on the door, and I don't care how great you are, how noble, how fantastic... because it's the oldest trick in the book" (54).

As Furtwängler continues his defense, arguing that Nazi control was impossible to resist and arguing that art made a difference, Arnold confronts him with the reality of the war and the Holocaust:

> Have you ever smelled burning flesh? I smelt it four miles away. Four miles away, I smell it. I smell it now, I smell it at night because I can't sleep any more with the stench of it in my nostrils. I'll smell it for the rest of my life. Have you seen the crematoria and the gas ovens? Have you seen the mounds of rotting corpses being shoveled into gigantic craters by the men and women who murdered them? Yes, I blame you for not getting hanged, I blame you for your cowardice. You strutted and swaggered, king-pin in a shithouse. (64)

War's realities fuel Arnold's determination to find the truth, to ask the one question they cannot answer: "You were their boy, their creature. That's the case against you, old pal. You were like an advertising slogan for them. . . . You may not have been a member of the Party because the truth is, Wilhelm, you didn't need to be" (62). Furtwängler profited from the Nazis' favors. He made a deal with the devil to play his music, to conduct, and to lead one of the most influential orchestras in the world.

John Gardiner, writing on the film, found that the "moral world of *Taking Sides* is at its deepest and starkest here" (105). And while Gardiner says that the open-ended conclusion works, earlier in his essay he calls Furtwängler not so much another side but an empty set, "a void or absence" (99). Such a conclusion seems accurate. Too focused on his art, his ego, and his prestige, the maestro does not speak out, does not resist effectively.

István Szabó's direction of the film highlights how the Nazis used Furtwängler and his work to inspire Germans. The film's opening "is a powerful moment, intensified and extended by Szabo's direction where a long majestic tracking shot slowly reveals the nature of the audience (many of whom are uniformed SS)" (Cunningham, 114). The film also includes some actual Holocaust camp footage, which offers moving confirmation of Arnold's speech in the play.

The play does not end neatly, with Arnold triumphant and Furtwängler defeated. Arnold may have rational and moral evidence for the conductor's guilt, but there is no actual evidence. In lieu of such facts, Arnold calls a journalist who, the play suggests, is known to implant rumor and innuendo in the news. Is Arnold behaving in much the same way as the Nazis? Bullying and misleading the public for what he considers the greater good? Is our flawed hero not a hero at all?

The Szabó film concludes with archival footage showing Furtwängler with Joseph Goebbels. As in the play's baton incident, the conductor does not salute but instead shakes hands. But a close-up repeated throughout the end of the film shows, "Furtwängler wiping his hands" (*The Pianist and Taking Sides* [*Screenplays*], 195). The act could indicate Furtwängler's resistance, but the repetition suggests that no matter how often he wipes his hands, he cannot remove the "raw sewage" of Nazi Germany.

Harwood's Furtwängler argues that his art made a difference to the German people during the Nazi regime, and whether it was his fault or not, that art was compromised and used as totalitarian propaganda. Arnold, while pursuing the truth, compromises it when he decides to call a "tame journalist" who will give Furtwängler "a hard time" (*Ronald Harwood: Plays 2*, 66). The play itself exists as a testimony to the power of art, or at least to our faith in it and its ability to inspire change and resistance. To live a life without art is untenable, but at the same time, dictatorships must be overthrown. Is art strong enough to overthrow a totalitarian regime? In the end, neither Arnold nor Furtwängler embodies satisfactory perspectives or choices; both are flawed in some way. Something is lost when one chooses one side or the other. Harwood's mastery as a writer leaves the two so perfectly balanced that we must engage with both sides—without taking sides. In effect, through the choice, and the losses both choices require, Harwood expertly places the audience in the position of the tragic hero. To choose art risks cooperation with the enemy; to choose only politics risks the loss of art. As Harwood asks audiences: Which would you choose?

The Handyman

Following the success of *Taking Sides*, *The Handyman* (1996) returns to issues surrounding the Holocaust and retribution. Set during the 1990s, a wealthy couple, Julian and Cressida, live a thoroughly modern and comfortable life in Sussex. He makes money off money, and she, on a lark, decides to pursue gender studies. Romka Kozachenko, their Ukrainian handyman, is a family fixture. Cressida's father brought him home after the war in 1945, and he has remained, long after her father's death, serving as a father figure, despite his role as a home worker. Their lush life is disturbed by detectives from the Scotland Yard war crimes bureau who appear on their doorstep one day to arrest Kozachenko. Like the real-life Nazi John Demjanjuk, Kozachenko is accused of killing over 800 Jews during the war. Changes in British law have allowed the British to prosecute non-British war criminals.

The play met with incredibly extreme reviews, some damning, some praise-filled. The appearance of Harold Pinter's *Ashes to Ashes*, as well as a revival of Edward Albee's *Who's Afraid of Virginia Woolf?*, resulted in comparisons that concluded the Harwood play was not in the same league. Simon Reade in his negative review in the *Financial Times* concluded that Harwood "renders tragedy bloodless." Others, such as Michael Billington, slighted the characters as "vehicles for moral debate," and concluded that "the argument itself, not least about the need to strike a balance between legal fairness and historical culpability, is gripping" ("First Night"). Benedict Nightingale praised the play for raising the question of whether, "given the right time and temptations" how many of us "would keep our humanity intact?" ("Netting the Village Nazi"). John Peter not only concluded that the play was Harwood's "best and finest," but, more importantly, he, unlike Reade, perceived the tragic trajectory of the drama: "Sophocles and Ibsen would have understood the bravery of this play, its insistent moral drive and, most of all, its refusal to dispense blame or acquittal. There are no tragic flaws here, only tragic events" ("Punish and Be Damned"). But the play is about more than the Holocaust and its tragic results and the manner of retribution, as was the case in Harwood's novel *The Guilt Merchants*. Instead, while presenting two sides to the matter of Kozachenko's guilt, the play uses his guilt to highlight not only his crimes but also the systemic anti-Semitism that persists in contemporary culture. The play's star couple are no longer comfortable, and, if all goes well, the audience will be uncomfortable, too.

Before discussing the play, I want to mention that a 2012 revival, which attracted British star Timothy West and illustrates Harwood's ability to attract high-caliber performers, received equally mixed reviews. The 2012 version, however, included an additional final scene, which Richard Stockwell says hindered the original play ("Handyman"). This version is not readily in print, so it is not included in this discussion.

The play highlights the existing anti-Semitism and the past atrocities of the Holocaust. Following the detectives' accusation, Julian, a Catholic, decides that the best defense for Romka would be a Jewish lawyer, but "all absolutely refused to have anything to do with" the case. One, however, "because he's a conscientious old stick," finds Marion Stone, a good lawyer who is married to a Jew, "the next best thing" (*Handyman*, 19), the couple concludes.

With legal counsel secured, the couple wonders about the efficacy of prosecution. After all, Kozachenko is old and near death anyway. Stone notes that prosecuting a criminal is essential, but on the one hand: "It can be argued that a trial is as good a way as any of a society proclaiming the standards by which it lives" (26). On the other hand, it can also release "the poison" of anti-Semitism or worse, those who argue that the Holocaust is "just another Jewish conspiracy" (27).

With the skill of a detective, Stone interrogates Cressida about Romka and his relationship with her father and the family. According to Cressida, her father worked for British intelligence during the war, was captured and wounded, and came home with Kozachenko. As we learn later, Kozachenko had information on the Soviets, and he needed help getting out of Ukraine, where he served the Nazis. The play suggests that Cressida's father had done the old man a favor in return for the intelligence documents and brought him to their home as a live-in servant. Romka, then, is handy for more than home improvement projects. Later, Cressida recalls her father "apropos of nothing . . . said, 'Odd about Romka. You'd think he'd show signs of remorse'" (61), indicating that she is also not so sure about his innocence in general. When Cressida presses for more information about the war and Kozachenko, her father says, "Nothing, nothing. Remorse about fighting for the Nazis, that's all" (61).

The evidence mounts against Romka, who denies everything, saying he worked for the Nazis as a cook. Nikita, a fellow Ukrainian SS Division soldier who is testifying against Romka, coldheartedly describes murdering "four or five hundred Jews" in Mikolja (55) with Romka by his side. He concludes by saying, "I'd do it all over again. I don't mind saying that in your court either. Give me Romka beside me and we shoot the lot. Good man, Romka. Good worker" (57).

The second witness, a Catholic nun living in Jerusalem, recounts the Jewish massacre in Starivka, her hometown, and Romka's. Sister Sophia and Romka's sister, Larisa, were roommates in an orphanage, both having lost their parents to the communists. While she did not see the actual shootings of the Jews, she saw the soldiers "sprinkling lime into a large, deep trench . . . I could not see into the trench. But I saw several human hands reaching out of the pit, clawing at the earth. And this is the most terrible thing. I saw Larisa's brother, Romka, walking up and down with his rifle and firing" (68). When asked about Larisa, who disappeared during the war, Sister Sophia says that she heard they killed her because she knew too much. Romka, of course, denies everything.

Recounting atrocities from the Holocaust is only part of the play's purpose, however. Cressida, who still wants to believe Kozachenko innocent, attempts to explain the war's events as evil, something aberrant, inhuman.

Stone counters such a perspective, noting that we are all capable of such actions: "What happened was human unfortunately and reprehensibly human.... Think of the numbers murdered, six million Jews, millions of others, just think of the numbers who had to be involved in their destruction. Thousands.... All of them evil? No. None of them. You are right. Mr. Kozachenko is not evil.... He is intensely, pathetically human" (75).

The play repeatedly demonstrates that while the Holocaust may be over, the beliefs, sentiments, prejudices, and biases that created it remain and undergird the social structure. Romka tells the story of going to a priest after he joins the Ukrainian SS militia. The priest tells him they are damned, suggesting that the devil controls the country and war. Sister Sophia tells another version of the story, this time with Romka running from the confessional. The priest shouts that Romka is damned, not just in general or because of the situation, but because he has in fact massacred hundreds of Jews.

But even Sister Sophia is not without sin. After her statement, she admits that she often prays about the Jewish condition: "Why have Jews been made to suffer so appallingly?" It isn't because they handed Christ over to be crucified. "It was because they rejected him" (71). The speech is shocking because she has been, up to that point in the play, one of the witnesses for the prosecution who represents Catholics sympathetic to Jews.

But the play makes clear that this sympathetic alliance is uneasy at best. As recently as June 2022, information regarding Pope Pius VI and his relationship with Hitler was revealed. Though Pius was neither "Hitler's Pope" nor a sterling example of Allied resistance, it is clear he sent lists of Jews living in Rome to Hitler (Nawaz). Relations outside of the war were also fraught, so much so that the Second Vatican Council included language addressing the goal of religious harmony between Catholics and Jews, presumably because such harmony was absent: "Jews, therefore, the Fathers caution, are not 'to be presented as rejected or accursed by God, as if this followed from Holy Scripture.'" The Passion of Jesus, moreover, "cannot be attributed without distinction to all Jews then alive, nor can it be attributed to the Jews of today." The Church, the statement declares, "decries hatred, persecutions, displays of anti-Semitism directed against the Jews at any time and by anyone" (United States Conference of Catholic Bishops, "Guidelines"). Such a declaration makes it clear that one was necessary.

War and organized religion aside, the play highlights systemic anti-

Semitism. Stone tells Julian, after he has said she does not look Jewish, that she is married to a Jewish man: "I always like to get that in as soon as I can. Saves embarrassment should anyone say anything untoward later" (19). As David in *Taking Sides* said, "Show me a non-Jew who hasn't made anti-Semitic remarks and I'll show you the gates of paradise" (49). But Stone's line is also one Harwood told me during one of our interviews, and it also appeared in an interview with the *Jerusalem Post* (qtd. in Tugend, "Waiting for Oscar").

Progress has been made, but anti-Semitism persists. Harwood punctuates the point with a final speech from Stone repudiating the argument of evil: "Hatred of the Jews was at the heart of Nazism. That was the poison. And most of them had already drunk deeply. . . . The hatred of the Jews is a cultural norm in our civilization" (80). Cressida responds by telling Kozachenko to deny everything, to resist the fantasy of the Holocaust. Stone "cracks Cressida across the face," and the play concludes with a tableau: Stone standing but far from triumphant and Julian and Kozachenko comforting Cressida who sobs (81). The Holocaust may be over, but Harwood's play illustrates that, even among those living plush lifestyles, systemic anti-Semitism persists.

Quartet

Quartet (1999) is a delightful comedy about a group of retired opera singers facing death that offers a reprieve from the somber Harwood canon. Filled with classic Harwood gallows humor, the play is, at heart, a fairy tale about art's power to change our world and selves, specifically our ability to face aging and death.

Set in a magnificent castle, the play quickly establishes the humiliations of old age through three main characters. Cissy is losing her cognitive functions; Reggie suffers from general weakness but, as we learn later, really suffers from a broken heart; and Wilf is simply old in the play, though the film defines him as a stroke victim. Rather than succumb, they decide to make the most of their time by preparing for their annual Verdi birthday party, which coincides with the re-release of their "hit" recording of *Rigoletto*. While they all agree to perform their masterwork, they miss their fourth singer. Magically, Jean appears to complete the quartet. She moved into the nursing home because her husband died and she can no longer care for herself. She, however, wants to refrain from participating in the performance for several reasons. First, her voice has failed her. And second, she has very mixed feelings about Reggie, with whom she had an affair years ago. He, of course, still loves her. In the end, the quartet devises a clever solution for the performance, Reggie and Jean reunite, and all ends happily ever after.

While fantastical, both film and play versions do not gild the lily regarding aging. Wilf, whose Dionysian spirit embraces life and any woman around, admits:

> I have hated growing old. Hated every bloody moment of it. First, it's your prostate and peeing three times nightly. If it's not your prostate, it's piles. Then your teeth fall out, and your hearing goes, and your eyes start watering, and it's cataracts. Then you can't remember anyone's name, and then you can't remember your own name. And the bloody doctors know bugger all. (*Quartet*, 18)

Reggie, on the other hand, finds his hard-earned retirement soothing: "It's been so calm here. . . . I have taught myself to live in the present . . . age helps one forget that which is best forgotten. In some perverse way, I've enjoyed the course of nature, the falling away of petty ambitions, the withering of ridiculous pride" (17).

Harwood highlights further degradations in the film through staff members who treat residents like infants. One character snarls at a nurse who talks to her as if she is a child. In another, two elderly residents are chastised for smoking by Dr. Cogan, who oversees the facility. Harwood, who hated this hypercritical health culture, gets revenge on such nicotine Puritans by having hypocritical Dr. Cogan sneak a cigarette of her own during a break.

Initially, the play presents Jean's reluctance to sing in terms of vanity. Jean says her voice is no longer beautiful, nor are the rest of the quartet's. With their voices gone, they are no longer artists, and to a certain extent no longer human. But as the play progresses, we learn the truth about Jean's voice; she is not merely hiding it, she has lost it. Despite interventions from doctors, psychologists, and vocal coaches, she just cannot sing. In the play, the intrepid singers decide to lip-sync the opera using their newly released album. The solution is brilliant for the characters and the play's production. With the lip-syncing part of the plan to accommodate Jean's disability, *Quartet* audiences will not fault its use. They will expect it, not see it as a gimmick to cover up the poor operatic skills of the dramatic cast. In this way, Harwood protects the opera from mediocre singing.

In the film, first-time director Dustin Hoffman and Harwood include a soundtrack so superb it could serve as an introduction to classical music. The film also expands the musical occupations of the retirement residents to include more opera singers, performers, and musicians, many of them real-life artists identified in the final credits by photographs depicting them both young and as they appeared in the film. Critics praised Hoffman, particularly his "sensitivity as a director [which] is evident in his ability to handle an ensemble work that turns upon subduing and orchestrating competing egos. He draws together its themes and characters into a satisfying whole during the climactic concert" (French).

The setting, however, a lush castle with beautiful grounds and houses, prompted Roger Ebert and others to fault the film for pushing the limits of verisimilitude:

> You can sit in a theater and hope the retirement home can be saved. But when you look at this film, you see a stately manor surrounded by pastoral beauty. The location, Hedsor House in Buckinghamshire, near London, obviously suggests a multimillion-pound budget and isn't going to be saved by a gala — especially not after we see how small the well-dressed audience is. Their tickets must have been really expensive. ("Sweet")

Though most critics enjoyed both the play and the film, Ebert's comment offers an interesting perspective.[1] On the one hand, the gala serves as Harwood's version of Hitchcockian McGuffin, just something to move and shape the plot. On the other, the setting and lush accouterments create the "fairy tale" atmosphere critic Deborah Young noted. This is not reality; it is an opera-lover's fantasy.

Music appears around every corner, making this fairy tale transformation possible. Everyone, no matter how young or old, participates. Small children come to take music lessons or offer a recital. In one scene, a novice pianist needs help with a woefully out-of-tune piano. Another older musician begins playing it in order to assist. Suddenly and magically, the music becomes beautiful. In this world, art transforms.

Harwood and Hoffman, however, are not naive enough to represent art and its production without complications and petty interactions. In the play, we learn Jean lost her voice due to childbirth. In the film, we see her pride and fear of public failure. Once she discovers that a rival opera singer is going to sing a solo during the gala, her competitive nature compels her to join the trio's project. With a musical montage akin to that of Rocky Balboa's boxing training sequence, the four rehearse for their big moment.

Despite the preparations, Jean hesitates, and Reggie encourages her to live in the moment:

> Let go, Jean, let go. There's no holding on to these things. Face reality for once in your life. We're alive now and not for very much longer. So make the most of it. Make the most of these days, these hours, this moment. To hell with what Jean Horton was. Live now, for God's sake. We're alive. . . . We're artists and we're meant to celebrate life. (51)

Ironically, when Jean and the others admit the realities of aging, the magic begins.

Thanks to the flexibility of the camera, the film ends literally on a high note: a reverse crane shot of the magnificent retirement castle with a recording of "Bella figlia dell'amore" from *Rigoletto*, sung by Sherrill Milnes, Huguette Tourangeau, Dame Joan Sutherland, and Luciano Pavarotti.[2] Lip syncing on film is unnecessary, so the film leaves us with the operatic soundtrack. The characters have adapted, and Harwood and Hoffman have adapted from stage to screen, creating a musical fairy tale that leaves us thinking about ways that we can "make the most of these days, these hours, this moment."

Mahler's Conversion

In contrast to the optimism of *Quartet*, *Mahler's Conversion* (2001) returns to the serious themes of anti-Semitism, the role of the artist in a totalitarian environment, the flawed tragic hero, and the ultimate outsider. As the Mahler character tells his friend Siegfried early in the play, "I belong nowhere" (*Mahler's Conversion*, 14). As recounted in the play, Mahler, a narcissistic and ambitious musical genius, needs an outlet, so he seeks the prestigious Vienna Court Opera directorship. No non-Christian may hold the post, so Mahler decides to convert. The play illustrates Mahler's rise and fall in the wake of these events. He held the post for ten years until the anti-Semitic complaints became too much and the board pressured him to resign. He finds other work, notably in the United States. However, after the death of one of his children and the discovery that his wife, Alma, is having an affair with a younger man, he faces a mental and emotional crisis, so he seeks counsel from Sigmund Freud. The play concludes with Mahler's death at a fairly young age.

Based on Mahler's life, the play is an important one in Harwood's canon for several reasons. First, never the critics' darling, Harwood was ravaged by the critical reception of the first production:

> The reviews . . . were so savage that [Harwood] was plunged into a depression and writer's block such as he had never known. . . . Because the play had opened in the aftermath of 9/11 and because, in response, many were pointing to Israel as the heart of the problem, his depression was fueled by a rumbling paranoia that, as a Jew, he had never really 'belonged' in England. (Fergusson, "Curtain Up")

In many ways, then, the play represents a crisis, one that forces Harwood to embrace his Jewish heritage even more. Harwood and Mahler are more than unfashionable. They are Jews in an anti-Semitic world, artists whose work is being blunted by bias. Harwood's Mahler expresses this perspective. He is triply marginalized. Once as a "native of Bohemia in Austria. Second, as an Austrian among Germans. And third, as a Jew in the rest of the world" (15). The play's production history further illustrates this marginalization. It has rarely been produced.

The play is also noteworthy because, while Harwood has dramatized Jewish identity in his other plays, he has not pitted it against Catholicism, which had influenced his tastes and had once even appealed to him as a possible alternative to his Judaism. Inspired by Catholic writers like Graham Greene and Evelyn Waugh, and married to a Greek Orthodox Catholic who converted to Roman Catholicism, Harwood here explored both his Jewish identity and his family's Catholic culture through the character of Gustav Mahler.

For Mahler scholars, Harwood is unusual because he takes the conversion seriously. According to Norman Lebrecht, Christian Mahlerians define it as a "perfunctory necessity," and Jewish Mahlerians "treat it as an embarrassing act of expedience" ("Who Was Mahler?"). Harwood, however, crafts the decision to convert as a tragic one. Egotistical and irascible, Mahler wants to be "defined as a musician. I want to be defined as a human being" (*Mahler's Conversion*, 6). He wants to eliminate religious labels to pursue his musical goals. Like Wilhelm Furtwängler, Mahler faces a totalitarian regime, not the Nazis, but "the Court of His Imperial Catholic Majesty, the Emperor Franz Josef" (9). If Mahler wants to work at the level his talent is capable of, he must convert.

Antony Sher, Harwood's South African cousin who played Mahler in the first production and who died of cancer soon after Harwood's death, explained that the play is about more than the conversion: "What makes it a great play is that Ronnie uses the Mahler incident to discuss questions of identity—how far you go to bury who you really are" (qtd. in Lebrecht). Sher also admitted that he, too, as a South African in Britain, a gay man, and a Jew, identified with Mahler's alterity (Lebrecht).

The play explores both the necessity of the conversion and anti-Semitism, not just in Vienna but throughout the world, and the nature of identity in general. The significant point about the play is that while it pits individual identity against a more universal understanding, it does not choose one over the other. It is not just about being a Jew or about being a human being. It is about both, and this double-vision challenges current cultural trends that focus on one or the other. Works of art must reflect the individual, not a culture or vice versa. Harwood began to explore this theme in *César and Augusta* and continued it in *Mahler's Conversion*. And like *César and Augusta*, this play presents an unusual and creative solution through which audiences may continue to ponder questions of identity, ethnicity, heritage, and spirituality.

Set during the turn of the century, a period of great social and cultural change, the play depicts all the characters as going through identity crises. While Mahler faces the conversion question, Siegfried Lipiner, a Jewish writer and poet who has converted to Protestantism, warns Mahler not to convert, because Lipiner, having done so, lost his artistic gifts. Natalie Bauer-Lechner, also based on a real-life individual, was a violist who kept a private journal about Mahler and dressed as a man. She appears late in Harwood's play, impoverished and sick, her search for gender articulation apparently over. Soprano Anna von Mildenburg also loved Mahler, but it was Alma Schindler who became Mahler's wife. Though Alma offers stability to Mahler initially, she, too, seeks redefinition. When they first meet, she is a bohemian composer, but Mahler insists she give up her career when they marry: "[Y]ou have only one profession now: to make me happy" (*Mahler's Conversion*, 61). The entire culture appears to be struggling with identity, so it is no surprise the Freud makes an appearance in the play as he did in fin de siècle Vienna.

Mahler's struggle is clearly tied to his Judaism and his attraction to Catholicism. It is not just the pressure from Viennese authorities. As he tells Siegfried, he has attended synagogues and Catholic churches, but he liked the Catholic services more: "[T]he music was better . . . I felt part of something then. And now, why am I, what am I, who am I?" (14). While Siegfried encourages him to enter Vienna "as a Jew. Become thyself" (21), to embrace his Jewish identity, Mahler decides to convert.

As he prepares for his baptism, he tells the priest of a dream he has had that includes an image that reflects a hybrid of the two religions: "I glimpsed a figure of, the figure of the terrifying Eternal Jew . . . but there was something else about him, something astonishing. He was carrying a gnarled, twisted staff, and on the top was a golden cross. He began to chase after me, trying to give me this staff, this staff crowned with the golden cross" (28). In anti-Semitic myths and legends, the Wandering Jew was a character out of the Crucifixion story, a man who somehow humiliated or abused Christ. He was then condemned to walk the earth until the Second Coming. Gustave Doré's images of the figure, perhaps the most familiar, depict him with a stick but without a cross. Mahler's addition reflects his anxiety over his conversion and the merging of the two religious traditions in his psyche.

While Mahler may have qualms of conscience about his conversion initially, his music, according to most music critics, was better after his baptism. Mahler enjoys popularity, and as Natalie predicted, "the world is" his

(21). But not for long. Through persistent and overwhelming criticism and attacks, the Christian authorities force him out of his position, which inaugurates his descent. His daughter dies, and he discovers his wife's affair.

Desperate, he seeks counsel from Freud. He feels that his music suffers from a childhood trauma that causes him to interrupt his "noblest passages" with the commonplace (73). Impressed, Freud compliments Mahler for his insight on this and other matters. Mahler also strikes a kind of postmodern stance, saying "to be human is to be uncertain" (75). And argues that his music is about and reproduces this existential situation.

While Mahler offers some insights into his own identity crisis, he overlooks the role that his Jewish religion, culture, and ethnicity play in it. Rather than analyzing his critics, he dismisses them when they "say my music is full of Jewish tunes" (73). Freud assists his understanding by separating Jewish religion from Jewish history, culture, legacy, and lineage:

> All religion suppresses the universal essence of humanity. But being a Jew has nothing to do with religious belief. Being a Jew is to possess a common mental construction, a radical rather than religious. Which is why, in your case, for example, your conversion of convenience, as one might call it, has not, cannot change your essential Jewishness, which is the inheritance of all the obstinacy, defiance, and passion with which our ancestors defended their temple. . . . The society in which you lived unfairly demanded that you deny your origins and beliefs in order to rise through its ranks . . . [you] were made to feel ashamed of being ashamed, and as a result reacted to this mass suggestion of your unjust society and allowed it to seduce you. But the common mental construction of the Jews is immutable, and that is why you suffer guilt. (78)

Earlier in the play, Harwood offers a similar explanation through a mildly humorous observation by Siegfried. Mahler says he is "sick of anti-Semitism." Siegfried says, "You mustn't be. It is absolutely necessary. It defines you as Jew" (6). Both the joke and Freud's explanation highlight the systemic bias against Jews as well as the formidable and immortal Jewishness of Jews, finally telling Mahler to "Become thyself." The scene concludes with Freud returning to his work on jokes, laughing as he reads through his papers, perhaps indicating Freud's solution to life's trials: a good joke.

In terms of the Harwood canon, however, the play and its conclusion are not a joke. Harwood addresses questions of identity and religion in the context of his Jewish heritage and faith. Previously he used the work of his favorite writer, Graham Greene, particularly the figure of the whisky priest in *The Power and the Glory*. Once one becomes a priest, can one change? Here, Harwood asks, once one is a Jew, can one change?

To a certain extent, the play suggests a negative answer, but like many of the issues Harwood addresses, the answer is not an easy one. During the play's final scenes, Mahler becomes ill and faces death. Alma is by his side, resentful of all those hypocrites who are crying over his impending demise, the same people who worked against him throughout his life because of his Jewishness. She offers Mahler the choice between a priest and a rabbi, but he calls only for her. As he dies, the stage directions specify that the last movement of Mahler's Ninth Symphony begin.

Given his answer to Alma, the play appears to promote human love as a response to the two religious options presented, but Harwood continues to complicate the question. He offers the director the choice to conclude the play with the appearance of a figure: "[T]he figure could be Father Swider [the priest who helped convert Mahler] or Sigmund Freud or the Eternal Jew" (86). No matter which figure appears, it "holds out a twisted staff . . . a plain staff without a cross" (86).

A priest. The Wandering Jew. Sigmund Freud. All offer a different perspective on the play. By choosing Freud, the play would portray Mahler as a modern hero facing self-definition in a changing world. With Father Swider or the Eternal Jew, Mahler would choose the two religious traditions he struggled with throughout his life. By leaving it open, however, Harwood suggests that in many ways it does not matter: the staff without the cross suggests Mahler's inherent Jewishness, no matter what he did. During an interview about the play, Harwood defended Mahler's conversion, commenting, "the only other option [for Mahler] would have been to say no to ambition. There may be people who do that, but we never hear of them again" (qtd. in Lebrecht). Here, Harwood suggests that art is what matters. Despite the uncertainty of life, Mahler embraces it and performs; despite the conversion, he cannot dismiss, deny, or destroy his essential Jewishness and his art.

An English Tragedy

Rebecca West's *The Meaning of Treason* (1947) and the release of some previously closed documents inspired Harwood's *An English Tragedy* (2008), a play that examines the capture, trial, and execution of British playboy-turned-traitor John Amery. Writing for the *Chicago Law Review* when West's book first appeared, Harry Klaven Jr. praised her book for its insight into treason through the detailed analysis of twenty conspirators. In what serves as a great example of the lost art of collegial criticism, Klaven says the book is "superb" and makes a contribution "to law, to psychology, to journalism, and, with the greatest distinction, to the contemporary writing of the English language" (Review, 378), before faulting the book for its insufficient analysis of three traitors, men no one expected would betray their country. He was particularly disappointed in the lack of full detail regarding John Amery, particularly "how so happy an environment could produce so perverse a son" (378).

Harwood's play provides an answer by once again examining self-hating Jews through his tragic vision. While the play focuses on Amery, in the end, Leo, his father, is the tragic figure of the play. As Harwood explains, "I'm interested in men of conscience. And Leo Amery was a good man. But he hid his Jewish origins because he was scared that it would damage his career" (Hemming, "Heart of the Matter"). The consequences of Leo's deceit are his son's self-loathing, which led him to collaborate with the Nazis. The play illustrates not only the far-ranging consequences of self-deception but also of anti-Semitism.

The play establishes Amery's guilt as a traitor to England through a radio broadcast at the play's opening. Like Axis Sally or Tokyo Rose, Amery speaks against his country, the communists, and Jews in particular. In the next scene, we meet his father, who worked for Winston Churchill and was a member of Parliament, his mother, and a legal representative who tells them the insanity defense is the only way they can save their son from hanging. At the end of the scene, Amery's presumably Christian parents, who are trying everything they can to save their son, agree to this course of action but also admit that a family secret may affect the trial—they are part Jewish.

While his sympathetic parents fret and suffer, Amery's personality is reprehensible. A nonchalant playboy and Jew-hater, Amery's attitude to his arrest oozes entitlement, privilege, and lack of concern: "nothing's going to happen to me. . . . Use your common sense. . . . My father was in Winston Churchill's Cabinet" (*English Tragedy*, 22). His tales of sex, high living, failed filmmaking, and work with Nazis make him completely unsympathetic despite his occasional charming moments. He admits that he has contempt for "everything" especially the British people who not only "thought the Führer was their enemy," but also "for not ridding us of the Jews" (26). He brags about his associations with Nazi celebrities and the fact that he started the British Free Corps, a group of British servicemen recruited to fight communists and support Nazi Germany. The play begs the question Klaven asks in his review: How did this upstanding family create such a creature?

With the help of Dr. Pimlott, a psychiatrist enlisted to help with the insanity defense, they reveal the answer. Leo's mother, Elisabeth, was "by birth Jewish. And no matter that my father was English born and bred, no matter what faith my mother professed, by Orthodox Jewish law her children were Jews. . . . I can't rid myself of the conviction that John has been driven into this present danger by that knowledge" (47). In other words, the internalization of anti-Semitism turned Amery into a monster.

Dr. Pimlott concedes that while Amery is not legally and technically insane, he suffers a "moral insanity . . . his conduct in life determined by diseased mental processes . . . and is devoid of moral sense by which normal people control their actions and utterances" (65). Unfortunately, the courts do not agree with this presentation, so Amery faces a trial.

Despite a last-minute detail that might free him, Amery pleads guilty, and in a matter of minutes, the court condemns him: "You now stand a self-confessed traitor to your King and country, and you have forfeited your right to live" (75).

In her version of the story, West suggests that Amery confessed to save his family embarrassment, and he says as much in the play. But following the release of family documents showing their Jewish heritage, Harwood said, "this didn't seem right to me. He'd embarrassed them [his family] all through the war. His father was a cabinet minister, and he was broadcasting from Germany. I have wanted to try to explain it since then" (qtd. in Thorpe). Amery had been an embarrassment to his family for years, so why would he do otherwise at this stage? For Harwood, the answer lies in his anti-Semitism and self-loathing as a Jew.

Using the metaphor of disease, Harwood describes anti-Semitism and Amery's self-loathing. Amery calls Jews and Jewishness a contagion. His ancestry breeds this disease, which he loathes. But there is another disease that Harwood exposes through the behavior of Amery's father, the disease of ethnic denial and assimilationism. Leo not only denied his Jewishness, he hid it and subsequently bred a beast. He recognizes his tragic error in the final scenes: "I wish now I had ended up a good Jew instead of an indifferent Englishman" (93).

But it is too late. His son's final words illustrate the extent of the infection:

> Why the fuck do you think I pleaded guilty? To save my beloved family embarrassment? Don't you believe it? It's a plague. And I carry it. And we know what it is, don't we.... And just think, Father, if we'd have been born in Germany, the Führer would have saved us a lot of trouble. Both of us.... Whole, half, one-quarter, the Führer was indifferent to fractions. (94)

The family secret and its cover-up created Amery. Throughout the play, we see the result of his father's tragic miscalculation. Harwood explains:

> The whole problem of identity in the period intrigues me. [Leo] Amery was a brilliant man: spoke seven languages, went to Harrow, was a fellow at All Souls—you'd think he would be able to say who he was. But he wanted more than anything else in the world to be thought of as entirely English. That's the heart of the matter. I would have thought that was the mainspring of the whole tragedy. (qtd. in Hemming)

The decision to focus on Amery rather than his father offers a new perspective to Harwood's tragic trajectory. The play highlights not just the miscalculation but its consequences not just to the tragic hero but to others. Here, anti-Semitism corrupts internally and externally.

Most of the reviews were positive: "Harwood has found in an odd footnote of English history a metaphor for our flawed national psyche" (Billington, "English Tragedy"). Charles Spencer praised it as a "gripping true story ... emotionally devastating" told "with simplicity and power" ("Emotionally Devastating").

Quentin Letts's lukewarm review, however, illustrates the problems with misunderstanding Harwood and his tragic vision. Letts identified Amery as the tragic hero and then criticized Harwood for it: Amery is "such an unpleasant piece of work" that "this is never properly a tragedy. More an 'unfortunate story'" ("Sympathy for the Devil"). The misreading takes him even further afield: "the anti-Jewish stuff is obviously important to the plot, but it is hard to listen to quite so much of it." The play makes it clear that this is exactly the point. To listen to the anti-Semitic monster Amery has become, to see the environment that fostered his growth, and to read commentaries like Letts's, not only illustrates that anti-Semitism persists but also challenges us to avoid such attitudes in the future.

In an interview with the *Jerusalem Post*, Harwood explains his interest in the Holocaust and the reason for so many Holocaust films. The answer also serves as response to the Letts's critique: "[I]n the context of six million Jewish victims, this has not been overdone. There will be more such films when they are needed" (qtd. in Tugend, "Waiting for Oscar").

Collaboration

Harwood returns to the matter of artistic production under a totalitarian regime in *Collaboration* (2008), a play about Richard Strauss's work with the Nazis. As Harwood notes in the foreword to the published play, it is a "companion piece" to his 1995 play *Taking Sides;* the two appeared together in repertory, at the Minerva Theatre, Chichester, in 2008. In both plays, an artist must choose between art and politics. In *Collaboration,* Strauss, like Furtwängler and the rest of the Western world at the time, underestimates the Nazis and overestimates his own influence. Harwood's presentation of Strauss is more sympathetic than his presentation of Furtwängler, however. While personal ambition and artistic reputation motivate Furtwängler's compromises, Strauss's family, which has Jewish members, motivates his negotiations. By pairing the two plays in repertory, Harwood forces us to examine these differing motives. Though Furtwängler's commitment to art is noble, it does not have the same impact as Strauss's dedication to his family and those who share his family's Jewish heritage. As Hitler's favorite and a free agent, Furtwängler has more agency and more freedom to resist, so his work with the Nazis seems less forgivable.

Based on a collection of letters exchanged between Richard Strauss and Stefan Zweig, who collaborated with Strauss on the opera *The Silent Woman*, *Collaboration* opens with Strauss eager to work on this new project. After a few discussions and some domestic details, Strauss and Zweig decide to work together. Although Zweig divorces his wife and marries his secretary during this time, the struggles Harwood presents are domestic and minor. All seems to be going as planned, so the appearance of Nazis at their door is all the more shocking and accurate. Few took the Nazis seriously, and few thought they would succeed in any way.

The play shatters this illusion when Goebbels accuses another writer, coincidentally also named Zweig, of violent anti-Nazi sentiments. The error, of course, not only makes Stefan Zweig a Nazi target but brings attention to him and his work. Zweig, who is Jewish, opposes the Third Reich but would never incite violence as the other author did, so he appeals to Strauss to intervene and clear his name. Strauss assures him that he has "influence" and can help resolve the matter. Zweig is not so sure: "Everything we hold dear is now valueless. You have a government of gangsters—and who cares, who protests? The outside world says it's happening beyond their borders, it's not their concern. But it is, it's everyone's concern. These criminals move slowly, slowly, bit by bit, one drop of poison at a time, until all the world will perish" (*Collaboration*, 40).

Undaunted, Strauss writes to Goebbels to clarify the identity of the Zweig he has condemned. Goebbels's response is to send Hans Hinkel, a thug from the propaganda ministry, to Strauss's door. Just as Zweig predicted, "bit by bit," Hinkel terrorizes Strauss and his wife. Strauss not only has no influence, he is in danger because he has written a letter denouncing anti-Semitism and his daughter-in-law and grandchildren are Jewish. Hinkel sugarcoats the threats by mentioning Furtwängler, who they are working with to "toe the line" more enthusiastically (47). The conductor's compliance, Hinkel notes, has earned him a new post, the presidency of the Reich Chamber of Music. If there is any doubt, he is now one of them.

Despite the Nazi pressure, Strauss and Zweig complete the opera, but when it opens, Zweig is not allowed to attend and receives no credit for his work. Disappointed, Strauss still urges Zweig to continue to collaborate with him surreptitiously. Zweig refuses: "I have no choice to be what I am" (62), a Jew and defender of Jewish life and lives. He and his wife leave the country and begin their exile.

While under the illusion that he has some personal and creative freedom, Strauss receives another visit from Hinkel. This time, there are no positions offered to facilitate complicity. They remove his posts and force him to write music for popular events such as the Olympics.

The play ends with scenes following the war. We learn that Zweig and his wife, who have moved from country to country, finally settled in Brazil, but they committed suicide, bereft by their exile from Europe. Strauss and his wife appear at denazification hearings where Strauss explains his actions. He wanted to save his family: "my motives may not have been pure, but at least they were human" (74). Strauss is no hero, but his choices are understandable.

The play toys with the representation of collaboration—how it works and how it does not—under totalitarian regimes. Both musicians compromised. Straus says of Zweig's decision:

> A man of his genius. How could he do such a thing? . . . Men of his integrity are to be numbered—(*Breaks off*)—I loved that man. . . . You accuse me of being a collaborator but what about Zweig? . . . You think they didn't want to add another Jew to the millions they murdered? Of course, they wanted him dead. And he obliged. He did their bidding. (74)

To varying degrees, all the musicians compromised, as the regime's insidious power grew imperceptibly, unnoticed before it was too late.

And perhaps this insidiousness is the focus of both plays, not merely the motives of two, even three, tragic heroes but the political context that the men find themselves in, a situation that Harwood also detected in contemporary culture. In a 2006 interview with Tim Walker of the *Spectator*, Harwood admitted:

> I am very Jewish. It is who I am. It worries me that people think it is okay to be antisemitic again these days. I think of the posters depicting Michale Howard as Fagin during the last election. They came out

at the same time that Ken Livingstone made his remarks to a reporter on the *London Evening Standard*. His comments comparing a Jewish reporter to a concentration camp guard showed the sorts of views that are in him. They were calculated to give maximum offence. (qtd. in Walker, "In Praise of the Patriotic")

The context remains. The potential remains. In *Taking Sides* and *Collaboration*, and particularly through their pairing, Harwood sends a cautionary message to his audiences. The Nazis rose to power and the Holocaust happened, and both could happen again. Our only defense is vigilance. Without it, we will have our own tragic decisions to make.

Public Servants

Once again addressing the Nazis' insidious rise to power, Harwood illustrates the British government's stubborn denial of the truth about German's armament in his 2009 *Public Servants*. Using *In Search of Churchill* by Martin Gilbert and Gill Bennett's *Churchill's Man of Mystery: Desmond Morton and the World of Intelligence* as his main sources, Harwood credits Hugh Whitemore's "brilliant screenplay" *The Gathering Storm* as one of the works that brought the story and its hero, Ralph Wigram, to his attention. Through Wigram, Harwood creates an everyday hero, a "public servant" with a conscience greater than those of his superiors, who makes a courageous decision that destroys him. He is a tragic hero who is almost too good.

Critics faulted Harwood for taking liberties with the details. However, Harwood defended himself, saying, "although I have observed the main facts of Ralph Wigram's story . . . I have also invented and imagined without restraint" ("Public Servants," acknowledgements). In other words, he writes fiction.

In both the play and reality, Wigram discovered hard evidence that Germany was arming itself for war. As a "civil servant," however, he had to obey confidentiality directives. Wigram disobeyed these orders and leaked the information to Winston Churchill, who believed the reports but who was not prime minister at that time. The information, then, was not public, and the delay effectively empowered the Nazis. Wigram died under suspicious circumstances, some pointing to a pulmonary hemorrhage as the cause, while others cited suicide brought on by his depression over the trials he faced and the carnage the delay resulted in.

Harwood sets the scene with Wigram's wife, who recites a passage from T. S. Eliot's *The Wasteland* that describes the fall of London:

> *What is that sound high in the air . . .*
> *Cracks and reforms and bursts in the*
> *violet air*
> *Falling towers*
> *Jerusalem Athens Alexandria*
> *Vienna London*
> *Unreal* (1)

In the next scene, we learn that Wigram has overdosed on his medication for no apparent reason. His wife explains that Wigram "bottles things up" (Public Servants," 5). To which Ava responds with typical Harwood humor, "The Foreign Office encourages its people to be reticent. It's called diplomacy" (5). The two women concluded the overdose was an accident. As the play progresses, it is clear that Wigram seeks relief from his tremendous pressure, so suicide is not out of the question. Sir Robert Vansittart, Private Secretary to the Prime Minister from 1928 to 1930 and Permanent Under Secretary of the Foreign Office from 1930 to 1938, known here as Van, encourages Wigram to reveal the evidence. Van, however, warns him, "Civil servants shouldn't have to make moral decisions." Wigram concludes, "We wouldn't have to if the ministers we served were honest" (22).

To release the information, Van introduces Wigram to a "cloak and dagger type," Desmond Morton. Harwood continues his political jabs during these interactions. Morton agrees to help. Wigram suggests "an honest reliable newspaperman" (35). Morris says, "Did you mean in this United Kingdom? . . . What a whimsical notion. An honest, reliable newspaperman. This would be rather like finding a piglet who has been trained to fly by the Royal Air Force" (35).

Instead, Morton suggests Winston Churchill. Once the news is released, the Wigrams celebrate, but the government exerts further pressure. Wigram undergoes interrogation. Sir Maurice Hankey reminds him, "is it not the case that civil servants are paid to be loyal to whomever is in power, to whomever the people have elected?" (22). Wigram agrees, but adds "there is always the matter of one's conscience" (22).

In the end, the decision brings no relief. Initially, the release changes nothing: "All we talk about is the Olympic Games" (35). He also questions his own motives. Did he do this for "self-aggrandizement or self-deception" (36). The pressure is too much for him, and the play concludes that he commits suicide, unable to cope following these events.

Realists Morton and Ava, however, discuss Wigram, who they think was too much of an idealist: "Did he really think he could turn a dishonest government into a brave champion of truth?" (40). But both applaud Wigram's decision. Despite the lackluster initial results, Morton reminds us that "we have to go on believing that every little helps, every drop eventually reduces great boulders to pebbles" (40).

In his final World War II play, in a play where people risk everything for the sake of truth, Harwood offers as the last word from Morton, ironically in Latin, a common Catholic utterance:

> My weakness is to believe that we should make the choice to side with good.... No dogma could be more ridiculous or laughable.... Yes, and it's a cause for great merriment. And you will say, how can you believe all that twaddle after participating in a war of unimaginable slaughter and believing there's going to be another one? I've no explanation. Can't help it. Credo. (41)

Harwood's final challenge in this unpublished work: Can we believe, despite what we have seen, despite ourselves?

Heavenly Ivy

Heavenly Ivy (2010) is the perfect way to conclude a discussion of Harwood's dramatic works. A celebration of theatre and food, it brilliantly captures Harwood's delightful sense of humor, a quality that appears in all his plays but is sometimes overshadowed by the moral conundrums his characters face. Here, Harwood offers a lighthearted tribute to the iconic West End London restaurant, the Ivy, and its companion eatery, the Caprice.

The play opens with a woman singing Noel Coward's "I'll See You

Again." As the lights come up, long-dead critic James Agate, played by Michael Pennington in the original production, and an unnamed man and woman suddenly realize they have been transported to the Ivy. Deceased Ivy founders Mario and Monsieur Abel, who now inhabit that "heavenly restaurant in the sky," have summoned them to celebrate the restaurant. Right on cue, the man asks, "[W]hat's it like . . . a heavenly restaurant?" To which Mario quips, "A heavenly restaurant is where you can hear what people at your table are saying" (*Heavenly Ivy*, 44).

Before moving much further, Harwood takes his revenge on the critics. If the restauranteurs have been in heaven, where has Agate been? While all other drama critics have been assigned to hell, Agate has been fortunate enough to live in purgatory "because he loved the game of cricket" (46). But purgatory certainly has its drawbacks because it is defined as "having to watch over and over again plays by Bertolt Brecht" (47).

With the afterlife hierarchy explained, Mario and Abel reminisce about their early glory days. As young men, they decide to expand their restaurant business and work together. Located in the West End theatre district, they attract famous clientele such as Sir Charles Cochran, Somerset Maugham, Tallulah Bankhead, Neville Chamberlain, Eleonora Duse, Pavlova, G. K. Chesterton, and "the greatest Englishman of all, Winston Churchill, who once practiced a speech here in this very room" (50). While celebrating a theatrical success, musical performer Alice Delysia, or Alice Lapize, gave the restaurant its name. During a conversation, she asks Mario about the restaurant's success. He says "actors seem to like us." She responds, "But, of course, actors cling together like ivy" (54).

In addition to some delightful gossip about events at the Ivy over the years, the play also includes a tribute to the restaurant's decision to stay open during World War II, serving Spam and other rations at the prices required by the war effort. In her review, Libby Purves compliments director Sean Mathias for "a surprisingly effective Blitz" and concludes by calling the play a "love song to the two professions"—theatre and the culinary arts.

The Ivy, then, is more than a restaurant. Mario clarifies:

It should not be anything like your home. No, no, a restaurant is not just a place where you eat, not just a room where food is served. A restaurant must be a magical world, just like the theatre that you of all people know so well. . . . A great restaurant casts its own spell of excitement and anticipation. A great restaurant should be a place where surprise, adventure, and pleasure are possible. . . . It's an old friend you're always pleased to see. (62)

Mario's speech could easily be applied to theatre, with Harwood and his works the old friend we are always happy to see.

Heavenly Ivy was performed in the restaurant, which is open to the public. But Harwood, thanks to his artistic work, received a lifetime membership to the exclusive Club at the Ivy. With his knighthood and this membership, Harwood, unfashionable until the end, made his way into the West End stratosphere. And yes, he still had his doubts. During an interview with Dominic Maxwell following the opening of *Ivy*, Harwood said that he did not "expect posterity to be kind to him," saying "I'm not a stylist in the sense that Harold [Pinter] was a stylist. I don't know if my language is particularly special. But I try to be true to the subject" (qtd. in "Ronald Harwood Graduates").

Heavenly Ivy underscores Harwood's dramatic talents, his joy in his work, his love of the theatre especially, and his faith in humanity's ability to overcome the suffering it creates for itself. There are challenges, and all of Harwood's plays indicate that more work needs to be done, but there is hope, and there are jokes. His plays force us to face moral dilemmas, challenge us to remain true to ourselves, demonstrate the need for justice, and warn us against the totalitarian impulses that persist in our world. For Harwood, art was the key to this hope, this resistance, and our future. He observes, "Totalitarian governments always have to control the arts because they know their power" (qtd. in Gore-Langton, "Moral and Political Dilemmas"). Art may have a lot to answer for, but life without it would have to answer for more.

CHAPTER FOUR
THE SCREENPLAYS

"I'm not doing it on stage."
—Anthony Hopkins, when asked to play in *The Dresser*

HARWOOD'S RESPONSE TO THE 2015 TELEVISION PRODUCTION OF *THE DRESSER*, starring Anthony Hopkins and Ian McKellen, was typical of his ambivalence about film and his preference for the stage. Harwood had always thought that Hopkins and McKellen would be perfect in the leading roles. But Hopkins, who left the stage in 1989 and had not been in a scripted television show for twenty years, refused to do the work live. Harwood thought he would never see it performed with those two celebrities, but media executives thought a television version would be possible, and they pitched the idea, arguing that it could serve as a reminder of the medium's golden age, the era that made Harwood's and other playwrights' careers through televised dramas. Ironically, Richard Eyre, former director of the National Theatre, a theatre that never produced any of Harwood's works, was engaged to direct. Harwood acquiesced. When the production appeared, Harwood was less than enthusiastic about it. Although he described it as a "master acting class" in a "majestic production," everyone read between the lines ("Production Notes: *The Dresser*"). A critical storm developed, and Harwood had to repeatedly acknowledge his support for the production that, ironically, only served to highlight his disappointment in the televised movie.

Harwood's entry into the film industry was a kind of Faustian bargain.

Given the revolutionary stylistic and political changes occurring in modern theatre when he first arrived in London—including the theatre of the angry young men, absurdism, and Brechtian politics—Harwood neither fit in nor wanted to, so he turned his artistic energies toward novels and film that supported his tragic vision. Most importantly, he needed money to support his growing family. Early in his career, he served as a "gun for hire" on many scripts and even worked with Italian producer Gianni Hecht to translate scripts into English. In a 2008 article for the *Guardian*, David Thomson described Harwood as "one of the hottest screenwriters in the world," and chronicled his many successes, among them screen adaptations of his own and others' works—including *The Dresser, Taking Sides, The Pianist*, and *The Diving Bell and the Butterfly*—but Thomson also characterized Harwood's earlier film career by saying, "he would do anything," mentioning less notable works such as *A High Wind in Jamaica* and *Arrivederci, Baby!*

While these early screenplays did not secure Harwood's reputation as a serious artist, they earned him a good living, good enough that later in life he could pursue his true calling as a playwright, and they brought him into contact with influential film performers, directors, and producers, some of whom became lifelong friends and colleagues. Robinson notes that Harwood even made money from Richard Burton who bought the rights to his novel *The Guilt Merchants* (104). During one of my interviews with Harwood, he offered this advice on screenwriting: "Never give back the money." And he never did.

Harwood's film career reflects the movie industry's chaotic production process, and he frequently wrote about the frustrations, failed projects, last-minute rescues, and other vagaries of the film industry. Thomson noted that "When Baz Luhrmann faced difficulties on his forthcoming epic *Australia* . . . and freely described [it] as the Australian *Gone With the Wind*, he called Harwood" (Thomson). In 2008, there were rumors he was working on a script of his novel *The Girl in Melanie Klein* (Thomson), and in 2010, Steven Spielberg hired Harwood to write a biopic about Martin Luther King (Sperling). Neither film ever appeared. In credits for *Love in the Time of Cholera* (2007) and *Australia* (2008), Harwood's name appears as screenwriter, but he personally disassociated himself from both films because the scripts he had written were not the scripts the filmmakers filmed.

Harwood was an avid defender of scriptwriters, saying during the writer's strike of 2008, "[I]f nothing else this dispute will have brought home our importance to the industry. Little, on a screen large or small, can be spoken without it first being written. By writers" ("I say"). His decision to write only adaptations for the screen stemmed from the industry's devaluation of writers. Not only do films need a tremendous amount of money to be produced, the process compromises artistic autonomy: "If you write an original script, you have to get a director on board, wait for the money to be raised. It's too daunting" (qtd. in Gritten).

Adaptation also afforded Harwood the opportunity to choose material that suited him and his style. In *Ronald Harwood's Adaptations,* a gathering of Harwood's responses to interviewers' questions on the art of adaptation, Harwood claimed to follow his intuition when choosing works to adapt: "Over the years, from childhood perhaps, a writer will, consciously or subconsciously, inform his creative mechanism—I hesitate to call it his conscience—as to what subjects and themes he or she responds. This response is essential to the screenwriter, and I now know immediately if the book or the play appeals to my creative process" (*Ronald Harwood's Adaptations,* 8). The choice of the term "conscience" as opposed to "intuition" suggests a level of moral complexity and a continuation of his tragic vision in the film medium.

Of course, adapting literary works to film has its challenges. The relationship between the original and the film is always subject to debate. And there is a decision to be made regarding how closely the screenplay will follow the original. One dramatic example of an adaptation that went far afield from the original is the 1946 movie version of Ernest Hemingway's short story "The Killers." Director Robert Siodmak and screenwriter Anthony Veiller (assisted by John Huston and Richard Brooks, both uncredited) used nearly two hours of running time to bring the less than ten-page story to the screen. To provide context for Hemingway's enigmatic piece, they expanded the script to include everything that had led to the scene recounted in the story and followed up with everything that happened afterward.

Like the work of Harold Pinter, Harwood's screenplays followed his sources closely, and both writers chose material consistent with their other works. Harwood, for example, adapted several books on the Holocaust or important political, musical, or artistic figures. The most common complaint Harwood received regarding his adaptations is that he used the source to create a new piece of art. He did not merely rewrite the source for film; instead, he used the source to create a new film with new meanings and themes. When he wrote about essential figures, surviving family members often resisted or faulted him for his characterizations or for including events that did not happen, just as Wolfit's family complained about his depiction of the actor-manager in *The Dresser*. Harwood responded that the story remained at the heart of his adaptations. In typical Harwood fashion, he explains that he avoided specifying camera angles and other such direction in his scripts "like the plague" because they detracted from his primary purpose—telling the story (*Ronald Harwood's Adaptations*, 27). But he remained true to what he called the truth of the original: "[A]nything is not fair game, but anything that feeds the story, leading backward or forward to the core, is fair game" (Harwood, "Ego").

An examination of Harwood's more successful screenplays shows that Harwood's tragic vision persisted even through the process of adaptation and film production. His film characters struggle, fail, and survive, leaving us with problems to consider and alternatives to choose among. Harwood's films are filled with outsiders, those unfashionables who seek to change their world and ours, as in his novels and plays.

One. Interior. Day: Adventures in the Film Trade

Harwood's collection of short stories, *One. Interior. Day: Adventures in the Film Trade* (1978), offers comic insights into his views on the movie industry by following the struggles of fledgling screenwriter Edward Lands. Because Harwood dedicated the book to Albert Finney, it is entertaining to assume they may have shared the collection's perspective on "the business." In the first short story, Lands "lands" a job translating Italian film scripts, something Harwood himself did. Of course, the script is a mess, and Italian emotional storms create chaos: one of the other writers has committed suicide over a failed love affair, and the remaining writer on the project, a world-famous Italian "scenarist," explains the film to Lands. At the same time, a naked young woman sits on the scenarist's lap like a pet.

Though Lands is not entirely naive, he is certainly inexperienced. He begins his work by quoting Shakespeare to describe his perspective on art: to hold a mirror up to nature, suggesting the young writer's comfort with verisimilitude. By the end, the mirror takes on a nightmarish quality, looking more like the endless repetition of images foretelling Banquo's succession. Lands concludes that he cannot stay in this environment for long because it brings out "the worst in him" (*One. Interior. Day,* 5). He wonders why he has been offered "a mirror on which much is written, but nothing understood" (32). The mirror symbolism highlights the spectacular nature of the industry while writing about it in a collection of short stories, and the interactions with the characters throughout question subjectivity and agency. Lands is clearly not in charge of the narrative or the image: the film machinery is. What we see is not the result of an artist, but a conglomeration.

The two final stories highlight Lands's powerlessness in this world, one conventionally and the other more subtly. In "Expenses," a clever secretary cheats Lands out of his expense account. "The Award Winner" documents the difficulties of adaptation in many senses of the word. Here, director-writer John Falkland offers Lands a screenplay opportunity because he needs help solving the problem of adaptation. As Harwood will do throughout his career, Lands focuses on the story to resolve the problem: "[H]alfway through . . . he saw a solution, a way of telling the story in cinematic terms that preserved the suspense until the very last shot. (It was a simple invention: the story should be seen through the eyes of the detective, a secondary character in the novel, who would then share the audience's dilemma)" (120).

Lands, however, must adapt more than the script; he must adapt to directors. Falkland lives by one motto, "the only creed is the creed of *l'auteur*, the One Creator. And anybody who tells you otherwise is lying" (132). Writers, he continues,

> occupy a nothing place. Limbo. All you can hope for is to tell the story in the right order, in the most economical way possible, with one or two lines of dialogue thrown in. But what you cannot say . . . is that it's anything to do with you, as a novel is, or a play. You've got to acknowledge that the final product is not of your making. . . . Not the view or the vision. (132)

Falkland clearly voices Harwood's perspective on directors and the position of writers in the moviemaking universe.

Much to his surprise, Falkland praises Lands's solution. He hosts an elaborate celebration for the cast and crew to celebrate. During the party,

Lands makes a tragic error—he flirts with Falkland's assistant. Lands leaves Italy, thinking that all has gone well. When the film is nominated for an Oscar, however, Lands sees that he has not been recognized in the credits. Falkland cheated him out of his "screenplay credit. . . . And an Oscar nomination" (140). Devastated, Lands attempts legal action, but his lawyer discourages him because the flirtation could be used against Lands. Lands does not pursue the lawsuit. Instead, he comforts himself by reminding himself that his film and writing career are about "the process . . . not the product. . . . Edward believed it would not be long before a particular mystery would again take place: a germ, an idea, a vision, a view, an insight. All he could do now was keep the faith" (146). The film industry, the art industry, and the life industry are unfair. They demand a tragic perspective. Challenges occur. Mistakes happen. Suffering results. Art and the work of art offer, if not the hope, the activity necessary to continue.

One. Interior. Day illustrates the kind of strength necessary to survive the frenetic film industry. It is a miracle that films get made at all, but here we will see a writer at work who did not merely endure but prevailed, illustrating the essential role of the screenwriter.

One Day in the Life of Ivan Denisovich

Aleksandr Solzhenitsyn's *One Day in the Life of Ivan Denisovich* (1962) recounts a day in the life of a Soviet political prisoner. Based on his own experiences, Solzhenitsyn chronicles the vagaries of totalitarianism, one of Harwood's common topics and themes. Working with colleagues from theatre and television, including Tom Courtenay, who would later immortalize the character of Norman in both the play and film versions of Harwood's *The Dresser*, Harwood illustrated not only the oppression and absurdity of the gulag, but also the coping strategies Ivan and the other inmates use to survive there.

Here, in his first major film adaptation, Harwood follows the original closely. As Harwood repeatedly said of adaptation, "[T]he screenplay, besides supplying all the information that it needs to supply, must be enjoyable to read. My advice is: just tell the story—which is not as easy as it sounds" ("Ego," 8).

Part of the challenge is working with a director who often focuses more on the visual than the narrative. A bit of dialogue from both Solzhenitsyn's book and Harwood's film script serves as a metaphor for the bifurcated relationship between the writer and director: "How can you expect a man who's warm to understand a man who's cold?" (*One Day in the Life*, 34). This binary also illustrates the contrasts that exist in the totalitarian regime, the lives of the prisoners, and their perspectives on their imprisonment. For example, both novel and film pit the hero's pragmatic secularism against the Christian faith of another inmate, Alyosha. In the end, the book and screenplay condemn totalitarian oppression, but both present varying ways of responding to the situation. And true to his other work, Harwood does not "take sides" on the varying responses.

The film (1970) immediately establishes the camp's terrible conditions. Through an establishing shot, we enter a void, then, very slowly, the camp appears, an island of incandescent light in the snowy darkness. As the camera penetrates the barracks, we meet Ivan, who is being punished for oversleeping. Three days "with work," sounds like a harsh punishment, but as we learn throughout the film, totalitarian regimes twist logical expression and expectation. Work duty is preferred here: "[T]hey gave you hot food and you had no time to start thinking. Real jail was when you were kept back from work" (21).

Though the food is atrocious, a kind of rancid cabbage oatmeal, its consumption, delivery, and absence occupy many scenes and many of the inmates' daily lives. The use of food is dualistic, too. As Dongmei Xu notes, eating is personal, a way to retain a sense of self ("Food and Homecoming,"106). But it is also used by the guards to control the prison population. As the men build a wall in the brutal cold, where mortar freezes if left out too long, Ivan's voice-over explains the rationale for the squads, a Soviet masterpiece of group manipulation: "A guard can't get people to budge even in working hours, but a squad leader can tell his men to get on with the job even during the break, and they'll do it. Because he's the one who feeds them. And he'd never make them work for nothing" (*One Day in the Life*, 90). Though eating is intensely personal, in the gulag it is used for group manipulation, fostering human automation.

The novel and screenplay present two heroes who resist this process of mechanization and homogenization. Ivan stands out as the narrator, but he also distinguishes himself through his work ethic. During a moment in the novel, Ivan reflects, referring to himself by his last name Shukov:

Wasn't it enough that Tiurin had told them himself not to bother with the mortar? Just throw it over the wall and fuck off. But Shukov wasn't made that way—eight years in the camp couldn't change his nature. He worried about anything he could make use of, about every scrap of work he could do—nothing must be wasted without good reason. (105–106)

According to Rimgaila Salys, for Ivan, "work is the most profound means of self-expression available to him in the repressive environment of the camp" ("Solzhenitsyn's *One Day*," 114). This dedication and persistence make him a tragic hero. Despite his situation, he retains something of himself.

Ivan's generosity also distinguishes him from others. At the film's end, he helps one inmate, a rather self-important Muscovite, hide a package of food and supplies he has just received. Ivan receives some of the food as payment, but he also shares some with other prisoners as they argue about the nature of God and faith. Through this ordinary day, we see the extraordinary in the individual, a clear contrast to the grubby conformity imposed in the gulag.

Actions of the Christian inmates stand in contrast to Ivan's humane individualism. To Ivan, their rituals are the same as those of the Soviets. He wryly observes that there is little difference between the Christians' prayers and the Soviet guards' morning exhortations that "every prisoner was heartily sick of: 'Attention, prisoners. Marching orders must be strictly obeyed. Keep to your ranks. No hurrying, keep a steady pace. No talking. Keep your eyes fixed ahead and your hands behind your backs . . . '" (Solzhenitsyn, *One Day in the Life*, 47). Later when the guards punish the inmates by taking away their "Sunday," Ivan wonders what Sisyphean tasks they will devise to fill the time (126).

While Harwood does not include these reveries, he makes it clear that Ivan is a secular humanist through his conversations with the pious Alyosha. Here, too, Harwood amends some of the lengthy discussions, but the novel's central question remains in his screenplay: How do we justify suffering? For Alyosha, there is a divine will at work. His time in prison is a time to rejoice, since "here you have time to think about your soul," the very thing Ivan wishes to avoid (155).

Unconvinced, Ivan mutters a prayer that reads more like a non sequitur, which Alyosha interprets as Ivan's soul yearning for God. Ivan comically responds, saying that his prayers are like his letters—unanswered (153). Like Harwood's Uncle Laban in his novel *Home*, Ivan may pray, but he will not "get too involved" (*Home*, 18). He considers Alyosha naive and "impractical ... [he] makes himself nice with everyone but doesn't know how to do favors to get paid back" (Solzhenitsyn, *One Day in the Life*, 158). Alyosha considers Ivan ignorant about religion and matters of faith, and tries to convert him by showing him how some of his actions are consistent with Christianity.

In some ways, both are heroes, adhering to their sense of themselves and their life purposes. But like all tragic heroes, they are not entirely successful. The film concludes with an outspoken prisoner being sent to the "cells" for ten days, a sentence that will surely lead to his death from exposure and hunger. Faith has its place, and secular community building may offer some relief, but in the end the regime triumphs here. After showing us the prisoner in his cell, the film returns to Ivan, who thinks about his day. The juxtaposition of these three images—the pious Alyosha, the generous Ivan, and the condemned man—creates a powerful image of the gulag's power, its ability to kill an inmate and to create a stalemate for personal choice.

In the novel, Ivan attempts optimism. It was "a day without a dark cloud. Almost a happy day. There were three thousand six hundred and fifty-three days like that in his stretch. From the first clang of the rail to the last clang of the rail. Three thousand six hundred and fifty-three days. The three extra days were for leap years" (Solzhenitsyn, 158).

Clearly, the human spirit resists, but can it survive such oppression? Both Ivan's and Alyosha's tactics seem impotent, but the film offers a third alternative. At several moments in both the novel and the film the prisoners discuss art. The scenes seem almost comical. During the struggle merely to survive, aesthetic discussions appear. While Solzhenitsyn faulted the film for its lack of humor (Harwood, "Ego"), these moments suggest art as an alternative to suffering and the threat of existential annihilation. The film's concluding shot highlights the power of art. Through a reverse zoom, moving from the barracks back into icy darkness, it highlights the invisibility of the men's suffering. Though the camera has the "final word," it suggests that without art—here, that of Solzhenitsyn, Harwood, and Wrede—the men in the gulag would never be seen, their stories never read, seen, or heard.

Mandela

Opening with some archival taken footage following the 1948 vote to codify apartheid in South Africa, Harwood's script for the HBO television film (1987) *Mandela* not only documents Nelson Mandela's rise to prominence in the African National Congress (ANC) and his subsequent incarceration, but also the life of his wife, Winnie. The choice is a unique in acknowledging women's contributions to the anti-apartheid movement, and it places a tragic, heroic couple at the center of the film.

Winnie was not thrilled with the results, however, and accused Harwood of capitalizing on her family's misery: "This film serves no political purpose and was made solely for commercial reasons. The producers are just cashing in on the name of the family." Though one of the producers assured her that the film was in fact losing money, "in the red," she was unconvinced (qtd. in Parks). ANC representatives praised the film, while Mandela remained silent. The quiet might be interpreted as criticism, but given the fact that Mandela approved Harwood's screenplay for a new, post-apartheid film version of Alan Paton's *Cry, the Beloved Country*, his response might have been focused more on keeping marital discord to a minimum. The couple separated five years after the film and divorced in 1996.

Critics saw the film's relationship and conclusion as idealized. The story could not be "the story of a triumphant struggle because the struggle isn't over, and triumph may be years away" (Shales). Such criticism is grounded not only in ignorance of Harwood's tragic vision and structure, it also taints the realities of historical fiction with the expectation for strict adherence to facts. Harwood, of course, was accustomed to this kind of critique from his work depicting his own family members and other historical moments and figures. Some in his family were unhappy about their representations in plays such as *A Family* and *Another Time*. Donald Wolfit's family members, too, were not entirely thrilled when Harwood included less than complimentary details about the great Shakespearean's life in *The Dresser*. These works are artistic pieces, however, not documentaries. Memory, details, and interpretations change as the materials of life and history are crafted into a new art form, and this is perhaps the best way to approach the film *Mandela*. As a film about the lives of Nelson and Winnie Mandela, it was a means by which Harwood continued his interrogation of totalitarianism and its effects on individuals and artists. Harwood tells the story of these anti-apartheid heroes in a tragic context, which required the adjustment of some facts.

Harwood said as much in a book he published to accompany the HBO film and that included script excerpts, South African history, and film commentary. In it he calls Mandela an "epic" hero. In light of our understanding of the years following the film, we can add the word "tragic." Harwood saw the film as revealing the epic struggle

> for justice and freedom in South Africa because it contains the essential element of an epic story, which is that the experience of one man represents and reinforces the experience of many. . . . All epics . . . seek to make a vast collective conflict intelligible in terms of one central figure or group. Nelson Mandela is such a figure. The danger of oversimplifying or inadvertently diminishing contributions of others is offset by the privilege of hearing an individual voice which speaks loudly, clearly, and often movingly for millions. (Harwood, *Mandela* [book], 3)

The description is consistent with Harwood's other outlier, unfashionable, and artistic characters. The comment recognizes that sometimes one individual represents the truth of a social situation better than a consensus can. Harwood, here and elsewhere, resisted the idea that contemporary culture cannot have or produce heroes or that heroism was a dying and elitist concept. Harwood throughout this and other works illustrated his belief that not only does heroism still exist, it remains necessary and essential, a key component to protecting consensus and democratic rule, not its antithesis. One person, one artist, one outsider, one unfashionable, can make a difference and inspire others. Unlike the dictator, however, this individual represents and protects the rights of the community members; they do not repress those rights.

In the film as in real life, Mandela represents an awareness of this responsibility and the role of a hero. When he announced his separation from Winnie in 1992, he observed that the marriage was a casualty of his political activism: "[J]ust as I am convinced that my wife's life while I was in prison was more difficult than mine, my own return was also more difficult for her than it was for me. She married a man who soon left her; that man became a myth, and then that myth returned home and proved to be just a man after all" (Mandela, "The Separation").

Mandela thus offers a perfect model for Harwood's tragic vision. He is a flawed over-reacher who resisted censorship, oppression, and totalitarianism. But Harwood wanted to expand this representation to include Winnie. Not only was Winnie a powerful force, but Harwood wanted to "balance Mandela's political activities with his personal life . . . to reveal something about the extraordinary bond . . . which sustained them through their struggle against a brutal and inhuman social system" (Harwood, *Mandela* [book], ix). At the time he was writing, the couple's public profile, at least, indicated a strong and committed marriage (Nelan).

The critic Michael Massing thought the script emphasized the relationship too much, showing how unusual Harwood's presentation was. Harwood acknowledges Winnie's importance and power, and demonstrates the sacrifices the couple made to the movement and does not idealize the couple or their life together. Winnie, for example, says that she married a "struggle," not a man, and the film offers her as a model for young women. She begins as a shy young woman and becomes a confident freedom fighter.

Though sometimes faulted by the critics for its stereotypical portrayal of the white majority, it is challenging to look for finer points of characterization when whites, both in the film and in reality, were killing so many innocent Blacks. In the scene depicting the 1960 Sharpeville massacre, there is a moment when the white soldiers, who look incredibly young and inexperienced, hesitate when given the orders to kill. But, in the end, they shoot. Similarly, the film depicts a massacre during the Soweto uprising in 1976. Such moments illustrate the power of mob mentality and serve as a cautionary tale for all.

In fact, the ANC had several white supporters, and Harwood chose to represent a friendly relationship between a character he named Benny, perhaps based on Mandela's relationship with a Jewish lawyer early in his career. Benny helps Mandela hide by disguising him as his white chauffeur. These scenes with Benny not only demonstrated that whites and Blacks had a good deal in common and could work well together, they undercut any lingering white supremacist ideas about Black inferiority. Mandela can outrun, outthink, and out-politic his white friend Benny. While this film strategy may seem myth-making, it served an important political purpose in

South Africa and the United States: the film shows that Mandela and Blacks are undeniably capable.

When faced with impossible situations, however, there are no perfect solutions. Harwood includes the ANC's relationships with the communists, the only group willing to work with them at a point when violence against them was escalating. In the film and in life, the ANC had few options. This plot detail, however, led Reverend Jerry Falwell, an ultra-conservative televangelist, to condemn the film and to urge a boycott of both the movie and HBO (Farber). Harwood illustrates Mandela and the ANC's difficult position in a scene in which Mandela and his colleagues discuss using force, concluding, "at the heart of the decision was the dismal realization that twenty years of non-violent protests had been answered with brutal force" (Harwood, *Mandela* [book], 87). When in the film Mandela and other ANC members are on trial for high treason, they meet with their lawyer and indicate that they are willing to admit to their use of violence because nothing else was working: "We've nothing to be ashamed of, we had no alternative" (*Mandela* [film], 108). They had to find allies like the communists, and they had to resort to violence. While the lawyer warns them, "You realize that's like putting the noose round your own neck" (108), they had no choice.

They are consequently arrested, but not killed, and after a trial they are sentenced to years of hard labor on Robber Island. After many difficulties and much time has passed, Mandela is finally permitted to have in-person visits with his family in a prison in Johannesburg. He is also offered his freedom on the condition that he agrees to no further violence and to forgo future political activism. His response is that of a hero, and whether we agree with the portrayal of Mandela in this film or not, this scene, based on Mandela's own words and decisions, is one of the film's most moving. In a speech delivered by his daughter, Mandela questions the kind of freedom the white hierarchy offers: "What freedom am I being offered while the organization of the people remains banned? What freedom am I being offered when I may be arrested on a pass offence? ... What freedom am I being offered when my very South African citizenship is not respected?" (Harwood, *Mandela* [book], 129).

The film concludes with a voice-over while Mandela looks up into the camera, physically silenced by the apartheid practices in his country. The irony is powerful. Though silenced, he speaks. Though incarcerated, he is free. Though invisible, art helps us to see him: "I cannot and will not give any undertaking at a time when I and you, the people, are not free. Your freedom and mine cannot be separated. I will return" (Harwood, *Mandela* [book], 129). Given that this statement was made in 1985, five years before Mandela's release, the words and the image are prescient. They also repeat Harwood's ending to his very first novel on the atrocities of apartheid. Like the main character in Harwood's early novel *George Washington September, Sir!*, Mandela is not physically triumphant, but he has the spirit of a hero. And while this spirit may not prevent others from dying or abuses from occurring, it endures, offering hope to those who fight against totalitarian oppression.

Cry, the Beloved Country

The lukewarm reception of *Mandela* did not prevent the choice of Harwood to write an updated version of Alan Paton's *Cry, the Beloved Country* (1995), which was the "first major film to be made in the newly democratic South Africa." And while Mandela was silent on the HBO film, he hailed *Cry* as a "monument to the future" (Holden, "Searching for Answers," 27).

At the time, the original novel appeared to have seen its day. Published in 1948, Alan Paton's work illustrated and critiqued racism in South Africa. Ironically, that was the year the National Party came into power and instituted strict apartheid laws. Under its leadership, "South Africans endured institutionalized racial discrimination and the intrusion of a security state on an unprecedented scale" (Gump, 1148). But in the 1990s, apartheid was overthrown, Mandela was about to become the first democratic president of South Africa, and many felt the struggle was over. James Earl Jones initially responded that the work was a "museum piece" when he was approached to star in the Harwood film version, but he eventually agreed to participate (Keller, "*Cry, the Beloved Country*," 11). Anant Singh, the South African producer who had hoarded the film rights for years, finally decided to make "it as a celebration" (Keller, 11). But given Harwood's tragic vision and his interest not only in South Africa but in oppression and totalitarianism more generally, as well as his belief in the role even one person can play in changing abusive situations, it seems more likely that Harwood was drawn to the work's application to all ages. In the 1987 edition of the novel, Edward

Callan notes, *Cry* "is not propaganda. It seeks no solace in utopian political schemes of the left or the right, but it does reveal a concern for nurturing the capacity for justice in individuals" (Introduction, 29).

The novel explores the almost mythic journeys of two fathers, Stephen Kumalo, a Black South African cleric, and James Jarvis, a white landowner. Both men have lost touch with their sons, but their searches reveal understanding of their commonalities. Unfortunately, the men come to this understanding too late. Kumalo's son kills Jarvis's son in a burglary, and Kumalo's son is then tried and hanged for the crime. Kumalo discovers that his son had repented, and Jarvis discovers the anti-racist work his son was completing. As a result, he commits himself to fight against apartheid and racial oppression. The novel does not end optimistically, however. While the two fathers seek and support justice, the entire population, Blacks and whites, resist the changes necessary for peace and justice.

Harwood's 1995 film version not only closely follows the novel but also the screenplay written by Alan Paton for the 1951 film. Both Harwood and Paton establish the comparison between the two patriarchs quickly. Rather than postponing the development of Jarvis as in the novel, both screenplays introduce him and his family in the film's opening scenes. The strategy works well for a visual text. While Paton's introduction to the Jarvis section of the book highlights the economic differences, the screenplays establish these differences through juxtaposed visual images.

One of the biggest changes in the Harwood screenplay accommodates changes in audience perceptions. Paton thought the 1951 film was plodding, but Harwood's script is much brisker and more efficient, and the director, Darrell Roodt, uses the camera to establish many issues that Paton's screenplay explained. Gone are the lengthy descriptions and moments of exposition. When Jarvis travels to Johannesburg, he takes a plane, while Kumalo travels by road. The economic division behind the choices between the two modes of transportation is clear. The 1951 film, however, shoots the plane arrival at night, so the discrepancy is not as apparent. Roodt's daylight shot contrasts shimmering luxury to poverty.

One of the most important changes that Harwood makes is the addition of several voice-overs that punctuate the action. The sonorous voice of James Earl Jones presents some of the most lyric and poetic passages from the novel, passages that were not included in the 1951 screenplay. The most notable invokes the title of the novel and film:

Cry, the beloved country, for the unborn child that is the inheritor of our fear. Let him not love the earth too deeply. Let him not laugh too gladly when the water runs through his fingers, nor stand too silent when the setting sun makes red the veld with fire. Let him not be too moved when the birds on this land are singing, nor give too much of his heart to a mountain or a valley. For fear will rob him of all if he gives too much. (Paton, 111)

Harwood's addition of the voice-over pays homage to the novel's beauty as well as highlighting the importance of the writing and language underlying this visual medium.

Kumalo's voice-overs establish him as the hero of the film, but they also give him an otherworldly quality. Yes, he is flawed. He, too, is on a journey. But the voice-overs make him the film's moral center. Ironically, and as is often the case in the tragic universe, all his powers cannot save his son, but they do redeem a white stranger, Jarvis. Robert E. Lauder praises director Darrell Roodt for situating the reconciliation between the two men in the rain, a decision that gives the scene a spiritual dimension: "While speaking with Kumalo, Jarvis is pelted repeatedly by rain coming through the worn roof. The baptismal montage that Roodt creates is marvelous. . . . In a long shot Roodt situates his camera so that Kumalo and Jarvis are seen on opposite sides of the church, with the crucifix on the wall between them; the outstretched arms of Christ seem to be trying to draw the two men together" ("Filming the Face of God," 25).

A series of scenes in both the novel and the 1951 film that Harwood omits from his version deserve some discussion, however. In the 1951 film, when Kumalo comes to Johannesburg, he meets a white priest, Father Vincent. When Vincent offers to help him find his family, Kumalo says he will do it tomorrow He quotes a proverb he attributes to Father Vincent's country, saying, "[W]hy do today what you can do tomorrow." Father Vincent laughs and says, "[N]ot from my country, not from my country." The jest implies the racial stereotype: Blacks are lazy, and whites are disciplined.

Later, Kumalo, growing increasingly impatient with his son and with Johannesburg's promiscuity, interrogates his son's pregnant mistress. He loses his temper and returns to the priests' residence filled with anger. Father Vincent preaches forgiveness. Kumalo agrees. The scene remains in the 1951 film, with Father Vincent's authority clearly augmented by low angle camera positions. While the scene honors Kumalo's flawed human nature, necessary to a tragic hero, the necessity of white intervention is troublesome. In the novel and the film, Father Vincent, not Kumalo, is the moral center. With these deletions, however, Harwood empowers Kumalo and emphasizes his agency in a way the novel and earlier film did not. Kumalo is wise, forgiving, and pious. So, in the final scene, when he prays on the mountaintop, he may be surrounded by God's grandeur, but we have seen his own heroic strength and determination as well.

The critical response to the Harwood film was mixed at best. Critics faulted the understated nature of the narrative. Leonard Klady in his review noted, "[T]he low-key tone eventually works against the material. Without seeing the events that change the lives of key characters, the audience is asked to believe that the story's incidents will make reasonable men better" (4). The weakness of this criticism is that it overlooks the variations possible in a hero and his or her journeys. Kumalo begins and ends as a man of peace. His commitment to non-violence is tested, and he does lash out at times, but he is a peacemaker. Jarvis changes from a complacent white man who enjoys the fruits of systemic racism to a white ally to the anti-apartheid cause when he reads his son's speeches and writings. Jarvis's transformation results from reading, not a particularly cinematic or dramatic activity (one reason Harwood often prefers to use music and musical metaphors when creating his heroes). In this way, the film, in addition to illustrating the abuses of racism, suggests a reevaluation of the tragic to include the values of quiet strength, reading, writing, language, and literature, and to exclude violent methods.

The Pianist

Based on Władysław Szpilman's 1999 translation of his 1946 memoir *The Pianist: The Extraordinary Story of One Man's Survival in Warsaw, 1939–1945*, Harwood's Oscar-winning screenplay closely adapts Szpilman's experience and miraculous survival under the Nazi regime. In many ways, the film inverts Harwood's play and film *Taking Sides*. In *Taking Sides*, the Nazis support and enable Wilhelm Furtwängler's musical career, while in *The Pianist* (2002) the Nazis silence the musical expression of the titular character. The two films offer varying perspectives on the Nazis and their relationship with art and artists.

The film creates an ironic situation. It is a work about a pianist who does not play, and a film about music with very little music. For Lawrence Kramer, the situation is akin to Theodor Adorno's comment "No poetry"—that is, no pretty fictions, no aesthetic alibis—"after Auschwitz" (qtd. in Kramer, "Melodic Trains," 67). But Kramer concludes that Harwood and Roman Polanski's film does not uphold the Adorno dictum. Instead, the film shows "that art, above all music, speaks a transcendental, universal language, and that art, and above all music is a profoundly civilizing force" ("Melodic Trains," 67). Such sentiments are consistent with Harwood's other works, but Kramer argues that the music itself, specifically Chopin and, more specifically still, the Chopin Nocturne in C-Sharp Minor that bookends the film, becomes the protagonist, not Szpilman. Others, such as David Denby and Michael Oren, misread Harwood's protagonist and fault him for his effete and passive nature. Viewing the film through the lens of Harwood's canon and the tragic trajectory of his characters and works reveals that Szpilman is a hero on a journey to protect, recover, and play the music necessary for survival during and after the Holocaust. Moreover, Szpilman's inability to play does not create emptiness. Instead, its absence creates desire, a desire that propels the film and its characters forward. The music is not lost. Its absence represents the opportunity for future fulfillment, which appears to be completed in the final scene, when Szpilman finally plays again.

The complications arise through the decision to tell the story through Szpilman. But choosing such a perspective, the conclusion is not entirely satisfying. Yes, Szpilman is free. Yes, the Nazis have been overcome. But there is still the remembrance, and both Harwood and Polanski want us to remember. So, in this way, here in this film, art may prevail, but it also recalls.

Both Harwood and Polanski struggled with the representation of the Holocaust for personal reasons. Both experienced the Holocaust, albeit in different ways. Harwood's experience was secondhand. He recalls, "Then in 1945, when the Nazi atrocities were revealed, I was taken with other Jewish schoolchildren to see the newsreels of Belsen and Auschwitz. Those dreadful images—the skeletons passing for human beings, the bulldozers shifting mounds of corpses in mass graves—have haunted me ever since. The war defined my childhood, the Holocaust my adolescence" ("Ego"). As Harwood documents in his play *A Family* and his novel *Home*, during one screening he identified one of his family members as one of the deceased prisoners. Polanski and his family, on the other hand, experienced the Holocaust firsthand. They lived in the Krakow ghetto, and early on Nazis killed his mother and later separated him from his father. Polanski narrowly escaped and was at first taken in by Catholics, but was on his own for some time before the war ended.

Polanski chose Szpilman's book because it was written immediately after the war. He wanted reportage, not memoir. Polanski, who turned down the opportunity to direct *Schindler's List*, admits that he had searched for a vehicle for this period in his life, but he could not find one that met his expectations. The Szpilman book offered him this opportunity because it described experiences that Polanski had had. Polanski admitted to using his personal experiences throughout the film, particularly the focus on young children yearning for their parents ("Bonus Materials," *The Pianist*, DVD).

But, as it stood, the Szpilman book was "unfilmable." After seeing Harwood's *Taking Sides*, Polanski reached out to Harwood about creating a script. The rest, as they say, is history. The two men worked incredibly well together. Unlike many other directors who take the "script and never see the writer again," Harwood says he and Polanski locked themselves up together in a "house outside of Paris for five weeks and hammered it out" (Muir, "He Changed My Life," 14). Both men appreciated the camaraderie and noted that they laughed a lot while working on this serious film, perhaps as a defense against the horrors both men witnessed during their childhoods and while viewing the archive footage they used to help them create the film ("Bonus Materials").

Both men took their responsibilities seriously. And both committed themselves to telling the story accurately. While Polanski approached the subject humbly, Harwood explains what telling the truth is: "As we all know, there is no such thing as an undeniable historical fact. All history is subject to dispute . . . [but] an important lesson when adapting for the screen: always be true to the source material, the original author's truth" ("Ego"). While liberties may be taken to create art, to craft the narrative, the "truth" that motivated both Harwood and Polanski was simple: the extermination of the Jews by the Nazis.

One of the reasons the men were so cautious was because they were both keenly aware of the role of film during the war, and so this film also cautions audiences about the use of the medium to manipulate. Both realize the Nazis were filming their "masterpiece," the establishment of the Nazi regime in the world ("Bonus Materials"). This goal required documentation of not only atrocities but of petty humiliations and jokes. Szpilman mentions several humiliating moments in his book. In one, the Germans "insisted that the chairman of the Jewish Council should hold a luxurious reception and invite all the prominent people in the ghetto" (Szpilman, *The Pianist*, 86). During this reception, they humiliated Jews by forcing them to shower together on film. Szpilman comments that "only much, much later did I discover that these films were intended for the German population at home in the Reich and abroad. . . . They would show how well off the Jews of Warsaw were—and how immoral and despicable they were too . . . immodestly stripping naked in front of one another" (86).

Given the Nazis' misuse of film as propaganda, Polanski and Harwood became obsessed with objectivity. Harwood struggled with this goal not in terms of content but in terms of style and structure. He finally decided to use what he calls his "epic" and what I call his tragic approach. As he says, "it is self-evidently impossible to tell the whole story of the Holocaust," so he admires what he calls the "epic form," the focus on one individual. More importantly, Harwood insists the character must be trustworthy: "in dramatizations of events concerning any historical subject, but especially Holocaust, the individual artists come to be trusted as a lens, and it is his or her integrity that is the filter" (*Ronald Harwood's Adaptations*, 9).

To create their tragic character and avoid using the propaganda techniques they witnessed the Nazis using, to attain the level of objectivity they both desired, Harwood and Polanski decided to use Szpilman as the "cam era" for the film. It is through Szpilman that audiences learn the truth about the Holocaust, as well as the truth about visual imagery. What is remarkable here is that Harwood accomplishes this perspective without a voice-over. We rely on Szpilman's actions and comments only. The effect is a firsthand experience. The rise of the Nazi regime happens to its audiences in a kind of filmic real time. And what we witness is the Third Reich's slow and seductive rise to power.

While this method of characterization and narrative offered the objectivity Harwood and Polanski desired, it also brings a kind of coolness to the character, because he is distanced from himself to a certain degree. This fuels the criticism that Szpilman is merely a recording device, not a hero. Underlying such criticism is the stereotypical expectation of a hero. Szpilman is not Superman; he is an ordinary individual with an extraordinary talent, but he, like the rest of the world, could not prophesy the Nazis rise to power or single-handedly fight them off with a musical performance. Instead, the film shows us the heroic actions of a survivor from his perspective.

Initially, Szpilman, like many of his friends, both Jew and non-Jew, cannot even entertain the idea that the Nazis could succeed. It is, in the words of one of his non-Jew friends, "absurd" (Szpilman, 23). They may be rude and abusive, but the ghetto could not, would not happen. And yet, it does. They would not, could not take Jews to concentration camps. And yet, they do. They would not, could not be killing Jews. And yet, they are. To prove it, we are given reliable information, just as Szpilman's family learns it. Trains carrying people to Treblinka return empty. "They're exterminating us" (Szpilman, 63), says one member of the Jewish resistance. And still people cannot believe the news.

In addition to the atrocities committed by the Nazis, the film shows how their appearance unhinges Warsaw's moral center. In the ghetto, with Nazi violence escalating and resources scarce, many Jews go mad, die in the streets, steal from one another, or grow rich on the black market. For a while, Szpilman and others practice evasive strategies, a depiction that Michael Stevenson argues is rare in Holocaust films ("*Pianist* and Its Contexts," 179). But even the Szpilmans cannot remain untouched for long. They, too, resort to the Jewish black market when their patriarch needs a work permit.

To illustrate the absurdity of the situation, Harwood creates Itzak Heller, supposedly one of the Szpilman family's distant relations. He has joined the Nazi police, sports a Hitler haircut and mustache, and thinks that his actions will do some good. He even encourages Szpilman and his brother to join. Ironically, Heller does save Szpilman from the camps and sets him on his life of hiding.[1] And while the film documents Nazi atrocities, it also shows that many other people during this time exhibited inhuman behavior. Jews and non-Jews both help and hinder Szpilman.

Music, however, appeals to all groups and serves a variety of purposes throughout the film. First, it highlights what has been lost because of the

Nazis' atrocities. At one point, after hearing only sounds of gunfire and screams, Szpilman hears a few notes from Beethoven's "Moonlight Sonata." The music is almost ethereal, heavenly, coming from some undetermined place and an unidentified pianist. In another scene, when Dorota shelters him, he hears her playing Bach and follows the music to see her, pregnant, focused on her playing; the music offers a moment of peace and beauty, but it also creates a vision of what Szpilman does not and cannot have.

Second, as in the early scene with the Beethoven notes, music represents immortality and omnipotence. When Szpilman finds an abandoned piano, he "plays" without touching the keys; the film produces the music nondiegetically. Despite the Nazis determination to silence him and others, the music is still available. It exists above and beyond the limitations inflicted upon Szpilman and his people.

Third, Szpilman's meeting with the Nazi captain Wilm Hosenfeld, suggests that not only is music eternal, but it can be transformative. In the scene, Hosenfeld finds Szpilman who is desperate, starving, and injured. As Szpilman tries to open a can of pickles, in one of his most humiliating moments, he looks up and sees, thanks to a low-angle pan, the familiar black boots and then the face of a Nazi. In answer to his question, "Who are you?" Szpilman says, "I am—I was a pianist" (Szpilman, 105). The response is significant. Szpilman is not Szpilman. At this moment, he is the embodiment of art, art in the face of the destructive totalitarian force.

Szpilman plays Chopin's Nocturne in C minor, the piece he played at the beginning of the film. It is difficult to determine whether or not the music changed Hosenfeld at this very moment. He has admitted that the Nazis are losing the war, so maybe he decided to help this lone Jewish man in the hopes it will buy him forgiveness. But it is also possible that the music transformed him, moved him to realize that they are both human. There is no difference worth killing another over. Whatever the case, Hosenfeld decided to help Szpilman, and the music symbolizes art's ability to counteract the destructive tendencies of human nature. The film, moreover, highlights the continued connection between the two men after the war. Szpilman attempts to help Hosenfeld, only to discover that he has been taken to a Russian war camp, where he dies years later.

Harwood and Polanski viewed the conclusion of the film as a "triumph," but it seems the triumph is not Szpilman's release alone. Of course, Szpilman's survival challenges the totalitarian regime of the Third Reich and illustrates his incredible will to survive, perhaps redefining our understanding of a hero, not as a warrior, but as an artist and survivor. Clearly, art and Szpilman have triumphed, but the final scene of the film reminds us of Hosenfeld. Szpilman may be free, art may prevail, but we must also remember.

The Statement

If *The Pianist* inverts the presentation of music and totalitarianism in *Taking Sides*, *The Statement* (2003) inverts the fugitive motif of *The Pianist*. Rather than running from the Nazis, a Nazi runs from justice. Based on a true crime, the film tells the story of Pierre Brossard, a French Nazi played by Michael Caine, who killed seven French Jews in a small town. A Jewish tribunal found Brossard guilty and sentenced him to execution, but he escaped. While in exile, he manages to obtain a pardon from the French government, but with passage of the Crimes Against Humanities Act, he is once again a fugitive who faces further prosecution. Though Brossard's crime is heinous, the murder of innocent Jews, his connection to a secret, anti-Semitic society makes him an especially important target. Assisted by the Roman Catholic Church, specifically a secret sect called the Chevaliers de Sainte Marie, Brossard had managed to escape prosecution and incarceration for years, but with a new detective on the case, Annemarie Livi, played by Tilda Swinton, his luck runs out. As she fearlessly pursues him, his comrades determine that he knows too much. Too many of them remain in the upper echelons of the French government, and they cannot have their anti-Semitic war crimes, activities, and attitudes exposed. They kill Brossard to silence him, staging the execution to place blame on a radical Jewish group by planting a revenge "statement" on Brossard's corpse. Brossard's evasive techniques may parallel Szpilman's, but he is no hero. Pursued by French authorities as well as by those who will betray him, his flight documents the journey of a committed Nazi and Catholic pursued by the real hero of the film, Annemarie Livi.

Based on the 1996 novel by Brian Moore, Harwood's close adaptation of *The Statement* draws on his lifelong interest in the Holocaust and the moral decisions made during that period by both Jews and non-Jews. According to Mel Gussow, Brossard "is a fictionalized version of Paul Trovier, the only French citizen convicted of crimes against humanity" ("Of War

Crimes"). Michael Dirda calls the film a "true intellectual thriller" ("Shadow of a Gunman"). In the book and the film, Brossard embodies a situation many French faced during Hitler's rise. As Hitler gained power, so did communism, and many Catholics thought the best choice was to support Hitler, who offered them sanctuary from the atheists. Killing a few Jews—77,000 in France—was seen as just the cost of doing business with the Nazis. So, in some ways, Brossard faces the no-win situation that characterizes tragic heroes, but he chooses wrongly.

Both Moore and Harwood interrogate Brossard's decision, but more pointedly, they explore the role of Catholicism behind it. The film repeatedly exposes Brossard's faith as little more than a belief in magic: if he says enough prayers, he will win the day or heaven or both. After killing an assassin, he retrieves his Saint Christopher medal, which he kisses and prays to throughout the film, hoping that the saint will protect him. It is unclear if Harwood expects the audience to know the complications regarding Saint Christopher: he had been considered a saint, but then was removed from the liturgical calendar, only to be returned due to public outcry. Whether you believe he is a saint or not, this on-again, off-again situation highlights the less than reliable systems for producing Catholic content. Brossard also seeks penance through the Catholic rite of reconciliation. Here, the penitent confesses to a priest who offers the sinner forgiveness as a representative of Christ. True repentance and the promise to sin no more are part of the ritual, but throughout the film Brossard goes through the ceremony several times with as much concern as getting on a bus. His confessors are also members of the secret cult, so their participation in the ritual is also compromised.

To ensure that audiences do not misread Brossard's prayers and penance, the film includes a scene with his ex-wife, played by Charlotte Rampling. We learn that he has mistreated her for years, abandoned her, and now appears ready for sex and a place to hide. She resists, but he then, in an incredibly menacing scene, threatens to kill her dog. To punctuate his cruelty, as he leaves, he kicks the dog. Brossard is no aging, repentant Nazi. Director Norman Jewison uses Caine's voice as an old man in the early scene during which Brossard kills the Jewish men to show that Brossard has not changed. He is the same man from beginning to end. His rituals, prayers, and repentance are false.

By impugning Brossard's piety and character, the film questions not only the efficacy of Catholic religious rituals but also interrogates the role of the Catholic Church in the Vichy regime. The result is a complex representation of the Catholic Church. On the positive side, the action of the film takes place after the period of reform in the Catholic Church known as Vatican II. The reforms challenged nearly every ritual Brossard participates in. The church wanted to move away from the practices of rote recitation of prayers, dogma, and rituals and instead focus on social justice and living like Christ. Catholics were encouraged to love and serve, not just pray to statues.

Brossard and the Chevaliers are clearly members of the old school and do not support these changes. The Saint Christopher medal specifically symbolizes Brossard's refusal to embrace the Church's new ways. Even his wife, Nicole, challenges his piety when he laments that he cannot go to daily services. He says it is because he worries about Jewish assassins, but she confronts him with the truth: he does not want to sit next to Black people.

So Brossard's faith is not only hollow, it also does not reflect the changes in the Church. He belongs to a rogue group, so the film might be seen as excusing the Catholic Church in some way. The problem is that the Church supported the rogue group, whether by directly funding them, as they did, or by allowing them to perpetuate anti-Semitism and commit and conceal war crimes. As one Jesuit priest says in the novel and film: "The Church is not monolithic. . . . Religious orders such as the Jesuits, Dominicans, the Cistercians, etcetera, are a law unto themselves. . . . They can decide to help someone like Brossard. . . . In addition, there's the medieval tradition of a churchly authority which puts itself above the laws of men" (Moore, *The Statement*, 77).

Admittedly, the Chevaliers are exceptions, but the fact that the Church permitted such sects and behavior makes it culpable. While the official Church may not have sanctioned these rogue group behaviors, they turned a blind eye. But when repercussions began to arise in the course of the narrative, the official Church representative removes all support for Brossard and the Chevaliers, ostensibly eliminating any connection. The hypocrisy, however, is undeniable.

In addition to exploring the culpability of the Church, the film explores the complicity of the average French citizen. While on the run, Brossard relies on a couple who own a bar in a small village. Even after he has been identified as the infamous Nazi Jew killer in the paper, they greet him warmly and offer to assist his escape. After he kills someone in their restaurant, they tell the police they never liked him to cover up their support of this Nazi and his crimes.

Into this moral morass, Harwood places Annemarie Livi, a minor character in the novel who becomes the hero of the film. Livi becomes involved as a result of her role as an investigative judge. After Brossard kills one assassin, they find a "statement," a copy of the original court document that found Brossard guilty and sentenced him to execution. The French government puts Livi in charge, thinking the murder was the result of a Jewish group seeking retribution. As the film progresses, Livi discovers that there is no Jewish conspiracy. In fact, a powerful member of the government is behind both the plot to assassinate Brossard and the plot to frame the Jewish community for the murder. The government official, played by John Neville, attempts to cover up his own anti-Semitic participation in the Milice française, the French police during the Vichy government.

Livi's family friend, Armand Bertier, played by Alan Bates in his last film role, is a high-ranking official who warns her to let the case go. In a scene between the two added by Harwood, Bertier cautions her about the Brossard case, saying that she has been handed a "poisoned chalice," and he advises her that she should hand it back. Livi will have none of it, storms out of his office, and continues the investigation, despite the possible cost to her career. One critic praised Swinton's performance as Livi, saying, "Never mind the scales of justice, this is the pit bull of justice. She cannot be frightened or cajoled out of her mission" (Bernard, "A Powerful Statement," 230). Harwood underscores Livi's power and persistence, highlighting the challenges she presents not only to totalitarianism and injustice but to patriarchy. When the Catholic priests treat her condescendingly, she persists, using her legal power to resist their stonewalling tactics. The film also contrasts Brossard's docile wife to Livi's agency, augmenting the sense of her power as a character.

Like both Major Arnold in *Taking Sides* and Szpilman in *The Pianist*, Livi embodies the qualities of Harwood's unfashionable outliers who operate with integrity in the world, in this case, a world that still carries the remnants of a totalitarian government. Undeterred by Bertier's advice, Livi and her partner Roux continue to dig and finally discover that there is no Jewish conspiracy, and that the Catholic Church, while complicit, is not the prime mover behind the Brossard case. It is, finally, a matter of politics, and the man behind the scenes in the film is a high-ranking official, unnamed, but clearly a member of the French ruling class.[2] He finally sends one of his close aides, Pochon, played by Ciarán Hinds, to kill Brossard; it was Pochon who had framed the fictional Jewish terrorist group for the murder. In a voice-over, he says he found the "statement" on the body, and the case is closed officially.

Livi, who had hoped to find Brossard alive and to bring him and others to justice, finds a member of the Chevaliers willing to betray the high-ranking official. With the Brossard case closed, it seems nothing can be done. In the film's final scene, however, Livi confronts her uncle and the high-ranking official. While Livi loses Brossard, the film ends in her triumph. She has discovered the truth, and the film's conclusion suggests that she will prosecute the senior members of government.

Moore's novel offered a different kind of justice. His novel does not include punishment for anyone but suggests that punishment may be meted out later. He describes Brossard's death:

> He fell forward, striking his head on the concrete walk. Pain consumed him, but through it, he struggled to say, at last, that prayer the Church had taught him, that true act of contrition for his crimes. But he could feel no contrition. He had never felt contrite for the acts of his life. And now, when he asked for God's pardon, God chose to show him . . . dead Jews. (Moore, *The Statement*, 250)

According to Moore, Brossard's punishment occurs after death. Without Livi, there is no one to avenge the death of the seven Jews. Harwood's screenplay, however, suggests that Brossard may have felt remorse at the moment of his death. He dies holding his defunct medal, seeing the eyes of the men he killed, and saying "May God forgive me." Whether this is sincere or not is open to discussion, but one matter is clear. For Harwood, justice occurs on earth. Individuals like Livi and Major Arnold can make a difference. For Moore, justice is in God's hands. For Harwood, it is in ours.

Being Julia

Being Julia (2004) offers a comic look backstage at a 1930s-era London theatre through the character of Julia Lambert, supposedly the greatest actress to ever walk across the British stage. Based on Somerset Maugham's short novel *Theatre*, *Being Julia* brings Harwood and director István Szabó together again. Szabó directed Harwood's *Taking Sides*, a serious film about serious issues of denazification, art, and politics, so the choice to pair the two for this lighthearted subject may come as a surprise. Anyone who studies or worked with Harwood, however, knows that he has written comic pieces but also, more importantly, that he had a delightful and wicked sense of humor. In this film, Harwood directs his sharp wit toward one of his earlier themes, the nature of theatrical illusion and the high cost of art to the individuals who create it. While Annette Bening won a Golden Globe and an Oscar nomination for her performance, many critics saw the film as a simple variation on the film *All About Eve* (1950), with Bening as Julia in the Margot Channing role (Ebert, "'Being Julia'"). Such judgments ignore Harwood's aim and his tragic vision. Ebert and other critics were puzzled by Julia Lambert. The film had quickly followed *The Statement*, however, in which Harwood created a strong female hero. Here, he builds upon that representation and incorporates his tragic perspective in comedy. By examining the film through Harwood's tragic lens, we see that Lambert is actually the hero, a female character with agency, on a tragic journey toward self-actualization, who disrupts conventional expectations about women, art, and aging.

Like many of Harwood's screenplays, *Being Julia* closely follows its source. Both novel and film illustrate the career of Julia Lambert and her husband-manager, Michael Gosselyn, played in the film by Jeremy Irons. The novel offers more details about the marriage, namely that Julia is much more interested in sex than Michael, but in both the novel and film, their libidinal differences seem to be managed, with both Lambert and Gosselyn focusing on their offspring and the theatre. At the film's opening, however, we learn that this fragile equilibrium is threatened. Julia is exhausted, and her performances are becoming perfunctory. Here, the film highlights how her audiences have objectified her. Julia's work is stale, but audiences continue to come to see her: just seeing her has become a kind of theatrical trophy.

She proposes a vacation but becomes distracted by a young American, Tom Fennel, who eventually seduces her and disrupts the marital status quo further. Tom's attention blinds Julia to the decline in her acting. After one performance, her husband confronts her about her weak performance. She counters, claiming the audience loves her, and they do, applauding wildly after every show. Michael, whom we have been told has been trained by one of the major actor-managers of the late nineteenth century, Robert Benson, counters: "The public are a lot of jackasses. If you yell and scream and throw yourself about, you'll always get a lot of damned fools to shout themselves silly. Just barn-storming, that's what you've been doing the last four nights" (213). After further argument, she realizes that, of course, he is correct. She has "let her emotion run away with her; she had been feeling, not acting" (Maugham, 213). Both Michael and Julia suspend performances while Julia rests, recuperates, and reassesses her career and Michael works on a new script. Refreshed, Julia returns to rehearsal to find both her lover and husband having an affair with ingenue Avice. Julia, however, gets her revenge, humiliates Avice during a performance, and reestablishes her power as Britain's great leading lady.

On the one hand, the film could be a story about an aging woman's foolishness. During a metatheatrical moment, Julia even pitches the idea to her good friend, Lord Charles, who not only confesses that he is gay but dismisses her idea for the play as a "farce." Here, the film alerts us to its genre, which is not farce or the comic onstage humiliation of a woman. Julia has her flaws, but she is also heroic, an exemplary woman struggling to make her way in an industry that values female youth over skill.

The Maugham novel establishes Julia's artistry through numerous flashbacks to Julia's early training. Like Michael's, her training was also grounded in the great actor-manager tradition, the tradition that Harwood experienced through his work with Wolfit. As Harwood notes, he could not have flashbacks in the film, so he made Julia and Michael's acting teacher, Jimmie Langdon, a ghostly mentor who offers Julia advice and reminders. Brilliantly played by Michael Gambon, Jimmie opens the film yelling at Julia: "What I don't know about the theatre isn't worth knowing." He advises her to tell the audience, "You pay attention to me," so that they know "the theatre is the only reality." Jimmie's pugilistic demeanor and demands illustrate what is at stake for Julia. This is not a film about an aging woman who needs her vanity fed. This is a film about an actress desperately seeking to reinvigorate her art.

The obstacles to reinvigoration are numerous. The cult of youth and beauty threaten her work. She must sacrifice food, drink, and even beer to the stage. The industry works against her and other women, too. For example, when Julia admits that she is afraid her acting career in the future will only offer tours to Australia and Canada, she laments: "Bugger playwrights. They can't write for women. That's because they are all men."

After years in the theatre, and thanks to Jimmie's constant intervention, she has her own arsenal to combat these challenges. Jimmie reminds Julia, "Don't *be* natural. . . . The stage is not the place for that. The stage is make-believe. But *seem* natural" (16). The film demonstrates her quick wit in an early restaurant scene in which a high society woman tries to embarrass Julia by mentioning that her father was a doctor, a classist dig. Julia politely responds that her father was a vet, and he visited the woman's house frequently because they had so many "bitches" to deliver.

After her brief retreat from the stage, Julia returns. Michael has written a new play, and he auditions Avice for a role that would upstage Julia. Rather than throwing a tantrum, Julia acquiesces and begins to give the performance of her lifetime. Thanks to interjections from Jimmie, Julia performs onstage and off to reclaim the premiere position in her marriage and on the stage.

The film defends her decision in an early scene in which her son accuses her of being a fake. He says, "I don't think you really exist." If we see Julia as spectacle only, as the aging foolish woman, her son's and the critics' assessment would be valid. But Julia is not an object; she is a hero struggling to find herself and her art. The title of the film highlights the two interpretations, as well. *Being Julia* could just refer to a stagey actress who, like Donald Wolfit, was dismissed for overacting and theatrical gimmicks. But by looking at Julia's journey, *Being Julia* reveals another perspective. Julia is trying to "be Julia," despite the cult of youth, despite the lack of roles for women, despite the theatre industry's male bias. Julia is "being Julia," a talented actress.

In the end, the film dismantles Julia's challenges. Youth may have its advantages, but experience prevails. Julia succeeds in upstaging Avice, thrilling the audience, and reasserting her prominence. The film concludes with a medium shot of Julia, alone, away from the crowds, sitting in a bar, ordering a bottle of well-deserved beer. This is "being Julia." She is an actress, a performer, an illusionist, and an artist. Under the guise of a romantic comedy, the film illustrates the art of acting. It is not just dress-up. Although trained by an experienced teacher, Lambert faces the diminution of her power with age. She seeks the source of art, and life experiences, but like many heroes, she misjudges before finally regaining control. Like Ulysses at the end of Tennyson's poem, Julia Lambert will not retire. Instead, she continues "to strive, to seek, to find, and not to yield."

In this Harwood film, artists experience challenges, sacrifices, successes, and failures that demand a hero's heart, a heart that Harwood possessed and understood.

The Diving Bell and the Butterfly

Based on the memoir of the same name, *The Diving Bell and the Butterfly* (2007) is a remarkable screenplay about a remarkable man, Jean-Dominique Bauby, a former *Elle* editor and *bon viveur*, who was struck by a cerebrovascular accident that left him completely paralyzed, with the exception of the use of his left eye. Suffering from "locked-in syndrome," Bauby was "the same" person internally, mentally, emotionally, and spiritually, but not physically. Through an incredible act of will and with the help of dedicated occupational therapists, Bauby recorded his experiences for the book by blinking his eye to indicate each letter, one at a time. The diving bell image refers to his bodily imprisonment, and the butterfly to his mind. Writing the memoir sustained Bauby, who died three days after completing it.

The plot is classic Harwood. Bauby, a flawed hero, struggles to respond to adversity in the pursuit of truth. Bauby persists, fights, and while he cannot triumph over death, achieves immortality through his writing. *The Diving Bell and the Butterfly*, then, is a fitting work to conclude this discussion of the work of Ronald Harwood, illustrating that while life ends, art does not.

The production history of this film is almost as complicated and tenuous as the transformation from caterpillar to butterfly. Harwood, having read the book on the recommendation of his wife, Natasha, never thought of it as a play or film. He joked that when he told an American audience this detail, they were shocked: "I suspect in much of the United States, many people read only to discover if the subjects will make movies." Two years later, however, Kathleen Kennedy, "who has produced many of Stephen Spielberg's films, including *Jurassic Park, Indiana Jones*, and *Munich,*" approached him about a screenplay for the book (Harwood, "How I Set the Butterfly").

He accepted but nearly backed out of the project. Harwood met with Bauby's long-term partner and the mother of his children, as well as Claude Mendibil, "the woman who took down Jean-Do's words." He met with neurologists to discuss the syndrome, and still, nothing: "I decided I had made a dreadful mistake. . . . I would return the [advance] money. Now, as I have said many times before, nothing concentrates the mind of a writer more than the thought of having to return the money" ("How I Set the Butterfly"). Just as he was about to call Kennedy, the idea came to him—he would tell the story from Bauby's perspective. Like Szpilman in *The Pianist*, Harwood decided to use the character as the camera for much of the film.

After he had the screenplay, Johnny Depp, who was slated to play Bauby, dropped out to make "films about pirates" ("How I Set the Butterfly"). Universal Studios dropped the project, and it was not picked up again for several years. Once Pathé and Schnabel took over the script, it was translated into French, which Harwood approved. The book was in French, then translated into English, then into an English screenplay, then into a French screenplay, and then, for most, accompanied by subtitles when it arrived in theatres. It survived to receive four Oscar nominations.

The film follows the memoir closely, but is particularly striking in the first thirty minutes, when we see the world from Bauby's perspective as a victim of locked-in syndrome. The firsthand experiences depicted his learning the nature of his condition, seeing objects unclearly, and realizing that although he could hear his voice in his head, he cannot speak. Punctuating those horrors is his loss of one eye and a painful eye surgery. As he comes to realize the truth about his situation, he faces other indignities: someone leaves the television on with no picture, only static; another turns off an important soccer game he is watching; telephone installers refer to him as a kind of monster; and he, not a particularly jovial fellow, must endure the incredible cheerfulness of the nursing and therapy staff.

We learn that his previous life had been a charmed and sophisticated one, filled with fashion, luxury, and fame. In the process of separating from his longtime lover and the mother of his children for another woman, Bauby had been living the high life before his illness.

With the stroke, he loses everything and must re-envision and reframe his life. He begins therapy sessions to assist in communication. One therapist devised a version of the French alphabet arranged in terms of frequency. As she sounds out the letters, Bauby indicates his choice through blinking. Harwood said he preferred this scene in French because the letters sounded like music ("How I Set the Butterfly"), offering some solace to the painfully slow method of communication endured by Bauby and the audience.

Though he can now communicate, Bauby struggles to accept his situation and wallows in self-pity. Some of the nurses sympathize with him, and one prays for him and even takes him to church for a blessing she hopes will heal him and bring him back to a normal life. The situation not only has no effect on Bauby, it prompts him to recall a "dirty weekend" he took with his new lover in Lourdes.

While God does not offer a change in Bauby, an argument with one of the staff does. Understandably frustrated, Bauby tells her that he refuses to work on his rehabilitation for the day and tells her he wants to commit suicide. The young woman loses her temper, reminding him that all of them are working for him and helping him, and he is being selfish. The interaction prompts Bauby to recognize what he does have—memory and imagination. The film commemorates the moment in a brilliant montage with a voice-over:

> There is so much to do. You can wander off in space or time, set out for Tierra del Fuego or for King Midas's court. You can visit the woman you love, slide down beside her and stroke her still-sleeping face. You can build castles in Spain, steal the Golden Fleece, discover Atlantis, realize your childhood dreams and adult ambitions. (Bauby, *The Diving Bell*, 3)

His realization, not God, inspires him to embrace the "butterfly," his memory and imagination, rather than the "diving bell," his physical limitations. With this scene and Bauby's change, the film affords perspectives beyond Bauby's; he and the film have literally opened up.

While Harwood's screenplay closely follows the memoir, he added more to this work than he had to other adaptations. Perhaps as a result of his interactions with the mother of Bauby's children, Sylvie de la Rochefoucauld, as he struggled to write the script, Harwood highlights the family in several ways. He adds a child and expands the role Sylvie played in Bauby's life after the stroke. In the book, Bauby mentions her and notes that they are separated. In the film, however, the relationship is much more complicated. Sylvie admits that Harwood asked her a lot of tough questions: "It was like a torture session at times, but I had to go through with it. There are many things I'd never addressed since Jean-Do's death, not even with my children. Ron brought them all out" (Allen, "How Jean-Do").

In the film, Sylvie, called Celine, frequently visits Bauby with their children and cares for him while she is there. The woman Bauby is obsessed with, however, never visits. To highlight the pain and tension of this love triangle, Harwood adds a scene during which the lover finally calls, her one and only moment of contact with the stricken Bauby. Because he cannot communicate on the phone, Celine, who has been reading him letters, must translate the lovers' discourse. It is a heartbreaking moment for both Bauby and Celine. He cannot ignore his feelings for his lover, and Celine cannot ignore her feelings for Bauby. The scene presents Bauby in a selfish light, and Harwood adds another nail to this situation by having Bauby's father chastise him for not marrying Celine.

But Harwood also presents Bauby's endearing qualities. Clearly, he is flawed. Clearly, he is a womanizer. But he is also charming, compassionate, and confused. In one scene, he visits his homebound father, brilliantly played by Max von Sydow. To highlight their level of intimacy, the film shows Bauby shaving his father as they talk.

Harwood highlights themes of guilt and forgiveness by expanding Bauby's relationship with Jean-Paul K, a friend to whom he gave up his seat on an airline trip. During that trip, Jean-Paul is taken hostage by Hezbollah and imprisoned and tortured for "several years." He survives by reciting wine classifications (Bauby, 94). In the memoir, Bauby mentions feeling guilty for not seeing his friend after his return from Beirut. In the film, Harwood has his friend visit and offer advice on how Bauby can survive his own hostage situation. In addition to thinking of wine, Jean-Paul tells Bauby he survived "by clinging to what makes me human . . . hold fast to what is human in you and you will survive."

The scenes regarding the development of a butterfly were also Harwood's:

> My approach also meant that the visual metaphors of the diving bell and the butterfly would mark Jean-Do's anguish and elation. Shameful to admit, but I had no idea of how a butterfly came into the world, and

I wanted very much to use that process. I had a piece of luck. We were staying with friends in Switzerland, and one of the other house guests was David Attenborough. Who better to teach me? Over breakfast, he explained to me in detail the emergence of the butterfly with appropriate drawings. I made notes and transferred them to the script. ("How I Set the Butterfly")

The image is an important one, particularly at the end of the film when Bauby finishes his memoir. In the memoir, Bauby downplays his accomplishment, asking of his efforts, "Do they add up to a book?" (116). The scene concludes with a description of his writing tools. He observes his caregiver's purse filled with symbols of locomotion: keys, a metro ticket, and money, and he wonders if "the cosmos contains keys for opening up my diving bell. . . . We must keep looking" (117). In the film, Harwood returns to the butterfly imagery to highlight Bauby's transformation. Bauby's journey has led him from self-pity to artistry. His recognition of memory and imagination sustain him, but his decision to write the memoir sustains others. The butterfly imagery suggests the new life Bauby experiences following his stroke and perhaps a new life he attains through his work. Neither the film nor the memoir, however, represents that transformation in a religious or even a spiritual way. Instead, both film and memoir exist as reminders of art's permanence. Bauby exists in his work, just as Harwood continues to exist in his.

Conclusion

RONALD HARWOOD'S PROLIFIC AND SIGNIFICANT CONTRIBUTIONS TO LITERAture, drama, and film earned him an Oscar, two Oscar nominations, one BAFTA, three BAFTA nominations, one Tony nomination, numerous other awards and nominations, and a knighthood. He wrote twenty major plays, eight successful novels, nearly twenty major screenplays, many television episodes, and numerous essays and edited collections on theatre. Some of the most outstanding performers of the twentieth century worked with him: Maggie Smith, Tom Courtenay, Alan Bates, Annette Bening, Tilda Swinton, Michael Gambon, Ian McKellen, Anthony Hopkins, and close friends Harold Pinter and Lady Antonia Fraser—to name just a few. And yet many spectators do not know his work or realize that Harwood wrote the work they are experiencing. The situation proves Harwood's claims about the role of the writer in society, particularly the role of the screenwriter in Hollywood—they are either presumed or ignored. More importantly for Harwood, the critics have often misunderstood his work. This study attempted to investigate the causes behind the critical disconnection between Harwood and many of the critics.

What I discovered was that Harwood's works all share what I call his tragic vision. Born in South Africa during a period when the British were revered, his parents, his education, and World War II also influenced his perspective on art and theatre. When he arrived in London in 1951, he studied acting at the Royal Academy of Dramatic Arts but for various reasons left to work with Sir Donald Wolfit's theatre company. As Wolfit's dresser, Harwood experienced the actor-manager tradition firsthand. Steeped in Shakespeare and the faith that theatre in general could improve the world, Harwood traveled around the United Kingdom performing the classics.

These experiences developed Harwood's perspective on narrative and storytelling structure. Based on the principles of Aristotle but adapted to his artistic skills, needs, assumptions, and development, many of Harwood's works contain flawed heroes who face obstacles, generally within the context of totalitarian regimes. For Harwood, the role of the hero and individual standing outside the norm, or what he calls an unfashionable stance, offers the greatest resistance to these oppressive systems that demand goose-step conformity.

This vision did not fit into the changes in the British dramatic world of the late 1950s and early 1960s when the theatres of the absurd and of the angry young men were "fashionable." An alternative strain, the political theatre of the day, also did not appeal to Harwood, who frequently reminded us that he would rather die than sit through Bertolt Brecht's work.

His politics and his origins as a South African Jew certainly marginalized him, too, but they did not silence him. Rather than succumbing to social pressures and systemic anti-Semitism, he embraced his marginalized status. He celebrated other unfashionables, those who did not fit into the popular British culture of the day. He revealed the talents, gifts, power, strengths, and weaknesses of his mentor, Sir Donald Wolfit and others like him. His works are filled with marginalized outliers trying to do the right thing, find the truth that Harwood cherished in all his efforts, and inspire audiences to do the same.

Like the actor-managers he admired, Harwood was an artist with vision and purpose. His first novel, *George Washington September, Sir!*, is a prototype for subsequent works. An unlikely and unfashionable tragic hero, a young Zulu is caught in a trap set by the White South Africans but enacted by fellow Blacks to incarcerate his uncle, a dissident who works against apartheid. George is a flawed hero, and experiences many losses, but he learns the truth about himself and his country along the way. The novel concludes, not with a solution to the problems of personal identity and apartheid, but with another journey, inspiring readers to consider their alternatives to the conflict. Harwood, who considered himself a dramatist first, continues using the structure throughout his dramas, from *Pinfold* to his unpublished manuscript *Public Servants*. The form changes, of course, and Harwood refines and amends the trajectory of the tragic hero in every work.

Harwood's humor often appears in the most desperate situations, particularly in his later dramas and screenplays. *The Dresser* is filled with asides, jabs, and teasers as the characters face the bombing of London, aging, and death. *The Pianist* and *The Diving Bell and the Butterfly* include witty gallows humor. His *Girl in Melanie Klein* is a fun romp through the psychiatric profession. And *Quartet, Being Julia,* and *Ivy* offer perhaps the best examples of his dry humor.

In the serious work, there is, if not a moral, then the pedagogical energy of tragedy. Harwood presents situations and conflicts that prompt thinking, not inhibit it, so resolutions are rarely given. He repeatedly said, "I don't want to do the thinking for them." In his introduction to *A Night at the Theatre*, he railed against the academic approach to theatre that focused on textual interest and message (7), ignoring the theatrical and emotional components. For him, as for the actor-managers, the theatre particularly, but art in general, affected audiences in ways beyond reason. Harwood wrote from and about the heart, and this perspective creates the moral energy in his plays. *Taking Sides* poses the question: What if the Nazis offered you everything you wanted and more to work with them? How much of yourself would you sacrifice to practice your art, work, livelihood?

Often dismissed as old-fashioned, Harwood still had access to some of the most influential personalities in stage and film. He received awards and adulation and even, at times, brilliant reviews. But he still considered himself an "outlier."

And perhaps this status is the status of the artist. As an outlier, Harwood observes and writes about some of the most critical issues of our day: racism, anti-Semitism, sexism, aging, classism, art, and politics. Harwood's tragic vision may be traditional, but it did not inhibit his ability to critique the most pressing contemporary issues.

In addition to establishing Harwood as a significant writer, this examination of his canon also demonstrates his growing insights into his Jewish heritage and faith. Initially ambivalent or neutral about his Jewish heritage, Harwood's work grows increasingly concerned with subjects related to his Jewish heritage, particularly anti-Semitism and the Holocaust. Some of his best works deal with those topics. A 2008 interview revealed the tension: "I approach everything as a writer, but everything I write is informed by my Jewish heritage. I am very proud of being a Jew" (qtd. in Tugend, "Waiting for Oscar"). While Harwood acknowledged his Jewish heritage and its important influence on his life and work, he resisted being categorized as a "Jewish writer." The sentiment is consistent with his work and his characters. As unfashionables, they are outside the box, outside the usual definitions. For Harwood, this was a requirement for their heroic journeys.

The characters Harwood casts in these situations are frequently artists because he saw that role as providing the emotional and moral barometers of culture. His unfashionables are those who, by their very marginalized status, have gained a better perspective on the situations they encounter. Their work is also their vocation, so the cost is high when they are asked to sacrifice their art to politics.

Even though art gives meaning to their lives, they see that it also has a lot to answer for. The demands of a life in the performing arts, which Harwood experienced on a personal level, can be exhausting, and yet the artists continue, driven to express their vision of the world. Sir, in *The Dresser*, sacrifices himself to art, offering all his physical and emotional resources to the stage.

Art, too, serves as a threat to totalitarian regimes, so dictators frequently silence its production. The individual stands as a testimony to their misrepresentations and oppression. Artists, unfashionables, offer alternative insights. They may sense the subtle changes in a culture, or they represent the horrific outcomes of humanity's selfishness in ways that no one else could. In Harwood's world, they all must speak their truth. And in doing so, inspire us to speak ours. Consequently, Harwood's heroes are artists. They read, play music, perform, and conduct in the face of insurmountable obstacles.

Those who miss Harwood's tragic vision misread his heroes. Like Oedipus, Lear, and Wolfit, they are larger-than-life over-reachers. As artists, too, they are driven and monomaniacal. They are far from democratic, though they often save or protect democracy or, if nothing else, protect the positive cultural values threatened by totalitarian forces. Admittedly, it is a tricky stance because heroes, these mighty figures, often obliterate diversity, but Harwood's heroes represent the others, the marginal, the unfashionable, the diverse. Further, his characters, even the pugnacious Wolfit, are not as domineering as other tragic figures. His heroes are single-minded, flawed, ambitious, but they come from the ranks of the ordinary. His characters illustrate that the very characteristics that make them so difficult are the characteristics that ennoble them. Harwood's heroes become extraordinary because the forces against them make them so.

Harwood's works and heroes defend diversity. His first novel casts a young Zulu man as a hero, which was unheard of at that time. In *Another Time*, he presents the complicated nature of boycotts, especially artistic boycotts, asking if change can happen if art silences itself? His screenplay for *Mandela* highlights the domestic cost of political resistance. And *Taking Sides*, *The Dresser*, and *The Pianist* investigate the possibility of artistic production in a totalitarian state. Despite Harwood's comments about women playing male roles, *After the Lions* and *Being Julia* present female heroes who must overcome patriarchal oppression.

Harwood's adaptations for film have introduced many to various authors, and while he talked about adaptation and remaining true to the source, he admitted that every adaptation demands something different. His struggles with *The Diving Bell and the Butterfly* show that even an experienced screenwriter can be stumped, at least for a time.

This book is an introduction to Harwood studies, and I hope that further analysis of his work will continue. There is more to be done on his representation of the family and on several plays I did not have time to discuss, including *Tramway Road*, *Reflected Glory*, and *Equally Divided*, specifically.

Harwood's use of comedy, music, and the theatre demands further study. With the publication of selected screenplays, further work could be completed on Harwood's skills at adaptation. New productions of his paired plays such as *The Dresser* and *After the Lions* or *Taking Sides* and *Collaboration* should be mounted, as well as productions of early plays and some that were not well-received when first presented, such as *J. J. Farr*, *The Handyman*, and *Mahler's Conversion*.

Richard B. Gidez notes that while Harwood was writing novels "he was also busy writing televisionscripts" (244). In addition to *The Barber of Stamford Hill* and *Private Potter*, Harwood produced a documentary on Evelyn Waugh, a work on Evita Peron that starred Faye Dunaway, and what Gidez considers Harwood's best, *The Guests* (1972), a one-person play about an old woman who thinks she has dinner guests: "Not only are they not there, but also at no time have they existed" (244).

Harwood's representation of Jewish identity and culture and his growing acceptance of his heritage are fertile topics for future discussion. Rabbi

Delphine Horvilleur has discussed her growing popularity among Jews and non-Jews in the post-pandemic world. Horvilleur, who had to officiate many funerals online during the pandemic, decided to use her online skills to create podcasts. Her explanation of why she is so interested in death may also shed some light on Harwood's tragic vision, a distinctly Jewish direction that could be explored in future works:

> I was brought into the world with an unspoken knowledge of tragedy. . . . I was clearly aware as a child that ghosts haunted my life. Often, I walk in cemeteries and wonder what I'm looking for. I think I am trying to attend funerals that never took place. It is definitely haunting that the Shoah left us with millions of unburied souls, and it should continue to haunt all of us. (Lieblich, "French Feminist Rabbi")

While Harwood attained great success and fame, he never felt fashionable. A gun for hire, a script doctor, a remnant from another age, Harwood nonetheless triumphed. The tension between being "in" and being "out," being part of the artistic elite and being excluded, in many ways represents the writer's role. As Harwood frequently pointed out, writers are invisible in our culture. Screenwriting is even more marginalizing because the writer's vision may not survive the collaboration among directors, producers, and designers. For Harwood, this was the nature of writing and of art in general. Artists may participate, like his pianist, but they must also bear witness. In this case, then, to study Harwood is to study the work, life, role, and purpose of the artist. Artists bear the cultural burden, and they serve to resist the ever-present threat of tyranny. So, as Harwood wrote, "Art has a lot to answer for."

Ronald Harwood was, above all, a writer. His daily routine included writing for hours, napping, and writing some more. His tremendous output not only shows that he was disciplined, but also that writing was a vocation, a calling, something he could not keep from doing. His position as an outsider, an unfashionable Jew in the British world, gave him his outlier perspective, which might define all writers worth reading.

Notes

Introduction

1. Harwood remained very proud of his time with Wolfit, and when we left our interviews, which occured in February 2010, he deftly helped me on with my overcoat.

2. In *The Hoosier State Chronicles*, Indiana's Digital Archive for Historical Newspapers, of all places, at the time Harwood made this deal a small note appeared in *The Jewish Chronicles* of Marion County in a section called "Jewish Enough." The report stated,

   > The debate over whether Richard Burton looks Jewish enough to play the role of a Jewish concentration camp inmate has been decided in the affirmative. The husband of Elizabeth Taylor, who converted to Judaism when she was married to Eddie Fisher in 1959, acquired the film rights to Ronald Harwood's novel, "The Guilt Merchants." Mr. Burton will play the role of Anido when the film is made next year. He told Mr. Harwood that "in certain lights I look Jewish."

3. Such neat distinctions rarely hold, and several studies complicate these divisions, Michael Billington's *State of the Nation* and Christopher Inness's *Modern British Drama*, for example. That said, the distinction between the absurd and the epic or political offers a reasonable representation of the changes occurring in the British theatre at the time and in subsequent years. Even those more recent analyses agree that the British theatre became much more political following World War II.

Chapter One: Sir Donald Wolfit

1. Harwood's description of Ayrton illustrates the tension between the London theatre and the regional theatre of the day:

Perhaps the most remarkable member of the company was the leading
man, Randle Ayrton, one of the strangest, most fascinating figures in the
theatre of the 1930s. Originally Benson's authoritarian stage-manager, he
had become an actor when well into his middle years. In 1936 he was
sixty-six years old, crochety and aloof, but the purveyor of compelling
dramatic power. He disdained London, but he gave, principally in Stratford,
a series of performances ... [which] many fellow-actors, judged to be
among the finest of the period. In those days, few of the London critics
made the pilgrimage to Stratford, but it is doubtful, having regard to
Ayrton's bias against the capital, that even if they had acclaimed him the
greatest actor since Irving (as was the critics' wont) it would have lured
him to the metropolis. Ayrton preferred to play in Stratford, to toil in
his market-garden. He was, by his own inclinations, a curiously isolated
figure and, to the London sophisticates, more or less unknown. It was ...
Wolfit's good fortune ... to play with Ayrton, and Wolfit never omitted to
acknowledge the debt. (*Wolfit*, 123)

CHAPTER TWO: THE NOVELS

1. In his introduction to *Ronald Harwood: Plays 2*, Harwood notes that he would get
together with Casper Wrede, Michael Elliott, James Maxwell, Malcolm Pride, and
Richard Negri.

We used to meet, all through the 1960s, to discuss the state of theatre,
to voice our discontents and our hopes to attempt to seek solutions.
Personally, during that decade I felt entirely isolated from the medium
I most loved—which is, I now suppose, why I mostly wrote novels then.
While I have always admired and marvelled at the great theatrical explosion
detonated in Sloane Square at the Royal Court Theatre in 1956 with John
Osborne's *Look Back in Anger*, I was not, nor could be part of it. I was not
and never had been a "committed" playwright—to use the buzz word
of that time—and I had no interest in writing about the English class
system that, as a foreigner, I barely understood, but which most of the
highly acclaimed plays of that period seemed to be about. (ix)

CHAPTER THREE: THE PLAYS

1. Nicholas De Jongh offered one of the most negative reviews of the play.
His perspective, however, is a great example of the kind of misreading
Harwood's more serious writings received and illustrates the attitude of the

"fashionable theatre" Harwood described as prevailing when he began working in London. De Jongh wrote in the *Evening Standard,* "Anyone hankering for those deadly 1950s country-house dramas, before Godot failed to arrive or Osborne looked back in anger, may find Ronald Harwood's *Quartet* is just their blast from the past."

2. This website identifies the various pieces in the film's soundtrack: https://www.classicfm.com/discover-music/periods-genres/film-tv/quartet-official-soundtrack/quartet/.

CHAPTER FOUR: THE SCREENPLAYS

1. In the film, as Szpilman makes his escape, he begins to run. Heller says, "Don't run." Polanski added that line because it is what the guard told him when he escaped from Krakow ("Bonus Materials," *The Pianist* [film]).

2. The novel identifies him as Maurice de Grandville, Paris Prefect of Police under General de Gaulle:

> Now eighty years old, with a record of past actions requiring judicial investigation that, over the years, had accumulated thirty tomes of evidence without his ever spending a night in prison, he had outlived the statute of limitations on his former deeds. Except for one, the one which had shadowed his long career.... [H]e had facilitated his SS colleagues by organizing a series of French deportation trains which sent sixteen hundred people, including two hundred forty children, to their deaths in Nazi extermination camps. For this action there was no statute of limitations. The crime against humanity. (*The Statement,* 212)

Works Cited

Alberge, Dalya. "Smoking Rules Could Exit, Stage Left." *The Times*, 27 April 2008, p. 33.
Allen, Peter. "How Jean-Do, My Butterfly, Escaped His Diving Bell at Last." *Daily Mail*, 3 February 2008, https://www.dailymail.co.uk/femail/article-511930/How-Jean-Do-butterfly-escaped-diving-bell-last.html.
Apartheid: Its Effects on Education, Science, Culture, and Information. UNESCO Digital Library, 1967, https://unesdoc.unesco.org/ark:/48223/pf0000002428.
Arditti, Michael. "Star Who Lacks Direction: Whatever Happened to Dorothy Tutin." *The Guardian*, 18 December 1991, Nexis Uni, https://advance-lexis-com.echo.louisville.edu/api/permalink/10058c28-be12-4878-91098c6e0a3ad0db/?context=1516831.
Aristotle. *Aristotle's Poetics: A Translation and Commentary for Students of Literature*. Translated by Leon Golden, commentary by O. B. Hardison, Jr. Florida State UP, 1981.
"Articles of Faith." *Kirkus Reviews*, 29 April 1974, https://www.kirkusreviews.com/book-reviews/a/ronald-harwood-2/articles-of-faith-2/.
Barbour, John D. "Tragedy and Ethical Reflection." *The Journal of Religion*, vol. 63, no. 1, January 1983, pp. 1–25.
Bartel, Dennis. "Franck's Fling-Woo F Minor Quintet." *Classical California KUSC*, https://www.kusc.org/culture/staff-blog/francks-fling-woo-f-minor-quintet/. Accessed 26 December 2023.
Bauby, Jean-Dominique. *The Diving Bell and the Butterfly*. Wheeler, 1997.
Bernard, Jami. "A Powerful 'Statement' Made." *Daily News*, 12 December 2003, Nexis Uni, advancelexis.com.echo.louisville.edu/api/document?collection=news&id=urn:contentItem:4B6V-C490-00T0-G13G-00000-00&context=1516831.
Billington, Michael. "An English Tragedy." *The Guardian*, 20 February 2008, Nexis Uni, https://advance-lexis-com.echo.louisville.edu/api/permalink/3172108c-2020-4746-9851-9145d8fd975f/?context=1516831.

———. "First Night: Genocide Gets Trial by Theatre." *The Guardian*, 25 September 1996, *Nexis Uni*, https://advance-lexis-com.echo.louisville.edu/api/permalink /c53ba16f-cc8a-49b2-b77c-dbd11d8d2078/?context=1516831.

———. *State of the Nation: British Theatre Since 1945*. Faber and Faber, 2007.

———. "When Guilt Is the Spur." *The Guardian*, 27 September 1989, *Nexis Uni*, https://advance-lexis-com.echo.louisville.edu/api/permalink/bd40bd40-5afe -4985-81e8-1cd88184eefd/?context=1516831.

Blau, Eleanor. "The Writer Behind 'The Dresser.'" *The New York Times*, 14 November 1981, *Nexis Uni*, https://advance-lexis-com.echo.louisville.edu /api/permalink/d1180c9a-3ff9-40d7-89e6-e01910669f19/?context=1516831.

"Bonus Materials." *The Pianist* [film]. Directed by Roman Polanski, Universal Studios, DVD, 2002.

Callan, Edward. Introduction. *Cry, the Beloved Country*, by Alan Paton. Scribner's, 1987, pp. 19–30.

Callendar, Newgate. Rev. of *Genoa Ferry* by Ronald Harwood. "Crime," *The New York Times Book Review*, 20 November 1977, *The New York Times Archive*, https: //www.nytimes.com/1977/11/20/archives/crime.html?smid=url-share.

Canby, Vincent. "Ronald Harwood's 'Dresser.'" *The New York Times*, 6 December 1983, *Nexis Uni*, https://advance-lexis-com.echo.louisville.edu/api /permalink/7ccd5b9c-b9a6-40eb-8fc2-da1c5bcaf6fd/?context=1516831.

Cavendish, Dominic. "Why the Dresser." *Telegraph*, 28 April 2020, *Nexis Uni*, https://advance-lexis-com.echo.louisville.edu/api/permalink/9afd310d-9fc5 -4222-ae11-f3d2d15ee5b0/?context=1516831.

"*César and Augusta*." *Kirkus Reviews*, 12 May 1980, https://www.kirkusreviews.com /book-reviews/a/ronald-harwood-3/cesar-and-augusta/.

Chothia, Jean. *English Drama of the Early Modern Period: 1890–1940*. Longman, 1996.

Coveney, Michael. "'After the Lions.'" *Financial Times*, 22 November 1982, *Nexis Uni*, https://advance-lexis-com.echo.louisville.edu/api/permalink/20e6476d -61a4-4ca3-89c0-8f8c89e67a6d/?context=1516831.

———. "Another Time." *Financial Times*, 26 September 1989, *Nexis Uni*, https: //advance-lexis-com.echo.louisville.edu/api/permalink/29c1db70-8e09-47b8 -be91-d22840acf70a/?context=1516831.

Cunningham, John. *The Cinema of István Szabó: Visions of Europe*. Columbia UP, 2014.

Davies, Laurence. *César Franck and His Circle*. Houghton Mifflin, 1970.

De Jongh, Nicholas. "This Quartet Fails to Hit the Right Note." *Evening Standard*, 9 September 1999, *Nexis Uni*, https://advance-lexis-com.echo.louisville.edu/api /permalink/4a459efe-7c47-4465-afda-728ecc6a7599/?context=1516831.

Denby, David. "Nocturnes: *The Pianist* and *25th Hour*." *The New Yorker*, 5 January 2003, *Nexis Uni*, https://advance-lexis-com.echo.louisville.edu/api/permalink/232c9795-cba1-4263-9ae8-ee66b5f02490/?context=1516831.

Diamond, Elin. "Churchill's Tragic Materialism or Imagining a Posthuman Tragedy." *PMLA*, vol. 129, no. 4, October 2014, pp. 751–60.

Dirda, Michael. "Shadow of a Gunman." *Washington Post*, 30 June 1996, https://www.washingtonpost.com/archive/entertainment/books/1996/06/30/shadow-of-a-gunman/6e469c7d-57ac-4729-be84-d6ee11b88511/.

"The Dresser." *Variety Movie Reviews*, 1, p. 25.

Eagleton, Terry. *Sweet Violence: The Idea of the Tragic*. Blackwell, 2003.

Ebert, Roger. "'Being Julia' Not All It's Cracked Up to Be." *Rogerebert.com*, 28 October 2004, https://www.rogerebert.com/reviews/being-julia-2004.

———. "Sweet. Needs More Marigolds." *Rogerebert.com*, 23 January 2013, https://www.rogerebert.com/reviews/quartet-2012.

Farber, Stephen. "Bringing Mandela to Television." *The New York Times*, 19 September 1987, *Nexis Uni*, https://advance-lexis-com.echo.louisville.edu/api/permalink/a21ae3c0-bbf0-4358-b118-7bfb04cd90c2/?context=1516831.

Felski, Rita. "Introduction." *Rethinking Tragedy*. Ed. Rita Felski. Johns Hopkins UP, 2008, pp. 1–29.

Fergusson, Francis. *The Idea of a Theatre: A Study of Ten Plays*. Princeton UP, 1949.

Fergusson, Maggie. "Curtain Up." *Sunday Times*, 26 April 2009, *Nexis Uni*, https://advance-lexis-com.echo.louisville.edu/api/permalink/611c4cd5-e470-4dc1-82e0-c65d8604c2db/?context=1516831.

———. "Maggie Fergusson Remembers Ronald Harwood." *Royal Society of Literature*, https://rsliterature.org/library-article/maggie-fergusson-remembers-ronald-harwood/.

Foley, Helen P., and Jean E. Howard. "Introduction: The Urgency of Tragedy Now." *PMLA*, vol. 129, no. 4, October 2014, pp. 617–34.

Forster, E. M. *Aspects of the Novel*. Mariner, 1956.

Freeman, J. "An Irreverent Look at a One-Legged Legend." (Australian) *Herald*, 1 October 1987, *Nexis Uni*, https://advance-lexis-com.echo.louisville.edu/api/permalink/3514e435-0217-4b36-a6f2-133a12856737/?context=1516831.

French, Phillip. "Quartet Film: Review." *The Guardian*. 5 January 2013, https://www.theguardian.com/film/2013/jan/06/quartet-review-film-dustin-hoffman.

Fullerton, Richard. "'I only know people in trouble': An Interview with Sir Ronald Harwood." *Theboar.org*, 3 July 2018, https://theboar.org/2018/07/sir-ronald-harwood/.

Gardiner, John. "Istvan Szabo's *Taking Sides* (2001) and the Denazification of

Wilhelm Furtwängler." *Historical Journal of Film, Radio, and Television*, vol. 30, pp. 95–109.

Genzlinger, Neil. "Review: In 'The Dresser' Ian McKellen and Anthony Hopkins Give Riveting Performances." *The New York Times*, 29 May 2016, https://www.nytimes.com/2016/05/30/arts/television/review-the-dresser-starz-ian-mckellen-anthony-hopkins.html.

Gidez, Richard B. "Ronald Harwood (9 November 1934–)." *British Dramatists Since World War II*, edited by Stanley Weintraub, vol. 13, Gale, 1982, pp. 243–47. Accessed at link-gale-com.echo.louisville.edu/apps/doc/EXIRWD790739937/DLBC?u=ulouisv_main&sid=bookmark-DLBC&xid=d20ba993.

Gilman, Richard. "The Dresser." *Nation*, 9 January 1982, pp. 26–27.

Gore-Langton, Robert. "Moral and Political Dilemmas." *Spectator*, 26 July 2008, *Nexis Uni*, https://advance-lexis-com.echo.louisville.edu/api/permalink/cf14ff61-cfac-4822-bc73-8a4acc17e717/?context=1516831.

Greene, Graham. *The Power and the Glory*. Vintage, 2004.

Gritten, David. "The Invisible Oscar Winner." *Telegraph*, 03 June 2003, *Nexis Uni*, https://advance-lexis-com.echo.louisville.edu/api/permalink/3eb138ac-51df-4d28-baac-bbcbc6713b1c/?context=1516831.

Gump, James O. "*Cry, the Beloved Country*." *American History Review*, vol. 101, 1996, pp. 1147–48.

Gussow, Mel. "Of War Crimes and Sanctuary." *The New York Times*, 18 August 1996, *Nexis Uni*, https://advance-lexis-com.echo.louisville.edu/api/permalink/36d4336b-626a-458b-adb2-77a6beab102b/?context=1516831.

Hardison, Jr. O.B. "A Commentary on Aristotle's *Poetics*." *Aristotle's Poetics: A Translation and Commentary for Students of Literature*, translated by Leon Golden, commentary by O.B. Hardison, Jr., Florida State UP, 1981, pp. 55–297.

Harris, Chris. "Ronald Harwood Obituary." *Times*, 9 September 2022, https://www.thetimes.co.uk/article/sir-ronald-harwood-obituary-526fl6rwh.

Harwood, Ronald. "Adaptation." British Library, London, manuscript, MS8881, n.d.

———. *After the Lions*. In *Ronald Harwood: Plays 2*, Faber and Faber, 1995, pp. 259–314.

———, ed. *The Ages of Gielgud: An Actor at Eighty*. Limelight, 1984.

———. *All the World's a Stage*. Little, Brown, 1984.

———. *Another Time*. In *The Collected Plays of Ronald Harwood*, Faber and Faber, 1993, pp. 195–278.

———. "Apartheid." British Library, London, manuscript, MS88881/6/28.

———. *Arrivederci, Baby!* [*Drop Dead, Darling* in the U.K.]. Directed by Ken Hughes, Paramount, 1966.

———. *Articles of Faith*. Holt, Rinehart, and Winston, 1973.

———. *Being Julia*. Directed by István Szabó, Sony, 2004.
———. *César and Augusta*. Little, Brown, 1978.
———. *Collaboration*. In *Collaboration and Taking Sides*, Faber and Faber, 2008, pp. 1–76.
———. *Cry, the Beloved Country*. Directed by Darrell Roodt, Miramax, 1995.
———, ed. *Dear Alec: Guinness at 75*. Limelight, 1989.
———. *The Deliberate Death of a Polish Priest*. Amber Lane, 1985.
———. *The Diving Bell and the Butterfly*. Directed by Julian Schnabel, Miramax, 2007.
———. *The Dresser*. In *The Collected Plays of Ronald Harwood*, Faber and Faber, 1993, pp. 63–138.
———. *The Dresser*. Directed by Peter Yates, Columbia, 1983.
———. *The Dresser*. Directed by Richard Eyre, STARZ, 2015.
———. "Ego? Forget About It." *The Guardian*, 6 July 2006, https://www.theguardian.com/film/2007/jul/06/2.
———. *An English Tragedy*. Faber and Faber, 2008.
———. *Equally Divided*. In *Quartet and Equally Divided*, Faber and Faber, 1999, pp. 85–154.
———, ed. *The Faber Book of the Theatre*. Faber and Faber, 1993.
———. *A Family*. In *The Collected Plays of Ronald Harwood*, Faber and Faber, 1993, pp. 1–62.
———. *The Genoa Ferry*. Mason Charter, 1977.
———. *George Washington September, Sir!* [*All the Same Shadows* in the U.K.]. Farrar, Strauss, and Cudahy, 1961.
———. *The Girl in Melanie Klein*. Holt, Rinehart, and Winston, 1969.
———. *The Guilt Merchants*. Holt, Rinehart, and Winston, 1963.
———. *The Handyman*. Faber and Faber, 1996.
———. *Heavenly Ivy*. Oberon, 2010.
———. *A High Wind in Jamaica*. Directed by Alexander Mackendrick, Twentieth-Century Fox, 1965.
———. *Home*. Orion, 1993.
———. "How I Set the Butterfly Free." *The Times*, 24 January 2008, https://www.thetimes.co.uk/article/how-i-set-the-butterfly-free-ndqhm9gqpd0.
———. "I Know What I Like." British Library, London, manuscript, 7/12/80, MS88881/4/48.
———. "I Say." *The Evening Standard*, 10 January 2008, Nexus Uni, https://www.advance-lexis-com.echo.louisville.edu/api/permalink/d9d9dcb6-ed2c-4c53-8717-d4a73b98e780/?context=1516831.
———. *The Interpreters*. Cotswold, 1986.

———. Interviews with Ann C. Hall. February 2010, Harwood residence, no transcripts.
———. Introduction. *A Night at the Theatre*, edited by Ronald Harwood, Methuen, 1982, pp. 7–10.
———. Introduction. *Ronald Harwood: Plays 2*, Faber and Faber, 1995, pp. vii–xi.
———. *Ivanov: A Version by Ronald Harwood*. Amber Lane, 1989.
———. *J. J. Farr*. In *The Collected Plays of Ronald Harwood*, Faber and Faber, 1993, pp. 139–94.
———. "Jewish Spirituality Lecture." British Library, London, handwritten notes, 1969, MS88881/4/53.
———. *Mahler's Conversion*. Faber and Faber, 2001.
———. *Mandela*. Directed by Peter Saville, HBO, 1987.
———. *Mandela*. New American Library, 1987.
———. "Memoir." Personal copy, unpublished manuscript, typescript, 2010.
———, ed. *A Night at the Theatre*. Methuen, 1982.
———. "Notes on Theatre." British Library, London, manuscript, MS8881/4/53.
———. *One. Interior. Day: Adventures in the Film Trade*. Martin Secker and Warburg, Ltd., 1978.
———. *One Day in the Life of Ivan Denisovich*. Directed by Casper Wrede, Group W. Films, 1970.
———. "The Ordeal of Gilbert Pinfold." *Ronald Harwood: Plays 2*. Faber and Faber, 1995, pp. 187–258.
———. "A Personal View of Contemporary Literature." British Library, London, manuscript, MS88881/7/18/10.
———. *The Pianist*. In *The Pianist and Taking Sides* (*Screenplays*), Faber and Faber, 2002, pp. 1–116.
———. *Poison Pen*. In *Ronald Harwood: Plays 2*, Faber and Faber, 1995, pp. 69–142.
———. "Pop Virus." British Library, London, manuscript, MS88881/4/54, 1999.
———. *Private Potter*. Directed by Casper Wrede, MGM, 1962.
———. "Public Servants." Personal copy, typescript, manuscript, 2009.
———. *Quartet*. In *Quartet and* Equally Divided [plays], Faber and Faber, 1999, pp. 1–84.
———. *Reflected Glory*. Faber and Faber, 1992.
———. *Ronald Harwood's Adaptations from Other Works into Films*. Edited by David Nicholas Wilkinson and Emlyn Price, Guerrilla Books, 2007.
———. *Sir Donald Wolfit: His Life and Work in the Unfashionable Theatre*. St. Martin's, 1971.
———. "Sir Ronald Harwood Clarifies Comments About BBC Drama 'The Dresser.'" *The Independent*, 23 October 2015, independent.ie, https://www

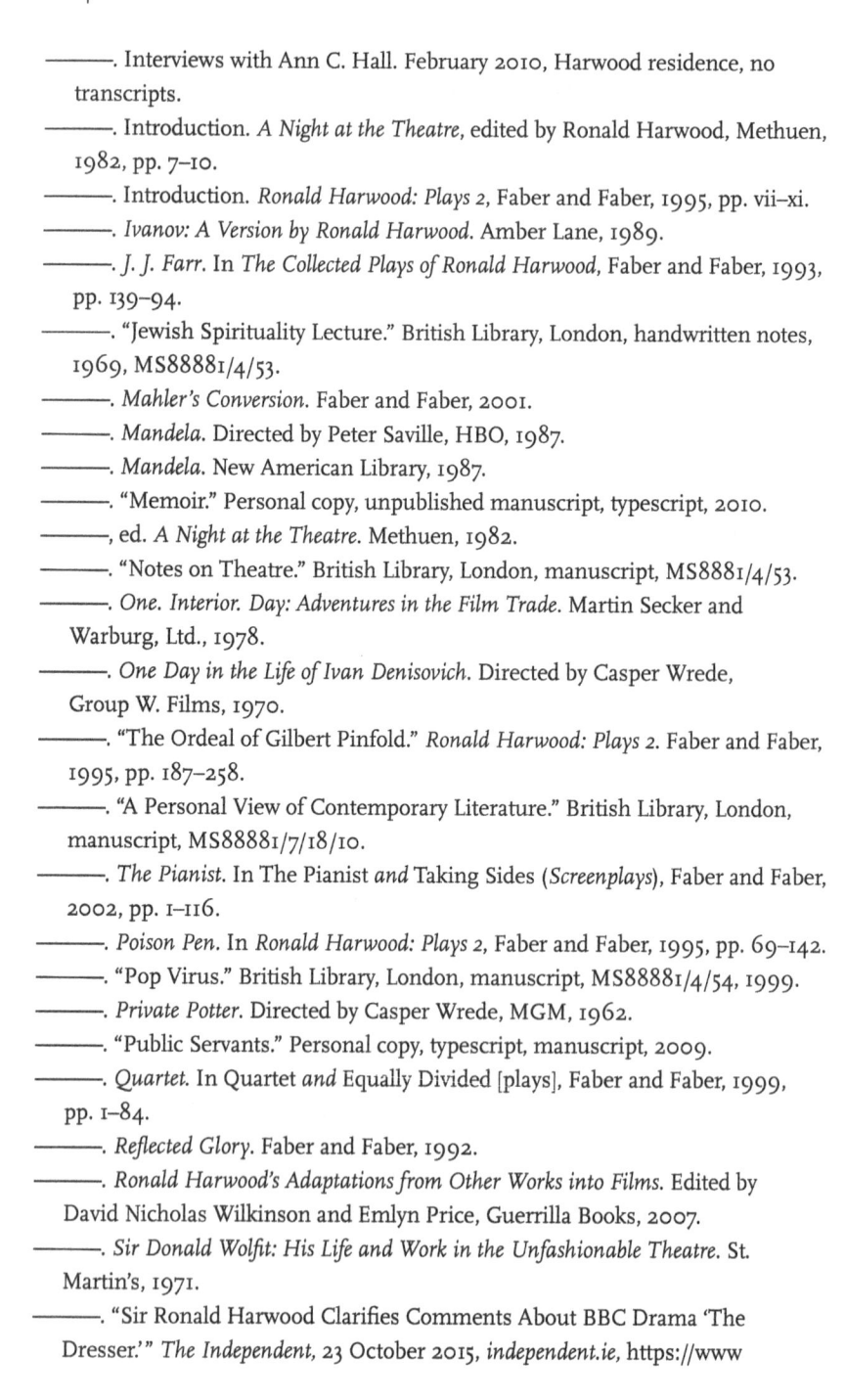

.independent.ie/style/celebrity/celebrity-news/sir-ronald-harwood-clarifies-comments-about-bbc-drama-the-dresser/34136139.html.
———. "Speech." British Library, London, manuscript, MS88881.
———. *The Statement*. Directed by Norman Jewison, Sony, 1996.
———. *Taking Sides*. In *Ronald Harwood: Plays 2*, Faber and Faber, 1995, pp. 1–68.
———. *Taking Sides*. In *The Pianist and Taking Sides* (*Screenplays*), Faber and Faber, 2002, pp. 117–95.
———. *Tramway Road*. In *Ronald Harwood: Plays 2*, Faber and Faber, 1995, pp. 143–86.
———. "Truth and Fiction: The Holocaust on Stage and Screen." *European Judaism: A Journal the New Europe*, vol. 38, no. 2, August 2005, pp. 4–16.
———. "Writers and Television." British Library, London, manuscript, MS88881/4/53.
Heilman, Robert Bechtold. *Tragedy and Melodrama: Versions of Experience*. U of Washington P, 1968.
Hemming, Sarah. "The Heart of the Matter." *Financial Times*, 16 February 2008, p. 16.
Hewitt, Phil. "West Sussex Mourns 'One of the Major Playwrights of the 20th Century.'" *Sussex World*, 10 September 2020, https://www.sussexexpress.co.uk/arts-and-culture/film-and-tv/west-sussex-mourns-one-of-the-major-playwrights-of-the-20th-century-2967799.
Hinchliffe, Arnold. *British Theatre: 1950–1970*. Rowman and Littlefield, 1974.
Holden, Stephen. "Searching for Answers in Yesterday's South Africa." *The New York Times*, 15 December 1995, https://www.nytimes.com/1995/12/15/movies/film-review-searching-for-answers-in-yesterday-s-south-africa.html.
"Home." Review. *Publisher's Weekly*, 4 January 1993, https://www.publishersweekly.com/9780297813682.
Howe, Marvine. "Fugard Opposes Playwright's Boycott of South Africa." *The New York Times*, 6 July 1970, https://www.nytimes.com/1970/07/06/archives/fugard-opposes-playwrights-boycott-of-south-africa.html.
Inness, Christopher. *Modern British Drama*. Cambridge UP, 1992.
Itzkoff, Dave. "Dustin Hoffman Graduates to Film Director." *The New York Times*, 13 September 2011, https://archive.nytimes.com/artsbeat.blogs.nytimes.com/2011/09/12/filming-begins-on-dustin-hoffmans-directorial-debut/.
Jacobs, Gerald. "Ronald Harwood." *Jewish Chronicle*, 9 June 2017, https://www.pressreader.com/uk/the-jewish-chronicle/20170609/282110636581393.
"Jewish Enough." *Jewish Post, Indianapolis, Indiana*, 6 December 1968, *Hoosier State Chronicles*, https://newspapers.library.in.gov/cgi-bin/indiana?a=d&d

=JPOST19681206-01.1.27&e=-------en-20--1--txt-txIN-------. Accessed 6 October 2022.
Kakutani, Michiko. "Lear, Shakespeare's 'Impossible' Role, Animates a New Play." *The New York Times*, 1 November 1981, sec. 2, p. 1.
Kater, Michael. *Culture in Nazi Germany*. Yale UP, 2020.
Kaufmann, Walter A. *Tragedy and Philosophy*. Princeton UP, 1992.
Keller, Bill. "*Cry, the Beloved Country*: A New Voice from the Past." *The New York Times*, 18 December 1994, https://www.nytimes.com/1994/12/19/movies/in-cry-the-beloved-country-a-new-voice-from-the-past.html.
Kimberley, Nick. "A Glimpse of God: Composers Exert a Powerful Hold on the Imaginations of a Small Band of Playwrights." *The Independent*, 27 October 1993, *Nexis Uni*, https://advance-lexis-com.echo.louisville.edu/api/permalink/9ca4b4ca-44da-44c0-9e78-2c393c25cfa1/?context=1516831.
Klady, Leonard. "Cry the Beloved Country." *Variety Movie Reviews*, 1995, *Nexis Uni*, https://advance-lexis-com.echo.louisville.edu/api/permalink/75c577f9-c31a-4597-9781-2cd3c8b5c418/?context=1516831.
Klaven, Harry Jr. Review of *The Meaning of Treason*, by Rebecca West. *University of Chicago Law Review*, vol. 16, no. 2, 1949, pp. 378–81.
Kramer, Lawrence. "Melodic Trains: Music in Polanski's *The Pianist*." *Beyond the Soundtrack: Representing Music in Cinema*, edited by Daniel Goldmark et al., 2007, pp. 66–85.
Kurnick, David. *Empty Houses: Theatrical Failure and the Novel*. Princeton UP, 2012.
Lauder, Robert. "Filming the Face of God." *America*, vol. 175, no. 11, 1996, pp. 24–25.
Lebrecht, Norman. "Who Was Mahler?" *The Daily Telegraph*, 26 September 2001, *Nexis Uni*, https://advance-lexis-com.echo.louisville.edu/api/permalink/0ff45bd5-ae84-4b08-9475-f0e1b19d2dbd/?context=1516831.
Letts, Quentin. "Sympathy for the Devil or a Nazi Piece of Work?" *Daily Mail*, 22 February 2008, *Nexis Uni*, https://advance-lexis-com.echo.louisville.edu/api/permalink/40ca0e93-98e8-4a81-8244-a05b485894f3/?context=1516831.
Levin, Bernard. "Bernard Levin's The Way We Live Now: The Soul Sniggered Off." *The Times*, 17 December 1987, p. 16, *The Times Digital Archive*, link.gale.com/apps/doc/IF0503147639/TTDA?u=viva_wm&sid=bookmark-TTDA&xid=b2c32709.
Lieblich, Julia. "French Feminist Rabbi Captivates Multifaith Crowds on Musings on Mortality." *The New York Times*, 30 September 2022, https://www.nytimes.com/2022/09/30/world/europe/delphine-horvilleur-rabbi-judaism.html.
Lockwood, Danielle. "*Without the Past, I could not have been the writer I am*":

Jewish Identity in the Life and Work of Ronald Harwood. 2009. University of Southampton, master's thesis.

Lynch, James. "Evelyn Waugh During the 'Pinfold Years.'" *Modern Fiction Studies*, vol. 32, no. 4, Winter 1986, pp. 543–59.

Mandela, Nelson. "The Separation." *Frontline*, www.frontline.org, https://www.pbs.org/wgbh/pages/frontline/shows/mandela/husband/book.html.

Massing, Michael. "Mandela." *The Nation*. 24 October 1987, Ebscohost, https://search-ebscohost-com.echo.louisville.edu/login.aspx?direct=true&db=fah&AN=11182536&site=ehost-live462–63.

Maugham, Somerset. *Theatre*. Vintage, 2001.

Maxwell, Dominic. "Ronald Harwood Graduates to the Ivy League." *The Times*, 1 November 2010, https://www.thetimes.co.uk/article/ronald-harwood-graduates-to-the-ivy-league-kmmlx8svxh2.

McGillick, Paul. "Evelyn Does Sarah Proud." *Australian Financial Times*, 16 October 1987, Nexis Uni, https://advance-lexis-com.echo.louisville.edu/api/permalink/3b2c4b36-e762-40ce-9a7e-939e460f2abf/?context=1516831.

Mendelsohn, Richard, and Milton Shain. *The Jews in South Africa: An Illustrated History*. Jonathan Ball, 2008.

Mikel-Arieli, Roni. *Remembering the Holocaust in a Racial State*. De Gruyter, 2022.

Miller, Arthur. "The Nature of Tragedy." *The Collected Essays of Arthur Miller*. Bloomsbury, 2000, pp. 11–14.

———. "Tragedy and the Common Man." *The Collected Essays of Arthur Miller*. Bloomsbury, 2000, pp. 8–10.

Moore, Brian. *The Statement*. Dutton, 1996.

Muir, Kate. "He Changed My Life." *The Times*, 11 February 2010, https://www.thetimes.co.uk/article/roman-polanski-changed-my-life-and-i-support-him-xnl6fc7lxpl.

Nathan, John. "Ronald Harwood: 'Having a Woman as King Lear Is an Insult to the Playwright.'" *The Times*, 31 August 2016.

Nawaz, Amna. "Vatican Documents Show Secret Back Channel Between Pope Pius XXII and Hitler." PBS News Hour, PBS.org, 7 June 2022, https://www.pbs.org/newshour/show/vatican-documents-show-secret-back-channel-between-pope-pius-xii-and-adolph-hitler.

Nelan, Bruce W. "Nelson and Winnie Mandela." *Time.com*, 5 January 1987, https://content.time.com/time/subscriber/article/0,33009,963172,00.html.

Nightingale, Benedict. "Netting the Village Nazi." *The Times*, 25 September 1996, Nexis Uni, https://advance-lexis-com.echo.louisville.edu/api/permalink/603e805b-6cde-42ca-8ba5-494278fbeca9/?context=1516831.

Oren, Michael. "Schindler's Liszt: Roman Polanski's Mistake About the Holocaust." *The New Republic*, 17 March 2003, pp. 25–28.
Parks, Michael. "Winnie Mandela Opposes HBO Movie." *Los Angeles Times*, 21 September 1987, https://www.latimes.com/archives/la-xpm-1987-09-21-ca-6056-story.html.
Paton, Alan. *Cry, The Beloved Country*. Scribner, 1948.
Peter, John. "Punish and Be Damned." *The Sunday Times*, 29 September 1996, Nexis Uni, https://advance-lexis-com.echo.louisville.edu/api/permalink/dff26de3-a037-4ce8-99d5-9dba4f5b3f12/?context=1516831.
———. "Theatre: The Mind Stays in Hiding." *The Sunday Times*, 24 November 1985, Nexis Uni, https://advance-lexis-com.echo.louisville.edu/api/permalink/ec5a9753-25db-4a32-a501-845658c69089/?context=1516831.
Pick, Robert. "Tragedy Born of Fear. Review of *George Washington September, Sir* by Ronald Harwood." *The New York Times Book Review*, 10 September 1961, https://www.nytimes.com/1961/09/10/archives/tragedy-born-of-fear-george-washington-september-sir-by-ronald.html?smid=url-share.
"Playwrights Against Apartheid." British Library, BL.UK., https://www.bl.uk/collection-items/playwrights-against-apartheid-with-letters-from-dennis-brutus-and-samuel-beckett.
Plunkett, John. "Ronald Harwood Insists He Is 'Proud' of BBC Adaptation of *The Dresser*." *The Guardian*, 23 October 2015, https://www.theguardian.com/media/2015/oct/23/ronald-harwood-bbc-the-dresser-ian-mckellen-anthony-hopkins.
Price, Matthew. "A Brilliant Crank at 100: Evelyn Waugh." *National Post*, 9 August 2003, PT6.
"Production Notes: *The Dresser*." *Starz*. 2015. https://www.starz.com/pressroomstatic/pr_thedresser/pdf/the_dresser_production_notes.pdf.
Purves, Libby. "Dainty morsel with a nostalgic flavour; Ronald Harwood's serving of theatrical history went down well with diners at the Ivy, says Libby Purves Theatre." *The Times* (London), 10 November 2010, advance-lexis-com.echo.louisville.edu/api/document?collection=news&id=urn:contentItem:51F7-MTG1-DYVC-J1DB-00000-00&context=1516831. Accessed February 29, 2024.
Reade, Simon. "Tragedy Rendered Bloodless." *Financial Times*, 25 September 1996, Nexis Uni, https://advance-lexis-com.echo.louisville.edu/api/permalink/194151f1-0ba0-4620-95d7-50ec5036fe36/?context=1516831.
Rich, Frank. "'Dresser,' Monarch and his Loyal Vassal." *The New York Times*, 10 November 1981, C7, https://www.nytimes.com/1981/11/10/theater/stage-dresser-a-monarch-and-his-loyal-vassal.html?smid=url-share.

Robinson, W. Sydney. *"Speak Well of Me": Ronald Harwood, The Authorized Biography*. Oberon, 2017.
Roche, Mark. "Introduction to Hegel's Theory of Tragedy." *PhaenEx*, vol. 1, no. 2, Fall/Winter, 2006, pp. 11–20.
"Ronald Harwood." *Contemporary Authors Online: 2007*. Gale Research Team, https://go.gale.com/ps/i.do?id=GALE%7CH1000043189&sid=sitemap&v=2.1&it=r&p=LitRC&sw=w&userGroupName=anon%7E48a57876&aty=open-web-entry.
Salys, Rimgaila. "Solzhenitsyn's *One Day in the Live of Ivan Denisovich*." *Explicator*, vol. 64, no. 2, 2006, pp. 112–15.
Shales, Tom. "Opportunities Missed." *The Washington Post*, 19 September 1987, p. D1.
Sobczynski, Peter. "The Dresser." *RogerEbert.com*, 27 May 2016, https://www.rogerebert.com/reviews/the-dresser-2016.
Solzhenitsyn, Alexander. *One Day in the Life of Ivan Denisovich*. Translated by Ralph Parker. New American Library, 1963.
Spencer, Charles. "Emotionally Devastating Tale of a Very English Fascist." *The Daily Telegraph*, 20 February 2008, p. 28, https://advance-lexis-com.echo.louisville.edu/api/permalink/8a79723a-7f97-4345-aca6-d0f90af3709f/?context=1516831.
Sperling, Nicole. "Oscar Winner Ronald Harwood to Write MLK script for Dreamworks." EW.COM, 19 January 2010, https://ew.com/article/2010/01/19/ron-harwood-mlk/.
Steiner, George. "Tragedy Reconsidered." *Rethinking Tragedy*, edited by Rita Felski, Johns Hopkins UP, 2008, pp. 29–45.
Stevenson, Michael. "*The Pianist* and Its Contexts." *The Modern Jewish Experience in World Cinema*, edited by Lawrence Baron, Brandeis UP, pp. 178–86.
Stockwell, Richard. "Handyman." *Cambridge Evening News*, 9 October 2012, *Nexis Uni*, https://advance-lexis-com.echo.louisville.edu/api/permalink/17b6d10f-ab1a-4fc1-bf3a-df16b4195f53/?context=1516831.
Szpilman, Wladyslaw. *The Pianist: The Extraordinary Story of One Man's Survival in Warsaw, 1939–1945*. Thorndike, 2000.
Thompson, Alice, and Rachel Sylvester. "The Saturday Interview: Ronald Harwood." *The Times*, 30 May 2009, https://www.thetimes.co.uk/article/the-saturday-interview-ronald-harwood-q78995pr769.
Thompson, Leonard. *A History of South Africa*, 4th ed. Yale UP, 2014.
Thomson, David. "Ronald Harwood Is Glamorous." *The Guardian*, 7 March 2008, https://www.theguardian.com/film/2008/mar/07/5.

Thornber, Robin. "Manchester/Poison Pen." *The Guardian*, 17 May 1993, *Nexis Uni*, https://advance-lexis-com.echo.louisville.edu/api/permalink/63a22d6f-fd35-4aca-9e95-8ef7da23133d/?context=1516831.

Thorpe, Vanessa. "Oscar Winner Reveals the Secret of Pro-Nazi Traitor." *The Guardian*, 16 February 2008, https://www.theguardian.com/stage/2008/feb/17/theatre.secondworldwar.

Tugend, Tom. "Writing for Oscar." *Jerusalem Post*, 17 February 2008, p. 24.

United States Conference of Catholic Bishops. "Guidelines for Catholic-Jewish Relations." National Conference of Catholic Bishops, 1985, https://www.usccb.org/prayer-and-worship/liturgical-year/lent/guidelines-for-catholic-jewish-relations.

Wainwright, Jeffrey. "*Poison Pen* in Manchester." *The Independent*, 1 June 1993, https://www.independent.co.uk/arts-entertainment/theatre-the-missing-link-jeffrey-wainwright-on-poison-pen-in-manchester-1489003.html.

Walker, Tim. "In Praise of the Patriotic Playwright." *Spectator*, 17 June 2006, *Nexis Uni*, https://advance-lexis-com.echo.louisville.edu/api/permalink/8622540f-bd72-4f55-b006-1db0be5a21d4/?context=1516831.

Ward, Victoria. "Sir Ronald Harwood Rules Out Women Taking Lead in Seminal Play." *The Telegraph*, 1 February 2016, https://www.telegraph.co.uk/news/celebritynews/12134069/Sir-Ronald-Harwood-rules-out-women-taking-lead-in-seminal-play.html.

Wardle, Irving. "Theatre: Echo of Truth." *The Times*, 18 October 1985, *Nexis Uni*, https://advance-lexis-com.echo.louisville.edu/api/permalink/dc997ad3-d0c1-4982-8e9c-ab6bcf8ae50b/?context=1516831.

West, Rebecca. *The Meaning of Treason*. Viking, 1947.

Wilkinson, Christopher. "Whatever Happened to the Actor-Manager?" Guardian Theatre blog, 16 July 2008, https://www.theguardian.com/stage/theatreblog/2008/jul/16/whateverhappenedtotheactor.

Worden, Nigel. *The Making of Modern South Africa: Conquest, Apartheid, Democracy*, 5th ed. Wiley-Blackwell, 2011.

Xu, Dongmei. "Food and Homecoming in Solzhenitsyn's *One Day in the Life of Ivan Denisovich*." *Explicator*, vol. 66, no. 2, 2008, pp. 104–8.

Young, Deborah. "Quartet Is a Lovely Salute to Classical Performing Stars." *Times Colonist*, 18 January 2013, *Nexis Uni*, p. C14, https://advance-lexis-com.echo.louisville.edu/api/permalink/be62fce7-bda5-4ece-b11c-db6cbad30ddb/?context=1516831.

Index

actor-managers, 26–29, 39, 61, 78
adaptation, 5, 9, 37, 71, 85, 99, 131–135, 149, 152, 162, 169
African National Congress (ANC), 40, 139, 141–142
After the Lions (1982), 2, 69, 84–88, 169
Amery, John, 119–125
Another Time (1989), 4, 7, 41, 66, 73, 93–99, 100, 103, 139, 169
anti-Semitism, ix–x, 6–7, 107–110, 113, 115, 119, 120–125, 154, 166–167
Arrivederci, Baby (Drop Dead Darling, 1966), 45, 48, 131
Articles of Faith (1973), 41, 50–56, 65, 94

Bauby, Jean-Dominique, 160–164
Beaumont, Binkie, 34
Beckett, Samuel, 15, 27, 37–38, 88
Being Julia (2004), 157–160, 169
Bernhardt, Sarah, 2, 69, 84–88
Boer War, 4, 6
Brecht, Bertolt, 15, 37, 128, 131
Burton, Richard, 48, 131

Catholicism, 6, 46–47, 90–93, 108–109, 114–115, 153–156
César and Augusta (1978), 5, 59–62, 94, 115
cigarette smoking, x, 69–70
Collaboration (2008), 122–125, 169–170

Country Matters (1969), 11, 67
Cry, the Beloved Country (1995), 41, 139, 143–146

The Deliberate Death (1985), 88–90
Diving Bell and Butterfly (2007), 1, 131, 160–164, 169
The Dresser (1983, 1993, 2015), 15, 24, 63, 69, 76–84, 93, 101, 130–131, 133, 135, 139, 167–169

Eagleton, Terry, 16, 19
Eichmann trials, 45–46
An English Tragedy (2008), 119–125
Eyre, Richard, 78, 130

Felski, Rita, 17, 101
Fergusson, Francis, 16, 23
Forster, E. M., 5, 36, 39–40
Frank, César, 59–62
Fraser, Antonia, 12, 63, 165
Freed, Donald, ix
Fugard, Athol, 95–96, 98
Furtwängler, Wilhelm, 100–106, 115, 122–123, 146

Genoa Ferry (1977), 56–59
George Washington, September, Sir! (originally published in Great Britain as *All the Same Shadows*, 1961), 9, 26, 36, 40–45, 143, 166

The Girl in Melanie Klein (1969), 48–50, 131, 167
The Good Companions (1974, musical), 67
Greene, Graham, 5
Guilt Merchants (1963), 10–11, 45–48, 100, 107, 131

The Handyman (1996), 106–110
Harwood, Deborah, 8, 23
Harwood, Ronald (née Horowitz): as anglophile, 4; apartheid, 3–4; awards, 1, 11–12, 69, 77, 100, 135, 146, 161, 165; biography, 2–12; Catholicism, 6, 8, 93; children, 8; cigarette smoking, x, 69–70, 111; critical reputation, 2, 12–15; edited collections, 1, 11, 70, 165, 167; friendship with Lady Antonia Fraser and Harold Pinter, 12; influences, 5, 39; Jewish identity, 2–3, 5–7, 8, 29, 48, 167–168; movie industry, 9, 10, 130–135; music, 4–5; name change, 7; novels, 36–66; plays, 67–130, 131–164; political theatre, 15, 37, 56, 69, 131, 166; screenplays, 1, 11, 69, 130–164, 165, 167, 169; Shakespeare, 5, 28, 32–33; South Africa, x, 2–4; spouse (Natasha Riehle), ix–x, 8–10, 12, 36, 45, 62–63, 160; tragic vision, 15–23; Donald Wolfit, 1, 8, 15–16, 19, 21, 37, 39, 61, 78–79, 158; work in television, 9–11; writing routine, 12
Havel, Václav, 88
Heavenly Ivy (2010), 127–129
Hegel, Friedrich, 16–18, 21–23
Heilman, Robert, 20–21
A High Wind in Jamaica (1965), 45, 48
Hoffman, Dustin, 12, 112–113
Holocaust, 7, 30, 167; and Harwood, 45, 48, 64, 68; *Collaboration*, 122–125; *The Dresser*, 76–84; *An English*

Tragedy, 119–125; *Guilt Merchants*, 45–48; *The Handyman*, 106–110; *The Pianist*, 147–150; *The Statement*, 152–156, 157; *Taking Sides*, 100–106
Home (1993), 2, 8, 63–66, 138, 147

International PEN, 12, 69
The Interpreters (1986), 88–90
introduction, 1–24
Islam, 92
Israel, 41, 45–47, 57, 114

J. J. Farr (1987), 90–93, 169

King of Hearts (1966), 49

Luhrmann, Baz, 131

Mahler's Conversion (2001), 5, 12, 113–119, 169
Mandela (1987), 9, 41, 139–143, 169
Mandela, Nelson, 40–41, 91, 139–143
March Hares (1964), 11, 67
Maugham, Somerset, 5, 39, 128, 157–160
Middle Eastern conflict, 47, 56–58, 59, 91
Miller, Arthur, 5, 20–21, 23, 44, 95
modern British theatre, 1–2, 12–15, 18, 26–29, 30–34, 37–39, 65, 68–71, 131, 166
Moore, Brian, 152–156
movie industry, 9, 10, 130–135
Muslims, 57–58, 91–92

A Night at the Theatre (1982), 11, 70, 167

One Day in the Life of Ivan Denisovich (1970), 135–139
One Flew Over the Cuckoo's Nest (1962), 49

Index | 189

One. Interior. Day: Adventures in the Film Trade (1978), 133–135
The Ordeal of Gilbert Pinfold (1977), 11, 71–72
Osborne, John, 7

The Pianist (2002), 1, 5, 11, 69, 94, 100–103, 105, 131, 146–152, 155, 161, 167, 169
Pinter, Harold, 12–13, 15, 26–27, 37, 63, 68–69, 85–86, 95, 100, 106, 129, 132, 165
Poetics (Aristotle), 16, 23, 166
pogroms, 3, 63
Poison Pen (1995), 99–100
Polanski, Roman, 69, 100, 146–152
politics, 2, 14, 15, 18, 37, 56, 57, 69, 93, 103–104, 106, 122, 131, 156, 157, 166–168
Popieluszko, Jerzy, 88–89
Power and the Glory (Greene), 5, 39, 118; and *J. J. Farr*, 90–92
Public Servants (2009, unpublished), 125–127, 166

Quartet (1999), 12–13, 110–113, 167

Riehl, Natasha (spouse), ix–x, 8–10, 12, 36, 45, 62–63, 160
Royal Academy of Dramatic Arts (RADA), 7–8

Sher, Anthony, 115
Sir Donald Wolfit: His Life and Work in the Unfashionable Theatre (1971), 11, 13, 24–35, 68, 81; Shakespeare, 28, 32–33
Snake Pit, 49
Solzhenitsyn, Aleksandr, 135–139
South Africa, x, 50–51, 139–145; African National Congress (ANC), 40, 139, 141–142; anti-Semitism, 6–7, 40–42, 46, 51; apartheid, 40–44, 46, 51, 94–97, 139–145; Bantus, 52–53, 55; Coloureds, 52, 55; Jewish community, 3–7, 41; Jewish migration to, 3, 6; Pan-Africanist Congress (PAC), 40; Sharpeville Massacre, 40–41, 141
SPAM (lunch meat), 128
Spielberg, Steven, 131, 161
The Statement (1996), 152–156, 157
Steiner, George, 16–17, 22
Strauss, Richard, 122–125
Szabó, Istvan, 105, 157
Szpilman, Wladyslaw, 146–152, 155, 161

Taking Sides (1995, 2002), 5, 94, 100–106, 110, 122, 125, 131, 148, 152, 155, 157, 167, 169
Taylor, Elizabeth, 48
totalitarianism, 2
tragedy, 15–23
tragic heroes, 16–35, 98, 168
tragic vision: defined, 2, 15–24; in works, 38–39, 40, 51, 66, 68, 72, 100, 119, 122, 131–133, 139, 141, 143, 157, 165, 167–168, 170

unfashionable theatre, 13–15, 23, 27, 40, 68, 71, 133, 166, 168

Warlock, Peter (aka Philip Heseltine), 99–100
Waugh, Evelyn, 5, 11, 39, 71–72, 114, 169
Weinstein, Harvey, 69
Wigram, Ralph, 125–127
Williams, Tennessee, 5
Wolfit, Donald, ix, 1–2, 8–9, 13, 19, 24–35, 81, 168; as actor-manager, 26–29; critical reception, 30–35; and *The Dresser*, ix, 1, 76, 78–81, 139, 165

Zweig, Stefan, 123–125